D1385067

What Shall I Cook Today?

Nika Hazelton's previous books include

Reminiscence and Ravioli
The Continental Flavor
The Art of Danish Cooking
The Swiss Cookbook
The Art of Scandinavian Cooking
The Belgian Cookbook
The Picnic Book
I Cook As I Please

WHAT SHALL I COOK TODAY?

Menus and Recipes for Every Day of the Year

by Nika Hazelton
with Marjorie P. Blanchard

BOBBS-MERRILL
Indianapolis/New York

Published by The Bobbs-Merrill Company, Inc.
Indianapolis/New York

ISBN 0-672-52098-2
Library of Congress Catalog Card Number: 74-21150
Designed by Lionhill Studios
Produced by Ottenheimer Publishers, Inc.
Phototypesetting by Mid-Atlantic Photo Composition, Inc.
Manufactured in the United States of America

First printing July, 1975

Contents

INTRODUCTION

This book is meant to help the person who has to cook every day, whether he/she wants to or not. It is based upon the experience that it is impossible and also undesirable to make a production of every course of every meal. But I feel that in every meal there should be something for which the family and guests praise the cook, thus keeping up everybody's morale.

So these menus are designed to give good, varied food for every day of the year, each with a starred dish for which the recipe is given — if it's a hamburger dinner, there's a special dessert; if the main course is rich or elaborate, the rest of the meal is simple.

Our other principle is to keep things as easy and as inexpensive as possible. Life is too short and food is too dear for anything else. For this reason, too, entertaining and parties have been kept within bounds, without the upmanship that has been known to creep into such affairs, whether you're giving a small, elegant lunch or a big all-day celebration.

All the food in this book is cooked from scratch, from seasonal and readily available ingredients. It is perfectly easy to do so, and infinitely less expensive than prepared convenience foods — not to mention the fact that the taste is superior, and that this kind of food is healthier.

As few of us cook always for the same number of people (on some days the children are out, or guests come in) we have included dinners for two, and family fare to accommodate varying numbers of people at the table.

Of course, there should be nothing iron-clad about these menus. We hope that you will use them, expand on them, return to them with your own variants. As parting advice, remember that cooking should be a pleasure, not a chore, and act accordingly.

JANUARY

Hail to the New Year! How marvellous it is, I always think in January, to have a whole year ahead in which to improve myself. However, experience has taught me to keep my ambitions small and within bounds, or they'll die unborn. I won't learn to spin sugar, but I will learn to bone a chicken or a leg of lamb. I won't try to reproduce a meal eaten in a good French restaurant, but I will learn to make perfect omelets every time. I will make a shopping list and stick by it to make better use of my food money, but I won't give up a bottle of good wine. I will use only fresh, seasonal foods, but the best I can afford. I won't feed my guests as if they worked on the Alaska Pipeline, but I'll give them carefully cooked small meals that won't fatten them. I won't fuss or show off when I entertain. I will cook a new dish twice a week — well, say, at least once a week. Above all, I will keep cool and not look back. Hail to the New Year!

JANUARY

FAMILY FARE

	LUNCHES	DINNERS
Sunday	Baked Apple Pancake* Bacon and Eggs Muffins, Hard Rolls, Fruit Danish	Baked Ham Creamed Spinach Baked Potato Sour Cream Banana Pecan Cake*
Monday	Black Bean Soup* Grilled Cheese Sandwiches Carrot Sticks Applesauce	Meat Loaf* Gruyere Potatoes Tossed Green Salad Chocolate Pudding
Tuesday	Cottage Cheese, Orange, Grapefruit, Apple and Grape Salad Apricot-Coriander Bread* A Piece of Chocolate	Norwegian Lamb and Cabbage* Boiled Potatoes Broccoli Vinaigrette Lemon Pie
Wednesday	Danish Bacon and Egg Pancake* Lingonberries Fruit Yogurt and Cookies	Fried Chicken Baked Rice and Cheese* Red Radish Salad Fruit and Cookies
Thursday	Hamburger on Buns Coleslaw Ella Elvin's Coconut-Almond Brownies*	Piquent Turkish Beef Stew* Buttered Noodles Glazed Carrots Apple Pie
Friday	Cheesy Swiss Eggs* Anchovy Toast Tossed Green Salad Fresh Pears	Creamy Shrimp Curry* Boiled Rice Chutney Sweet Pickle Relish Chopped Salted Almonds Sliced Oranges in Sherry
Saturday	Cold Cuts Noodle Pancake* Carrots and Celery Fruit and Cookies	Chicken Breasts in Cream Chez Moi* Yellow Rice Sautéed Zucchini Ice Cream with Rum Sauce

QUICK & EASY Dinners For Two	BUDGET DINNERS	ENTERTAINING
Little Steaks Braised Artichokes and Peas* Belgian Endive Salad Chocolate Pudding	Roast Chicken Potatoes Green Vegetable Thrifty Waldorf Chocolate Cake*	Belgian Waterzooie of Chicken* Brown Bread and Butter Tossed Green Salad with Capers and Anchovies Rum Parfait
Broiled Ham with Raisin Sauce Black Bean Casserole* Cornbread Green Salad Orange, Grapefruit and Banana Fruit Salad	Lima and Beef Stew* Buttered Rice Coleslaw Applesauce	Onion Soup Chablis* Caviar Omelets Bread Sticks Avocado and Grapefruit Salad Lemon Sherbet Cookies
Quick Madeira Stew* Buttered Rice or Noodles Watercress Ginger-Flavored Homemade Applesauce	Spaghetti with Zucchini Beef Sauce* Green Salad and Cheese	Country Captain* Rice Chutney Persimmon, Avocado, and Grapefruit Salad Brandy Cream Pie
Polish or Italian Sausages Green Beans and Potatoes* Waldorf Salad Apple Pie	Cranberry Pork Chops* Baked Potatoes String Bean Salad Fruit Salad	Clear Consomme with Sherry Cheese Sticks Roast Pheasant Ragout of Mushrooms and Eggs* Green Beans Vinaigrette Guava Shells with Cream Cheese and Crackers
Cream of Mushroom Soup Finocchio and Shrimp Salad* Broccoli Vinaigrette Fresh Fruit and Macaroons	Dried Beef and Corn on Buttered Biscuits or Toast* Green Salad Brownies	Fresh Spinach Soup Wiener Schnitzel Flemish Carrots* Brussels Sprouts with Chestnuts Sliced Oranges with Grand Marnier Almond Cookies
Oyster Stew* Pilot Crackers Cheese Tray Watercress, Apples, Pears Brownies	Tuna Fish with Noodles and Cheese* Waldorf Salad Cake and Fruit	Oeufs a la Russe Trout with Cream and Almond Sauce* Boiled Potatoes Tossed Green Salad Brie Cheese Hot Deep-dish Apple Pie with Cream
Spaghetti and Meatballs Boiled Artichokes with Piquant Green Sauce* Fresh Pineapple and Kirsch	Stuffed Flank Steak* Sauteed Onions Home Fried Potatoes Fruit	All-Day Open House

FAMILY FARE LUNCHES

January

Sunday

Baked Apple Pancake

Baked Apple Pancake
Bacon and Eggs
Muffins, Hard Rolls, Fruit Danish

2 eggs, separated
3 tablespoons milk
3 tablespoons flour
⅛ teaspoon salt
¼ teaspoon baking powder
5 tablespoons sugar
1 cup finely diced, peeled, and cored apples
1 tablespoon fresh lemon juice
1 teaspoon ground cinnamon
lemon wedges

Twenty minutes before serving the pancake, preheat oven to 400°F. Generously butter a 10-inch griddle or frying pan. If the handle is wooden or plastic, wrap it in foil. Place the pan in the oven to heat.

Beat the egg yolks until thick. Beat in the milk. Combine flour, salt, and baking powder in a strainer; sift into the egg mixture. Beat until smooth. Beat the egg whites until foamy. Gradually beat in 3 tablespoons of sugar; beat until stiff. Fold apples, lemon juice, and egg whites into the egg mixture. Turn the batter into the hot pan. Spread evenly. Mix the remaining 2 tablespoons of sugar with the cinnamon. Sprinkle over the pancake. Bake for about 10 minutes or until the top is glazed and the pancake is cooked through. Cut into quarters and serve hot with lemon wedges. Serves four.

Monday

Black Bean Soup

Black Bean Soup
Grilled Cheese Sandwiches
Carrot Sticks
Applesauce

1 pound black beans
¼ cup bacon fat or butter
¼ cup minced onion
1 garlic clove, minced
2 stalks celery, minced
2 quarts water
salt
freshly ground pepper
Tabasco to taste (optional)
1 thinly sliced lemon
or 6 tablespoons sour cream

Wash and pick over the beans. Soak overnight in water to cover. Drain and rinse. Heat the fat in a skillet and cook the onion, garlic, and celery until they are soft. Place the beans in a large kettle; add the water and vegetables. Mix well. Bring to a boil. Simmer, covered, until the beans are tender. If the beans get too thick, add a little more hot water. Strain the soup through a food mill or sieve; or, puree in a blender, but this mixture will be tougher because of the bean skins. Season with salt, pepper, and Tabasco to taste. Heat through. Serve with a slice of lemon or a tablespoon of sour cream on each serving. Makes four to six servings.

Tuesday

Apricot-Coriander Bread

Cottage Cheese, Orange, Grapefruit, Apple, and Grape Salad
Apricot-Coriander Bread
A Piece of Chocolate

¼ cup butter
1¼ cups sugar
1 egg, beaten
2 cups flour
½ teaspoon baking powder
½ teaspoon baking soda
½ teaspoon salt
1 tablespoon ground coriander
1 cup mashed canned drained apricots
2 tablespoons sour cream
½ teaspoon almond extract
½ cup chopped pecans
½ cup maraschino cherries (optional)

Cream the butter until soft. Gradually beat in the sugar, ¼ cup at a time, beating well after each addition. Beat in the egg. Sift together the flour, baking powder, soda, salt, and coriander. Beat flour into the creamed mixture alternately with the apricots and sour cream, beginning and ending with flour. Stir in the almond extract, pecans, and maraschino cherries. Grease and line with waxed paper two 7 × 4½ × 3-inch loaf pans. Turn the batter into the pans. Bake in a preheated 350° oven for about 1 hour. Cool. Wrap in foil or plastic wrap; store in the refrigerator. Let the bread ripen at least 24 hours before cutting. Makes about 2 pounds.

Wednesday

Danish Bacon and Egg Pancake

Danish Bacon and Egg Pancake
Lingonberries
Fruit Yogurt and Cookies

½ pound bacon
6 eggs
½ cup milk or light cream
2 tablespoons flour
½ teaspoon salt
3 tablespoons chopped chives or finely chopped green tops of spring onions

In a large, deep frying pan, cook the bacon until golden brown. Drain it on kitchen paper. Keep all but 3–4 tablespoons of the fat in the frying pan. Crumble the bacon into small pieces. Beat the eggs with the milk, flour, salt, and chives. Reheat the bacon fat; pour the egg mixture into it. Cook over low heat until the pancake begins to set, then sprinkle the bacon on the pancake. Lift the pancake edges with a fork so that the liquid part can run into the frying pan and cook. When the eggs are set and golden brown, fold, and serve hot. For a firmer pancake, place a plate over the frying pan and slide the pancake onto it. Then return it to the frying pan uncooked side down and finish cooking. Serves four.

Thursday

Ella Elvin's Coconut-Almond Brownies

Hamburger on Buns
Coleslaw
Ella Elvin's Coconut-Almond Brownies

2 eggs
1 cup sugar
⅔ cup flour
½ teaspoon baking powder
¼ teaspoon salt
⅓ cup melted butter
⅓ cup flaked coconut
½ teaspoon almond extract
1½ ounces unsweetened chocolate, melted

These brownies have baked-on coconut layer on top.

Beat the eggs until light and frothy. Gradually beat in the sugar, ¼ cup at a time, beating well after each addition. Sift together the flour, baking powder, and salt. Stir the melted butter into the egg mixture. Beat in the flour. Transfer ½ cup of batter to a small bowl; stir in the coconut and almond extract. Blend well. Stir the melted chocolate into the first (egg-flour) batter. Spoon this (chocolate) batter into a well-greased 8-inch square baking pan. Drop the coconut mixture over the chocolate batter by teaspoonfuls. Using a spatula or knife, spread the coconut mixture to form a thin layer over the chocolate batter. Bake in a preheated 350° oven for 30 minutes or until the cake shrinks away from the sides of the pan. Cool in the pan on a rack. Cut into squares and store in a container with a tight top. Makes about 20 brownies.

Friday

Cheesy Swiss Eggs

Cheesy Swiss Eggs
Anchovy Toast
Tossed Green Salad
Fresh Pears

½ pound sliced Swiss cheese
4 eggs
salt
freshly ground pepper
⅓ cup light or heavy cream or undiluted evaporated milk
4 tablespoons grated Swiss cheese

Butter a shallow baking dish generously. Line it with the sliced cheese. Break the eggs over the cheese. Season with salt and pepper. Pour the cream or milk over the eggs. Sprinkle with grated cheese. Bake in a preheated 350° oven for about 10–15 minutes or until the eggs are set. Serve with toast. This dish can also be made in individual shallow baking dishes. Makes two to four servings.

Saturday

Noodle Pancake

Cold Cuts
Noodle Pancake
Carrots and Celery
Fruit and Cookies

1 pound wide noodles
2 eggs
⅓ cup milk
salt
freshly ground pepper
4 tablespoons butter or margarine

Cook the noodles in plenty of salted water until just tender but still firm. Drain. Beat together the eggs and milk. Season with salt and pepper. Heat the butter or margarine in a large frying pan — preferably Teflon. Add the noodles and pour the egg-milk mixture over them. Stir with a fork to mix. Cook over low heat until the eggs are set and the bottom of the pancake is crusty. For crusts on both sides, put a serving plate over the pan and flip the pancake onto it. Flip it back into the pan with the browned side on top. Serves four.

Note: Leftover cooked pasta can be used.

FAMILY FARE DINNERS

January

Sunday

Sour Cream Banana Pecan Cake

Baked Ham
Creamed Spinach
Baked Potato
Sour Cream Banana Pecan Cake

¼ cup butter
1⅓ cups sugar
2 eggs
1 teaspoon vanilla extract
2 cups flour
1 teaspoon baking powder
1 teaspoon baking soda
¾ teaspoon salt
1 cup sour cream
1 cup mashed ripe bananas (about 2 medium)
½ cup chopped pecans

Beat the butter until soft. Gradually add sugar, ¼ cup at a time, and beat until light and fluffy. Beat in eggs, one at a time; beat well after each addition. Beat in vanilla. Sift together flour, baking powder, baking soda, and salt. Beat flour into the creamed mixture gradually, alternating with sour cream, beginning and ending with flour. Stir in bananas and pecans, mixing until just blended. Turn into a well-greased and floured 13 × 9 × 2-inch pan. Bake in a preheated 350° oven for about 45 minutes. Cool and add frosting of your choice.

Monday

Meat Loaf

Meat Loaf
Gruyère Potatoes
Tossed Green Salad
Chocolate Pudding

1 tablespoon butter
1 medium onion, minced
1 garlic clove, minced
¼ cup minced parsley
2 pounds ground chuck or round *or* a mixture of beef, pork, and veal
4 slices bacon, diced small
2 eggs
2 slices white bread, soaked in water and squeezed dry
½ cup grated Parmesan cheese
1–2 teaspoons anchovy paste (optional)
½ teaspoon allspice
salt
freshly ground pepper

Grated Parmesan and a little anchovy flavor improve a meat loaf to no end, as do diced bacon and sautéed onions and parsley. If a meat loaf is to be eaten hot, a mixture of meats is fine; if it is to be eaten cold, do not use pork, because it is gummy in a meat loaf. For a firm, easily sliced meat loaf, pummel and toss the raw mixture from hand to hand like a ball.

Heat the butter in a frying pan. Cook the onion, garlic, and parsley until the onion is soft but not brown. Turn the meat into a big bowl. Add the onion mixture and all remaining ingredients. Blend well first with a spoon and then with your hands. Shape the mixture into a loaf. Bake in a preheated 350° oven for about 1¼ to 1½ hours, depending on how well-done a loaf is desired. Use pan juices that will ooze from the meat for spaghetti and other sauces. Serves six.

Tuesday

Norwegian Lamb and Cabbage

Norwegian Lamb and Cabbage
Boiled Potatoes
Broccoli Vinaigrette
Lemon Pie

4 pounds lamb breast or riblets or other inexpensive cuts
1 medium cabbage
1 cup diced celery
1½ tablespoons salt
⅓ cup flour
boiling bouillon or water
2 tablespoons black peppercorns tied in a cheesecloth bag
½ cup sour cream

A national dish. Since lamb has considerable fat that must be trimmed off, you'll need about 4 pounds to get about 3 pounds of lean meat.

Trim all fat from the lamb. Cut meat into 2- to 3-inch serving pieces. Core the cabbage and cut it into 1-inch wedges. Place a layer of meat in a large, heavy saucepan or Dutch oven. Top with cabbage wedges and sprinkle with some of the celery, salt, and flour. Repeat the process; there should be at least 3 layers of meat and vegetables. Add enough boiling bouillon to cover lamb and cabbage halfway up. Add the peppercorns. Cover tightly and bring slowly to a boil. Cook over low heat until meat is tender, about 1½ hours. Check occasionally for moisture; if necessary, add a little more bouillon. Remove the peppercorns and stir in the sour cream before serving. Serves four to six.

Wednesday

Baked Rice and Cheese

Fried Chicken
Baked Rice and Cheese
Red Radish Salad
Fruit and Cookies

2 cups medium white sauce
½ teaspoon Worcestershire sauce
¼ teaspoon ground thyme or marjoram
3 cups cooked rice
1½ cups grated Swiss or Cheddar cheese
paprika
2 tablespoons room-temperature butter, cut into small pieces

Stir the Worcestershire sauce and thyme into the white sauce. Generously butter a 2-quart baking dish. Place a layer of rice on the bottom. Spoon some of the white sauce over the rice; sprinkle generously with some of the cheese. Repeat until all the rice, white sauce, and cheese are used up; 3 layers are best. Sprinkle with paprika and dot with the butter. Bake in a preheated 350° oven for about 15 minutes or until golden brown and bubbly. Makes four or five servings.

Thursday

Piquant Turkish Beef Stew

Piquant Turkish Beef Stew
Buttered Noodles
Glazed Carrots
Apple Pie

2 tablespoons butter
2-3 pounds lean stewing beef with all fat removed and meat cut into 1½-inch cubes
¼ cup water
salt
freshly ground pepper
½ teaspoon ground allspice
1 pound small whole white onions, peeled
2 garlic cloves
¼ cup vinegar
4 medium tomatoes, peeled and chopped
⅓ cup minced parsley

Heat the butter in a heavy saucepan or casserole. Add the meat and water. Cover; simmer over lowest possible heat for about 45 minutes. (An asbestos pad may be needed to keep the heat low.) Stir occasionally; if necessary, add a tablespoon of water at a time to prevent scorching. The meat should be dry. Season with salt, pepper, and allspice. Add the onions, garlic, vinegar, tomatoes, and parsley; mix well. Cover and simmer over lowest possible heat for about 30-45 minutes or until the meat is very tender. The sauce should have cooked down to thick pancake-batter consistency; if it has not, cook without a cover to let it reduce. Stir occasionally. Makes four to six servings.

Friday

Creamy Shrimp Curry

Creamy Shrimp Curry
Boiled Rice
Chutney
Sweet Pickle Relish
Chopped Salted Almonds
Sliced Oranges in Sherry

2-3 pounds raw shrimp
4 tablespoons butter
1 large onion, minced
1 tart apple, peeled, cored, and minced
1 cup celery, minced
1 cup hot water
salt
freshly ground pepper
¼ teaspoon ground thyme
2 tablespoons mild curry powder or curry powder to taste
2 cups light cream

Drop the shrimp in boiling water. Bring again to the boiling point. Lower heat; simmer for 5 minutes for medium shrimp, 2-3 minutes for baby shrimp. Drain, cool, shell, and, if the shrimp are large, remove the black vein with the point of a knife or a skewer. Heat the butter in a large skillet. Add the onion, apple, and celery. Cook, stirring constantly, for about 3 minutes. Add the water. Simmer over low heat until the vegetables are tender and almost dry. Season with salt and pepper and stir in the thyme and curry powder. Stir in the cream; add the shrimp. Mix well. Simmer over low heat, stirring frequently, until the cream has cooked down to the consistency of thin-to-medium white sauce. Makes four to six servings.

Saturday

Chicken Breasts in Cream Chez Moi

Chicken Breasts in Cream Chez Moi
Yellow Rice
Sautéed Zucchini
Ice Cream with Rum Sauce

2 tablespoons butter
2 tablespoons salad oil
4 large chicken breasts, halved, skinned, preferably boned
salt
freshly ground pepper
⅓ cup brandy
½ pound mushrooms, thinly sliced
1 tablespoon Dijon mustard
1 cup heavy cream
juice of ½ lemon

Heat butter and oil in a large, heavy frying pan. Add chicken breasts bone-side down, side by side. If the pan is not large enough, do 4 pieces, then add a little more butter and do the other 4. Cook the chicken over medium heat for about 5-7 minutes or until golden brown, turning once. Lower the heat and cook without a cover for about 10 minutes, turning once, or until chicken is about three-quarters cooked. Transfer to another frying pan and sprinkle with salt and pepper. Reserve the first pan and juices until needed again. Heat the brandy in a large spoon by holding it over the heat in the stove, pour over the chicken pieces, and flame. Keep chicken warm in a very low oven or at the back of the stove. Cook the mushrooms in the juices of the pan in which the chicken was first cooked. When mushrooms are golden but still firm, sprinkle them over the chicken. Stir the mustard into the cream. Pour over the chicken. Cover; cook over low heat 5-10 minutes or until chicken is tender; do not overcook. Check the seasoning and stir in the lemon juice before serving on a hot platter. Serves four to six.

QUICK & EASY DINNERS FOR TWO

January

Sunday

Braised Artichokes and Peas

Little Steaks
Braised Artichokes and Peas
Belgian Endive Salad
Chocolate Pudding

2 big artichokes, thinly sliced
water or beef bouillon
olive oil (it *must* be *olive* oil)
salt
freshly ground pepper
1 teaspoon dried basil *or*
½ teaspoon ground thyme or marjoram
1 to 1½ cups fresh shelled peas or frozen peas

Basic recipe for preparing artichokes: have ready a bowl of acidulated water; that is, combine 1 quart water and 2 tablespoons lemon juice or vinegar. Drop the artichokes into this as they are being cut up to avoid discoloration. A lot of artichoke is waste matter because it is tough and bitter. Remove the tough outer leaves of the artichoke. Stop when the leaves are greenish-white, two-thirds up from the artichoke's base. Dip artichoke in acidulated water and lay on its side. With a sharp knife, cut off green parts of leaves, with spikes, in one stroke, leaving only the light part. Again dip artichoke in acidulated water. Cut off stem, leaving about ¼ to ½ inch, depending on its condition. Peel the base and the remaining stem. Cut artichoke into 4 parts, as you would an apple. Drop these into acidulated water. Take out one and core it like an apple; cut off all fuzz in the middle. Drop into acidulated water immediately and work on the next pieces. Drain and dry before using in the recipe.

Small tender artichokes may be cooked cut in quarters. Larger, not so tender ones (the majority) should be cut into thin slices, the tougher the artichoke, the thinner the slice. Work quickly, slicing them directly into acidulated water to prevent discoloration.

Put artichokes into a heavy saucepan. Add an equal amount of water or bouillon and olive oil to come halfway up the artichokes. Season with salt and pepper and add the basil. Bring to a boil. Reduce heat to very low. Simmer, covered, until artichokes are about half done. If necessary, add a little more water to avoid scorching; if too soupy, cook uncovered. Add the peas. Cook, covered, until vegetables are tender.

Note: Minced leftover ham or prosciutto may be added to the artichokes.

Monday

Black Bean Casserole

Broiled Ham with Raisin Sauce
Black Bean Casserole
Cornbread
Green Salad
Orange, Grapefruit and Banana Fruit Salad

1 1-pound can black beans
4-6 slices bacon, shredded
1 small onion, minced
1 small garlic clove, minced
salt
freshly ground pepper
¼ teaspoon ground thyme

Drain the beans, leaving about 3 tablespoons of liquid on them. Combine the bacon, onion, and garlic in a small casserole. Cook over medium heat, stirring frequently, until the bacon looks glassy and is about to crisp. Add the beans, salt and pepper to taste, and the thyme; mix well. Simmer, covered, for 10 minutes or until the beans are heated through.

Note: Other canned beans may be treated in the same manner. The casserole can be kept for hours on a very low flame covered with an asbestos flame cover. Stir occasionally. Good reheated.

Tuesday

Quick Madeira Stew

Quick Madeira Stew
Buttered Rice or Noodles
Watercress
Ginger-Flavored Homemade Applesauce

1 tablespoon butter
1 tablespoon oil
2-3 large shallots *or* 1 small onion, minced
¾ pound top or bottom round, cut into 1 × 3-inch strips
1 medium tomato, peeled and diced
salt
freshly ground pepper
¼ teaspoon ground marjoram or thyme
¼ cup dry Madeira or Sherry

Heat the butter and oil in a frying pan. Cook the shallots or onion in it until soft and barely golden. Add the meat. Over medium heat, stirring constantly with a fork, cook until the meat is browned on both sides. Turn heat to low and add the remaining ingredients. Simmer for 10-15 minutes. Serve with rice or noodles.

Note: If a thicker sauce is desired, sprinkle 2 teaspoons of flour over the browned meat before adding the other ingredients. Then stir to avoid flour lumps.

Wednesday

Green Beans and Potatoes

Polish or Italian Sausages
Green Beans and Potatoes
Waldorf Salad
Apple Pie

2 tablespoons butter
1 medium onion, minced
½ pound green beans
 cut into 1-inch pieces
2 medium potatoes, peeled
 and cut into ¼-inch slices
¾ cup chicken bouillon
salt
freshly ground pepper
¼ teaspoon dried thyme

Heat the butter in a saucepan with a tight lid. Cook the onion until soft. Stir in the beans. Mix well so that the beans are coated with the buttery onions. Place the sliced potatoes over the beans. Add the chicken bouillon. Season lightly with salt (the bouillon may be salty) and pepper and add the thyme. Bring to a boil and turn heat to very low. Cover tightly. Simmer for 15 minutes or until beans and potatoes are tender. Check occasionally for moisture; if necessary, add a little hot water, one tablespoon at a time.

Thursday

Finocchio and Shrimp Salad

Cream of Mushroom Soup
Finocchio and Shrimp Salad
Broccoli Vinaigrette
Fresh Fruit and Macaroons

1 large or 2 small heads
 finocchio (fennel)
juice of 1 small lemon
¾ pound cooked, shelled,
 and deveined shrimp
salt
freshly ground pepper
homemade mayonnaise to taste
salad greens
3 tablespoons minced parsley

Cut off the green tops and "fingers" of the finocchio; remove the hard outer leaves; cut off the hard stem. Cut each finocchio in half; cut each half into thin slices. Place the slices in a mixing bowl and sprinkle with lemon juice. Add the shrimp and toss with a fork. Season cautiously with salt and pepper — the mayonnaise may be highly seasoned. Add mayonnaise to taste. Toss again with fork. Line a serving dish with salad greens. Pile the finocchio and shrimp salad on top. Sprinkle with minced parsley.

Friday

Oyster Stew

Oyster Stew
Pilot Crackers
Cheese Tray
Watercress, Apples, Pears
Brownies

1 cup milk
1 cup light cream
1 pint oysters, picked over to remove bits of shell
⅓ cup cold water
2 tablespoons butter, cut into small pieces
salt
freshly ground pepper

Combine the milk and cream in a saucepan; scald. In another saucepan combine the oysters and water. Cook until the oysters are plump and beginning to curl at the edges — about 2 minutes. With a slotted spoon, transfer the oysters to the milk mixture. Strain the oyster liquid into the saucepan with the oysters. Stir in the butter; season with salt and pepper. If necessary, heat through but do *not* boil. Serve in heated soup plates or bowls, with pilot crackers.

Saturday

Boiled Artichokes with Piquant Green Sauce

Spaghetti and Meatballs
Boiled Artichokes with Piquant Green Sauce
Fresh Pineapple and Kirsch

2 large boiled artichokes
salad greens
Piquant Green Sauce

Piquant Green Sauce

2 tablespoons drained capers
1 tablespoon minced onion
1 large garlic clove, minced
2 cups parsley heads without stems, tightly packed
1 teaspoon dried or fresh basil
1 hard-cooked egg, cut into quarters
¾ cup olive oil
juice of 1 large or 2 small lemons
1 teaspoon salt
freshly ground pepper

Combine all ingredients in a blender. Blend to a puree.

Note: This sauce is excellent for hot or cold broiled meats, seafood, hard-cooked eggs (as antipasto), and other cooked vegetables, such as cauliflower and broccoli.

BUDGET DINNERS

January

Sunday

Thrifty Waldorf Chocolate Cake

Roast Chicken
Potatoes
Green Vegetable
Thrifty Waldorf Chocolate Cake

2 cups sifted flour
1 cup sugar
½ teaspoon salt
⅓ cup cocoa, preferably Dutch-processed cocoa
1 teaspoon baking soda
1 cup water
2 teaspoons vanilla flavoring
⅔ cup mayonnaise

This is a famous old cake — very good and easy. Unless you tell, no one will know that it's made with mayonnaise.

Sift the flour, sugar, salt, cocoa, and baking soda together into a bowl. Mix thoroughly. Add the water, vanilla, and mayonnaise. Blend thoroughly. Beat the batter 100 strokes or until it is smooth. Grease and line with waxed paper two 8-inch layer pans. Spoon the batter into the pans. Bake in a preheated moderate 350° oven for 30 to 35 minutes or until the cake shrinks away from the pan, or, make a single layer in a 9 × 9 × 2-inch pan; bake about 45 minutes. Frost in any desired way.

Monday

Lima and Beef Stew

Lima and Beef Stew
Buttered Rice
Coleslaw
Applesauce

1 pound dried lima beans
3 tablespoons butter
1 tablespoon olive oil
1 pound chuck or round, cut into 1-to 1½-inch cubes
1 or 2 garlic cloves, minced
1 stalk celery, cut into 1½-inch pieces
1 teaspoon coriander seeds (optional)
salt
approximately 6 cups hot water
juice of 1 lemon

Soak the beans overnight; drain. Heat the butter and oil in a heavy saucepan. Brown the beef on all sides. Add the garlic, celery, coriander, and salt. Add the hot water and bring to a boil. Reduce heat, cover, and simmer over low heat for about 2–3 hours. Check for moisture; if necessary, add a little more water. The liquid and beans should be cooked down to almost a puree. To serve, remove meat pieces and keep warm. Stir the lemon juice into the beans and place in a serving dish. Top with the meat. Serve with a pilaf of rice. Serves six.

Tuesday

Spaghetti with Zucchini Beef Sauce

Spaghetti with Zucchini Beef Sauce
Green Salad and Cheese

2 tablespoons olive oil
1 pound ground chuck beef
1 garlic clove, crushed
1 pound small zucchini, sliced
1 cup diced green peppers
2 medium tomatoes, quartered
salt
freshly ground pepper
¼ cup water
2 tablespoons flour
½ to 1 pound spaghetti or other pasta, freshly cooked
freshly grated Parmesan cheese

Heat the oil in a heavy saucepan. Add the beef and garlic. Cook over medium heat, stirring occasionally, for about 5 minutes. Add the zucchini, peppers, tomatoes, and salt and pepper to taste. Cover; cook over low heat, stirring frequently, for about 20 minutes or until the zucchini is tender but not mushy. If necessary to prevent scorching, add 2 tablespoons of the water. For a thicker sauce, blend 2 tablespoons water with the flour. Stir into the sauce. Cook, stirring constantly, until thickened.

While the sauce is cooking, cook the spaghetti or other pasta in plenty of boiling salted water. Do not overcook. Drain, place in deep serving dish, and pour sauce over the spaghetti. Serve with plenty of freshly grated Parmesan cheese on the side.

Wednesday

Cranberry Pork Chops

Cranberry Pork Chops
Baked Potatoes
String Bean Salad
Fruit Salad

6 large pork chops
salt
freshly ground pepper
4 cups raw cranberries, ground
  or chopped very fine
¾ cup honey
½ teaspoon ground ginger
  or cloves

Trim surplus fat from the pork chops. Heat a heavy frying pan. Quickly brown the chops on both sides over high heat. Place 3 pork chops side by side in a greased baking dish. Season with salt and pepper. Mix together the cranberries, honey, and spice. Spoon half of this mixture over the pork chops. Top with the remaining 3 chops; sprinkle these with salt and pepper. Spread the remaining cranberry mixture over the meat. Cover the baking dish with a lid or tie foil over it to cover. Bake in a preheated 350° oven for about 1 hour or until tender. Makes four to six servings.

Thursday

Dried Beef and Corn on Buttered Biscuits or Toast

Dried Beef and Corn on
Buttered Biscuits
or Toast
Green Salad
Brownies

1 #2 can whole-kernel corn or
  about 2-3 cups whole-kernel
  corn with liquid
2 tablespoons butter
1 2½-ounce jar shredded beef,
  cut into strips
2 tablespoons flour
¼ teaspoon ground thyme
1 can cream of mushroom soup,
  undiluted
salt
freshly ground pepper

This recipe can easily be doubled or tripled. If the beef is very salty, soak in cold water for 5 minutes, then drain.

Drain the corn and reserve the liquid. Heat the butter in a heavy saucepan. Add the corn and the beef. Cook over medium heat, stirring constantly, for about 2–3 minutes or until dried. Stir in the flour. Cook for 1 minute longer, or until golden brown. Add thyme. Stir in the liquid from the corn and the soup. Cook over medium heat, stirring constantly, until thickened. Check the seasoning; if necessary, add a little salt and pepper. Serve over hot biscuits, hot toast, or buttered rice. Makes two or three servings.

Friday

Tuna Fish with Noodles and Cheese

Tuna Fish with Noodles and Cheese
Waldorf Salad
Cake and Fruit

1 13-ounce can tuna fish, drained
2 cups medium cooked noodles
2 tablespoons finely chopped olives or parsley
1 recipe Cheese Sauce (see below)
½ cup buttered bread crumbs

Cheese Sauce

3 tablespoons butter
3 tablespoons flour
salt
freshly ground pepper
2 cups milk
¾ cup shredded Swiss or Cheddar cheese

Flake the tuna. Make alternate layers of tuna and noodles in a greased baking dish. Sprinkle each layer with olives or parsley and top with some of the Cheese Sauce. Sprinkle the top with the buttered bread crumbs. Bake in a preheated 350° oven for about 20 minutes or until browned and bubbly on top. Makes four or five servings.

Cheese Sauce: Heat the butter in a heavy saucepan. Stir in flour, salt and pepper. Cook over low heat, stirring constantly, for about 2 minutes. Stir in milk. Cook, stirring constantly, for 3 to 5 minutes or until the sauce thickens and is smooth. Stir in the cheese. Cook, stirring constantly, until the cheese has melted.

Saturday

Stuffed Flank Steak

Stuffed Flank Steak
Sautéed Onions
Home Fried Potatoes
Fruit

1 flank steak (about 2–3 pounds)
1 teaspoon salt
freshly ground pepper
⅛ teaspoon ground ginger
stuffing of your choice
2 tablespoons shortening or salad oil
½ cup boiling water

Score the flank steak. Pound it with a meat mallet, wooden potato masher, or the edge of a heavy plate, making it as thin as possible. Rub the salt, pepper, and ginger into the meat. Spread stuffing on the meat. Roll the meat lengthwise and tie securely with string in 5 places, or sew it together. Heat the shortening in a heavy casserole with a cover and brown the meat roll on all sides. Add the water; cover. Lower heat; simmer for about 1½ hours or until meat is very tender, turning occasionally. To serve, remove the string or thread and carve diagonally against the grain of the meat. Makes four to six servings.

ENTERTAINING

January

Sunday

Belgian Waterzooie of Chicken

Belgian Waterzooie of Chicken
Brown Bread and Butter
Tossed Green Salad with Capers and Anchovies
Rum Parfait

4 tablespoons butter
4 large leeks, white parts only
4 celery stalks, chopped
2 carrots, chopped
1 onion, chopped
⅛ teaspoon ground nutmeg
⅛ teaspoon ground thyme
1 bay leaf

2 3-pound chickens, cut into pieces
6 to 7 cups chicken bouillon
3 egg yolks
½ cup heavy cream
salt
freshly ground pepper
juice of 1 lemon
⅓ cup minced parsley

Heat butter in a large, heavy saucepan or casserole. Cook, stirring constantly, all vegetables and herbs, except parsley, in the butter for about 5 minutes, or until vegetables are semisoft but not browmed. Lay the chicken pieces over the vegetables. Add enough bouillon to cover meat. Bring to a boil; cover; reduce heat to low. Simmer for 30 to 40 minutes or until the chicken is tender but not overcooked. Remove the chicken from the broth. Strain the broth, reserving both the liquid and the veretables. Chill liquid; remove all fat that accumulates on top. Puree the vegetables in a blender. Skin the chicken pieces and discard the skin. Cut off meat in as large pieces as possible. Keep in a warm place. Heat broth in a large saucepan over high heat, reducing it to about 4 cups. Beat together egg yolks and heavy cream. Away from the heat, stir egg mixture into hot broth; stir constantly to avoid curdling. Add the chicken. Over very low heat, heat broth and chicken but do not boil. Taste for seasoning and add salt and pepper. Remove from heat. Stir in lemon juice and parsley. Turn into a deep serving dish or soup tureen. Serve each guest with both chicken and sauce, which should have the consistency of heavy cream. Serves six.

Monday

Onion Soup Chablis

Onion Soup Chablis
Caviar Omelets
Bread Sticks
Avocado and Grapefruit Salad
Lemon Sherbet
Cookies

2 pounds small white onions
½ cup butter
2 tablespoons salad oil
8 cups chicken bouillon
2 cups Chablis or dry white wine
salt
freshly ground pepper
2 cups light cream
½ cup grated Swiss cheese

Peel the onions and slice them very thin. Heat together the butter and oil in a heavy saucepan. Cook the onions in it over low heat until they are soft and transparent but not browned. Add the chicken bouillon. Simmer, uncovered, until the mixture is reduced by half. Add the Chablis and season with salt and pepper. Salt lightly because the bouillon may be salty. Bring to the boiling point. Lower heat and simmer, covered, for about 10 minutes. Stir in the cream. Heat through, but do not boil. Serve the soup very hot in warmed soup plates or bowls and sprinkle each serving with cheese. Serves four to six.

Tuesday

Country Captain

Country Captain
Rice
Chutney
Persimmon, Avocado, and Grapefruit Salad
Brandy Cream Pie

¼ cup flour
1 teaspoon salt
½ teaspoon pepper
2 3-to 3½-pound frying chickens, cut into serving pieces
2 tablespoons butter
1 tablespoon salad oil
3 medium onions, minced
2 green pepper, seeded and diced
2 garlic cloves, minced
3 to 4 teaspoons curry powder, or to taste
1 teaspoon dried thyme
4 cups canned plum tomatoes, chopped
⅓ cup dried currants or seedless raisins
½ cup chopped toasted almonds

Put the flour, salt, and pepper into a paper bag. Add the chicken pieces, a few at a time, and shake the bag to coat them evenly. Shake off excess flour. Heat the butter and oil in a large frying pan or Dutch oven. Brown the chicken pieces on all sides, turning frequently. Remove from pan. Add onions, peppers, and garlic to the fat in the pan. Cook for about 5 minutes, or until tender but not browned, adding more butter if necessary to prevent sticking. Stir in curry powder and thyme; cook 2 minutes longer. Add tomatoes. Simmer, uncovered, for 15 minutes. Put the chicken back into the sauce; simmer, covered, for about 25 minutes. Add the currants during the last 10 minutes of cooking time. Before serving, sprinkle with chopped almonds. Serves six.

Wednesday

Ragout of Mushrooms and Eggs

Clear Consommé with Sherry
Cheese Sticks
Roast Pheasant
Ragout of Mushrooms and Eggs
Green Beans Vinaigrette
Guava Shells with Cream Cheese and Crackers

2 tablespoons olive oil
2 tablespoons butter
2 big shallots, minced, or 2 tablespoons minced onion
¼ cup minced parsley
1 pound fresh mushrooms, sliced
2 tablespoons flour
⅔ cup dry white wine
salt
freshly ground pepper
6 hard-cooked eggs, coarsely chopped

Heat the olive oil and butter in a wide, rather shallow saucepan. Cook the shallots, or onion, and the parsley 3 to 4 minutes or until they are soft but not brown. Add the mushrooms. Simmer, covered, for about 10 minutes, stirring frequently. Stir in the flour; cook, stirring constantly, for 2 minutes. Stir in the wine. Simmer for about 5 minutes. Season with salt and pepper to taste. Add the eggs; heat through thoroughly. Serve very hot. Serves four to six.
Note: One favored herb, such as thyme or tarragon, may be added, to taste.

Thursday

Flemish Carrots

Fresh Spinach Soup
Wiener Schnitzel
Flemish Carrots
Brussels Sprouts with Chestnuts
Sliced Oranges with Grand Marnier
Almond Cookies

8 large carrots, peeled and cut into matchsticks
½ cup hot water
½ cup butter
salt
freshly ground pepper
1 teaspoon sugar
2 egg yolks
½ to ⅔ cup heavy cream
2 tablespoons melted butter
2 tablespoons fresh lemon juice
2 tablespoons minced parsley

Put the carrots into a saucepan and add boiling water to cover them. Cook over high heat for 2 minutes. Drain the carrots. Put them into a heavy buttered casserole. Add the water, butter, salt, pepper, and sugar. Bring quickly to a boil and reduce heat to very low. Cook, covered, for about 10 minutes or until still crisp. Shake the casserole every 3 or 4 minutes to prevent sticking; if necessary, add a tablespoon or two of hot water. If soupy, cook without a cover. Beat together the egg yolks, heavy cream, melted butter, and lemon juice. Pour over the carrots, mix well, and heat through without boiling. Sprinkle with the parsley and serve immediately. Serves four to six.

Friday

Trout with Cream and Almond Sauce

Oeufs à la Russe
Trout with Cream and Almond Sauce
Boiled Potatoes
Tossed Green Salad
Brie Cheese
Hot Deep-dish Apple Pie with Cream

4 fresh trout, about 1 pound each, prepared for cooking
salt
flour
1 cup butter
½ cup slivered blanched almonds
½ to ¾ cup heavy cream
¼ cup minced parsley

Wash and dry the fish. Sprinkle the cavity of each with a little salt. Coat them on all sides with flour and shake off the excess. Heat the butter in a large, deep frying pan. Cook the trout over medium heat in the butter for 4 to 5 minutes on each side, or until golden brown. The fish should flake easily when tested with a toothpick. Remove the cooked trout to a hot platter and keep warm. Cook the almonds in the same frying pan until golden, stirring constantly. Stir in the cream. Cook, stirring constantly, for about 2 minutes. Pour the sauce over the trout and sprinkle with the parsley. Serves four.

Saturday

All-Day Open House

Fish

Different varieties of canned herring, sardines, anchovies, sliced smoked salmon, salmon mousse, tuna fish salad, shrimp in beer, shrimp salad, seafood salad, cold lobster with mayonnaise, jellied trout, cold bass, smoked eel

Meats

Sliced ham, sliced cold roast beef, beef tartare, assorted cold cuts, cold roast chicken, chicken in aspic, chicken salad, sliced smoked turkey, jellied veal loaf, sliced cold tongue, sliced cold meat loaf, patés

Salads

Marinated cucumbers, pickled beets, marinated mixed-vegetable salad, cauliflower with mayonnaise, shredded carrots with raisins, knob celery remoulade, trays with carrot and celery sticks, raw cauliflorets, green pepper and turnip strips, tomato wedges, black and green olives, to be dipped in different mayonnaises such as horseradish mayonnaise, mustard mayonnaise, and curry mayonnaise, white bean and chick-pea salads

Hot dishes

Veal casserole with Water Chestnuts*, Swedish meatballs, seafood Newburg, chicken or turkey has, yellow rice pilaf, creamed potatoes, baked beans, baked hominy grits

Cheeses

Sharp cheddar, Swiss, Port Salut, Bel Paese, Boursin, any kind of cheese, including creamy cheeses

Desserts

One's own pet cakes and cookies, pineapple with rum or kirsch, cut-up oranges, grapefruit, and bananas, any available fresh fruit, almonds (shelled) and raisins mixed, box of fancy candy, Swiss bitter chocolate (Lindt, Tobler)

Drinks

So many flavors occur in smorgasbord foods that it would be far too complicated to serve a wine suited to each. Do as the Scandinavians, who consume theirs with akvavit and beer. For people who don't like akvavit and beer, have some good-quality chilled rosé. Do not serve your finer wines, since they would be wasted.

Aalborg akvavit, well chilled, imported beers, Rosé wines: Almadén Grenache Rosé, Concannon Zinfandel Rosé

**Recipe in book*

A smorgasbord lends itself well to an open-house party. It can be as simple or as elaborate as desired, is not an expensive form of entertaining, can be produced for any number of people, and the foods keep well.

The table should look colorful and inviting. The foods must be arranged in a neat, orderly manner, so that they can be eaten in their proper order; that is, in courses, beginning with fish. The best way to arrange a smorgasbord is on a long table, displaying the dishes at different heights.

To set the table, place the plates, silverware, and napkins at one end. There should be enough plates and silver to enable people to change plates between courses. Not all the guests turn up at the same time, so it is possible to wash plates and silverware between guests.

The food can be arranged either in rows or in related groups. Hot dishes are usually placed at one end of the table on hot plates, candle warmers, and hot trays, to keep them hot. Cakes, desserts, coffee, and tea are best served from another table.

The smorgasbord must include several kinds of bread, such as white, light and dark rye, pumpernickel, rye crisp, and Norwegian flat bread. There should be plenty of butter, sliced, or if the hostess has the patience, shaped into rolls or curls. Each butter dish should be garnished with a sprig of fresh parsley. There should also be many different cheeses, served in large chunks.

Making the foods look attractive is an important part of a smorgasbord. Canned fish can be served in its own can, provided the lids are rolled back neatly to show the contents of the can. Each can is set on its own little plate, and the plate is garnished with a little lettuce, parsley, or dill and a radish rosette or a lemon slice, to make the can look as pretty as possible. Cold cuts and ham and roast beef slices should be arranged on platters, in overlapping slices. The pâtés may be surrounded with chopped aspic; salmon slices can be topped with a twisted lemon slice; and salads should be bedded on lettuce. The whole should look like a colorful food painting.

A smorgasbord, for our purposes, need not be an exercise in Swedish authenticity, but a product of the hostess' imagination.

Veal Casserole with Water Chestnuts

½ cup butter
4 tablespoons salad oil
3 pounds trimmed boneless veal, cut into 1-inch cubes
2 medium onions, thinly sliced
1 large garlic clove, minced
2 teaspoons salt
freshly ground pepper
¼ teaspoon Tabasco or cayenne
2 pounds fresh mushrooms, thickly sliced
¾ cup beef bouillon
⅓ to ½ cup thinly sliced fresh peeled ginger
½ teaspoon ground cardamom
2 bay leaves, crushed
4 5-ounce cans water chestnuts, drained and sliced
½ cup brandy
2 cups heavy cream
⅔ cup minced parsley

The veal must be trimmed of all fat and gristle. From 4 pounds of boneless veal, there will be a little over 3 pounds of meat after trimming. If a double quantity of this dish is desired, it is easier and better to make up two batches than to double the ingredients.

Heat half of the butter and 2 tablespoons of the oil in a large, deep frying pan. Over high heat, in batches, brown the veal on all sides. Using a slotted spoon, transfer the veal into a 3-quart oven-proof casserole. Add the onions and the garlic to the frying pan. Cook, stirring constantly, until the onion is just soft and barely golden. Stir in the salt, pepper, and Tabasco. Add the onions to the meat; mix well. Heat the remaining butter and oil in the same frying pan. Over high heat, stirring constantly, cook the mushrooms for 2-3 minutes. They must remain firm and white. Using a slotted spoon, add the mushrooms to the meat. Mix well. Pour off any excess fat in the frying pan. Deglaze the bottom of the frying pan with ¼ cup of the bouillon. Add this to the casserole with the remaining bouillon. Add the ginger, cardamom, bay leaves, and water chestnuts. Mix well. Cover the casserole. Cook in a preheated 350° oven for about 1 hour or until the meat is just tender. Check the seasoning and the moisture content. The liquid should reach halfway up the meat. If necessary, add a little more bouillon. After ¾ hour cooking time, stir in the brandy. Check the seasoning again. After 55 minutes cooking time, stir in the cream. Cook uncovered for about 10 more minutes. Sprinkle with parsley before serving. Makes eight to ten servings.

Note: If fresh ginger is not available, use the ginger canned in water that is available in oriental stores. Do not use sweetened ginger. The consistency of the sauce should be on the thin side. But if it is too thin and will not reduce sufficiently, combine 1 tablespoon of flour with 2 tablespoons cold water and make a paste. Stir this paste into the casserole after the addition of the cream and cook 5 minutes longer.

FEBRUARY

One of the very best ways of saving money is not to cook too much; that is, cook only what you expect will be eaten up — unless you are deliberately planning to have some leftovers for other meals, or you're cooking ahead for freezing. Haphazard leftovers all too often age in the refrigerator because the cook isn't quite sure what to do with them, or because, after all, she can't be bothered. Few leftovers are as attractive as they were when freshly cooked. The foods that actually improve on their second time around, such as stews and curries, have to be treated carefully when heated up or they will be vastly overcooked; slow heating does it.

Another way of saving is to serve small first helpings and ask people to come back for more, if they want it. Almost every cook overestimates the appetite of her public, with the result that much food is left on plates, a total waste unless there is a pig to feed. Now that we know we Americans must not waste food, let us begin with cooking less and serving smaller portions.

FEBRUARY

	FAMILY FARE	
	LUNCHES	DINNERS
Sunday	Grapefruit with Honey Onion Eggs* French Bread, Cheeses	Egg Noodles and Sauerbraten* Green Salad Baked Mocha Custard
Monday	Thick Barley Soup* Cheese Sandwiches Carrot Sticks Nuts and Raisins	Beef Goulash* Wheat Pilaff Cucumbers in Sour Cream Applesauce with Ginger
Tuesday	Egg Salad Sandwiches Radishes Blitz Torte*	Chicken Enchiladas with Sour Cream* Mexican Beans Lettuce and Tomato Salad Apricot Pie
Wednesday	Meatball Soup* Apple, Orange and Banana Salad	Pork Fillet with Prunes and Apricots* Braised Celery Brown Rice with Almonds Meringues and Ice Cream
Thursday	Homefried Spaghetti* Green Salad Chocolate Pudding	Boiled Beef with Vegetables and Horseradish Sauce* Cucumber Salad Cherry Pie
Friday	Cold Cuts Baked Mushrooms* Fruit and Cheese	Shrimp Gumbo* Rice Carrot and Celery Sticks Bavarian Cream
Saturday	Onion Omelet* Sliced Tomatoes Apples and Cheese	Pork Chops with Herbs and Wine* Mashed Squash Tomato Aspic Fruit Salad of Oranges, Grapefruit and Bananas

QUICK & EASY Dinners For Two	BUDGET DINNERS	ENTERTAINING
Piquant Beef Stew* Mashed Potatoes Buttered Carrots Avocado Vinaigrette Chocolate Cake	Smoked Boneless Butt Belgian Red Cabbage and Apples* Hashed Potatoes Lemon Chiffon Pie	Tortino of Artichokes* Peas with Prosciutto* Orange and Onion Salad Brownies
Bob Holleron's Crema Azteca Bean Soup* Chef Salad Hot Garlic Bread Cherries Jubilee	Lasagne Verdi Bolognese* Tomato Aspic Salad Vanilla Pudding	Scalloped Oysters Ham Biscuits* Brussels Sprouts with Buttered Crumbs Pecan Pie
Leeks with Lemon Juice* Broiled Ham Steak Rice with Cheese Sauce Brownies	Potato, Sausage and Cabbage Casserole* Green Salad with Roquefort Dressing Baked Apples with Cream	Fillet of Beef* Baked Stuffed Mushrooms Amber Onions* Endive Salad with Avocado Dressing Coffee Jelly with Whipped Cream
Belgian Pork Chops* Red Cabbage Boiled Potatoes Coffee Sponge	Hamburger Soufflé* Molded Vegetable Salad Canned Peaches and Cupcakes	Cream of Lettuce Soup* Ham Slices in a Sherry-and-Raisin Sauce Gratin Dauphinois Broccoli Puree Lemon Meringue Pie
Thick Potato Soup Margarethe Schanne's Hamburgers* Tossed Green Salad Broiled Grapefruit with Honey	Chicken and Rice Pilaff* Coleslaw from Red Cabbage Jellied Dark Sweet Cherries	Spinach Soufflé Russian Braised Veal* Heart of Palms Salad Chocolate Mousse Almond Cookies
Coquilles St. Jacques* Rice Pilaff Mixed Green Salad Baked Apples	Chow Mein Fried Rice* Carrot Salad Chocolate Pudding	Cold Celery Remoulade Italian Baked Rice Timbale* Mushroom or Tomato Sauce Grilled Tomatoes Cheese Tray, Apples and Pears
Lamb Chops Finocchio Au Gratin* Yellow Risotto Grapes in Sour Cream and Brown Sugar	Baked Chicken and Biscuits Green Salad Quick Applesauce Cream* Cookies	Malay Curry* Indian Pilau* Mango Chutney Lemon Chutney Any Fresh Homemade Chutneys Little Bowls with Chopped Salted Peanuts, Fried Plaintain Rounds, Crumbled Crisp Bacon, Fried Chopped Eggplant and Finely Chopped Green (Spring) Onions Cucumbers in Yogurt or Sour Cream Dressing Caramel Custard or Bavarian Cream or Fresh Fruit Salad

FAMILY FARE LUNCHES

February

Sunday

Grapefruit with Honey
Onion Eggs
French Bread, Cheeses

Onion Eggs

1 tablespoon butter or cooking oil
2 medium onions, sliced
¼ cup water
salt
freshly ground pepper
¼ teaspoon nutmeg or allspice
2 eggs

A good dish when you don't know what to have, made from ingredients always at hand. It is attractive to cook the Onion Eggs in individual metal or china baking dishes.

Heat the butter in a frying pan or an individual baking dish. Add the onions. Cook over medium heat, stirring constantly, for 2-3 minutes or until the onions begin to turn golden. Add water, salt, pepper and nutmeg. Cover and simmer over very low heat until the onions are extremely soft and mushy — at least 10 minutes. Stir occasionally and if the onions show signs of scorching, add a little more water, one tablespoon at a time. Make 2 little wells in the onions and break one egg into each. Cover and cook until the eggs are set. Serve immediately, with French bread. Recipe makes one serving.

Note: You can cook as many onions and eggs at one time as your skillet will hold. Increase quantities accordingly.

Monday

Thick Barley Soup

Thick Barley Soup
Cheese Sandwiches
Carrot Sticks
Nuts and Raisins

3 tablespoons butter
½ cup medium barley
1 celery stalk, minced
1 large onion, minced
1 large carrot, minced
1 tablespoon flour
8 cups hot chicken or beef bouillon
salt
freshly ground pepper
½ cup heavy cream or more to taste

Melt the butter in a large, heavy saucepan. Over medium heat add barley, celery, onion and carrot and cook until the barley is golden. Stir in the flour and cook for 1 minute longer. Add the hot bouillon. Simmer covered for about 30 minutes or until the barley is tender. Season with salt and pepper to taste. Just before serving, stir in the cream. Makes four to six servings.

Note: This soup can be made ahead of time and reheated with perfect success. Only the cream must be added at the last moment, after the soup has been reheated.

Tuesday

Blitz Torte

Egg Salad Sandwiches
Radishes
Blitz Torte

1⅓ cups flour
1⅓ teaspoons baking powder
½ cup butter
1½ cups sugar
4 eggs, separated
5 tablespoons milk
½ cup chopped blanched almonds
½ cup strawberry or raspberry jam

Sift together the flour and baking powder. Sift once more. Cream the butter until soft. Add ½ cup of sugar, a little at a time, and beat well after each addition. Add the egg yolks, one at a time. Beat in the flour and milk alternately, beginning and ending with flour. Beat the egg whites until stiff and beat in the remaining cup of sugar, 2-3 tablespoons at a time. Beat until the egg whites are very stiff and glossy. Spoon the cake batter into 2 well greased and floured 8-or 9-inch cake pans. Spread the beaten egg whites evenly over the cake batter in the 2 pans. Sprinkle almonds over the egg whites. Bake in a preheated oven 325° for 25 minutes. Turn up the heat to 350° and bake for 25 minutes longer. Cool the cakes in their pans. When cool, turn out and sandwich together with the jam on the meringue side. Makes one 8-or 9-inch cake.

Note: This Torte should be made and eaten on the same day. It does not "hold" well.

Wednesday

Meatball Soup

Meatball Soup
Apple, Orange and Banana Salad

6 cups beef bouillon
1 2 lb. 3-ounce can Italian-type tomatoes, undrained
2 green peppers, coarsely chopped
2 carrots, cut into ½-inch slices
2 onions, coarsely chopped
1½ to 2 pounds lean ground beef
salt
dash of Tabasco
2 tablespoons minced parsley
4 tablespoons butter
½ cup freshly grated Parmesan cheese

Pour the beef bouillon into a large saucepan. Add the tomatoes, peppers, carrots and onions. Bring to boil. Lower heat, cover and simmer for 10 minutes or until the vegetables are tender but still retain their shapes. Combine the beef with a little salt, Tabasco and parsley. Shape into marble-sized balls. Heat the butter in a frying pan and use to brown the meatballs. Ten minutes before serving, drop the meatballs into the soup. Simmer for 5-10 more minutes. Serve in deep soup plates with cheese sprinkled over the soup. Serves six.

Thursday

Homefried Spaghetti

Homefried Spaghetti
Green Salad
Chocolate Pudding

8 ounces spaghetti
4 eggs
2 teaspoons salt
freshly ground pepper
2 teaspoons instant minced onion
½ cup grated Parmesan cheese
¼ cup butter

Cook the spaghetti in plenty of salted boiling water until just tender. Drain thoroughly. Beat together the eggs, salt, pepper, onion and Parmesan cheese. Heat the butter in a frying pan and add the spaghetti. Pour the egg mixture over the spaghetti and mix well with a fork. Cook until the eggs are set and the mixture is golden brown and crisp at the bottom. Makes four to five servings.

Variation: Add 1 cup diced Mozzarella cheese to the egg mixture.

Friday

Baked Mushrooms

Cold Cuts
Baked Mushrooms
Fruit and Cheese

4 canned artichoke bottoms, drained
1 pound fresh mushrooms
½ pound cooked ham, cut into ¼-inch cubes
2 cups tomato sauce
¼ cup currant jelly
2 teaspoons curry powder
4 tablespoons grated Parmesan cheese
4 tablespoons fine dry bread crumbs

Generously butter a shallow baking dish. Slice the artichoke bottoms into narrow strips and place them on the bottom of the dish. Separate the mushroom caps from the stems and reserve the stems for another use, such as soup or sauces. Place the mushroom caps, capside down, on the artichoke strips and sprinkle the diced ham over them. Heat the tomato sauce and stir in the currant jelly. Cook, stirring constantly, until the jelly dissolves. Then stir in the curry powder. Cool the sauce and pour it over the mushrooms. Sprinkle the cheese and bread crumbs over the sauce. Bake in a preheated 350° oven for about 20-30 minutes, or until the mushrooms are just tender. Four servings.

Saturday

Onion Omelet

Onion Omelet
Sliced Tomatoes
Apples and Cheese

½ cup butter
2 tablespoons olive oil
1 pound onions, minced
6 eggs, beaten
salt
freshly ground pepper

Heat the butter and the olive oil in a frying pan. Add the onions. Cook, stirring constantly, until they are soft and golden. Season the eggs with salt and pepper. Pour the eggs over the onions and mix well. Cook over low heat until the omelet is golden and set at the bottom. Turn and cook until set and golden. Makes four to six servings.

FAMILY FARE DINNERS

February

Sunday

Egg Noodles and Sauerbraten

Egg Noodles and Sauerbraten
Green Salad
Baked Mocha Custard

2 cups red wine vinegar
3 cups beef bouillon
3 medium onions, sliced
2 carrots, sliced
1 celery stalk, chopped
2 tablespoons salt
¼ tablespoon freshly ground pepper
10 peppercorns
2 tablespoons light brown sugar
4 bay leaves
6 whole cloves
4-pound beef rump roast
flour
2 tablespoons butter
1 tablespoon oil
½ cup dry red wine
⅔ cup finely crushed gingersnaps
1 pound medium egg noodles

Combine the vinegar, 2 cups of bouillon, onions, carrots, celery, 2 teaspoons salt, ¼ teaspoon pepper, light brown sugar, peppercorns, bay leaves and cloves in a large bowl; do not use aluminum. Place the meat in bowl and turn over several times so that it is wet with marinade. Cover and refrigerate for 3 days, turning on the second day. Remove meat from the marinade, reserving 2 cups of marinade and vegetables. Dry meat well and coat with flour. Heat butter and oil in a Dutch oven and brown meat on all sides. Pour off excess fat. Add the reserved marinade, vegetables and wine. Cover and simmer over low heat for 2½-3 hours or until meat is tender. Remove meat to a platter and keep warm. Strain the juices and add the remaining 1 cup bouillon and enough water to make 4 cups. Return to Dutch oven and add gingersnaps. Heat until gravy reaches boiling point, stirring constantly. Slice meat, overlapping slices on a heated serving dish. Dribble gravy over the slices and serve remaining gravy separately. While making the gravy, cook noodles in plenty of rapidly boiling salted water until tender. Drain in colander, place in heated serving bowl and toss with a few tablespoons of the gravy. Serves six.

Monday

Beef Goulash

Beef Goulash
Wheat Pilaff
Cucumbers in Sour Cream
Applesauce with Ginger

2 pounds beef, round or chuck, trim off all excess fat
3 tablespoons butter
2 large onions, sliced
1 tablespoon paprika
1 garlic clove, minced
freshly ground pepper
1 teaspoon ground marjoram
2 teaspoons grated lemon rind
1 8-ounce can tomato sauce
½ cup beef bouillon
salt

Cut meat into 2-inch cubes. Heat 2 tablespoons of butter in a heavy frying pan and brown the meat over high heat. Transfer the meat to casserole which can go to the table. Add the onions and the remaining tablespoon of butter to the frying pan. Cook, stirring constantly, until the onions are golden. Stir in the paprika and cook for 2 minutes longer. Add the onions to the meat, together with garlic, marjoram, lemon rind, tomato sauce and the beef bouillon. Taste and then season with salt and pepper. Bring to the boiling point, reduce heat to very low and cover the casserole. Simmer for about 1 hour or until the meat is tender. Do not overcook. Check for moisture; if the gravy looks too thin, cook without a cover. Skim off the fat as it rises to the surface of the goulash. Makes four to six servings.

Tuesday

Chicken Enchiladas with Sour Cream

Chicken Enchiladas with Sour Cream
Mexican Beans
Lettuce and Tomato Salad
Apricot Pie

2 4-ounce cans hot green chili peppers
2 tablespoons vegetable oil
1 large garlic clove, minced
1 1lb. 12-ounce can tomatoes
2 cups minced onion
2 teaspoons salt
½ teaspoon oregano
3 cups shredded cooked chicken
2 cups dairy sour cream
2 cups (½ lb.) shredded Cheddar cheese
⅓ cup vegetable oil
15 corn tortillas

Drain and rinse the hot chili peppers and remove every seed; the seeds are very hot. Chop peppers finely. Do not touch your face while handling peppers; wash hands thoroughly when finished. Heat the oil and saute the chopped chili peppers and garlic. Drain tomatoes and break them up; reserve ½ cup liquid. Add the tomatoes, onions, 1 teaspoon of salt and oregano to the hot pepper mixture and stir in the reserved tomato liquid. Simmer over very low heat for about 30 minutes or until thick. Set aside. Combine chicken with sour cream, shredded cheese and remaining teaspoon of salt. Heat ⅓ cup of oil and dip in the tortillas one at a time long enough to become limp (they must not be crisp). Drain well on paper towels. Fill each tortilla with a little of the chicken mixture. Roll up and arrange seam side down in a greased shallow baking dish. Pour the sauce over the enchiladas. Bake in a preheated oven 250° for about 20 minutes or until heated through or bake in an electric frying pan. Fifteen enchiladas.

Wednesday

Pork Fillet with Prunes and Apricots

Pork Fillet with Prunes and Apricots
Braised Celery
Brown Rice with Almonds
Meringues and Ice Cream

½ pound dried pitted prunes
½ pound dried apricots
2½ cups dry white wine
2 pork fillets, each weighing about 2 pounds
¼ cup flour
1 teaspoon salt
freshly ground pepper
4 tablespoons butter
2 tablespoons Bourbon
1 cup heavy cream
1 tablespoon cornstarch or potato starch
½ teaspoon paprika

Combine dried fruits in saucepan. Add wine. Cook covered over low heat for 20 minutes or until tender. To butterfly the fillets: with a sharp knife, cut the fillet crosswise (as in sawing a log) into ½-inch thick slices. Cut each slice *almost* through to the bottom, making two round ¼-inch thick slices joined at the bottom. Opened up and flattened, this will roughly resemble a butterfy. Dust slices with flour mixed with salt and pepper. Heat butter in frying pan; use 2 frying pans (and more butter) if necessary to accomodate pork slices side by side. Cook meat until medium browned on both sides, turning over once. Heat the whiskey and flame the meat. Cover pan(s) and cook on low heat for 30 minutes. Then overlap the slices on a heated ovenproof platter and keep hot in very low oven. Drain and reserve the fruit and return wine to frying pan. Stir, scraping up the brown bits from bottom. Combine cream, cornstarch and paprika to a smooth mixture and stir into wine. Cook, stirring constantly, until the sauce is thickened and smooth. Pour sauce over pork slices. Arrange the fruit down either side of the meat. Serve very hot. Serves 6.

Thursday

Boiled Beef with Vegetables and Horseradish Sauce

Boiled Beef with Vegetables and Horseradish Sauce
Cucumber Salad
Cherry Pie

1 3-pound beef brisket
1 leek, cut into halves lengthwise, white and green part
1 large onion stuck with 4 whole cloves
7 carrots
1 bay leaf
½ teaspoon dried thyme
4 parsley sprigs
8 whole peppercorns
4 large potatoes, peeled and cut into quarters
12 small white onions, peeled
1 cup sour cream
1 tablespoon horseradish
salt

Put the beef into a deep kettle and add enough boiling water to cover. Add the leeks, the onion with cloves, 1 carrot cut into large pieces, bay leaf, thyme, parsley sprigs and peppercorns. Bring to boil. Reduce heat to low. Simmer covered for 2-2½ hours or until meat is tender but not mushy. Skim as needed. During the last 30 minutes cooking time, add potatoes, the remaining carrots cut into halves and onions. To serve: slice meat and place on heated serving dish in overlapping slices. Surround the meat with potatoes, carrots and white onions.

Horseradish Sauce: combine 1 cup sour cream with 1 tablespoon freshly grated or drained bottled horseradish and salt to taste. Serves six.

Friday

Shrimp Gumbo

Shrimp Gumbo
Rice
Carrot and Celery Sticks
Bavarian Cream

½ pound lean bacon, cut into small strips
1 cup minced onion
1 10-ounce package frozen okra, thawed
1 small green pepper, seeded and finely chopped
1 cup finely chopped celery
6-8 cups cold water, depending on how thick a gumbo is wanted
3 medium ripe but firm tomatoes, peeled and coarsely chopped
1½ cups kernels of 3 large ears of corn *or* 1½ cups frozen corn kernels, thawed
1½ to 2 pounds raw shrimp, peeled and deveined
½ cup minced parsley
freshly ground pepper
½ teaspoon dried thyme
1 bay leaf
salt
1 10-ounce package frozen lima beans, thawed

The thickener in this Creole dish is okra rather than file powder. Cook the bacon in a large heavy saucepan or casserole until it just begins to crisp. Remove the bacon strips and reserve. Pour off all but 4-6 tablespoons of bacon fat. Add the onion, okra, green pepper and celery. Cook over low heat, stirring frequently, for 5 minutes or until vegetables are soft but not brown. Add the water, tomatoes, corn and the reserved bacon and bring to boil. Lower heat to minimum. Simmer covered for 20 minutes. Add the shrimp, parsley, thyme and bay leaf. Season with salt and pepper. Simmer for 3-5 minutes, depending on the size of shrimp. Add the lima beans and cook for about 3-5 minutes longer, or until just tender. *Do not overcook this dish.* To serve, put about ⅓ to ½ cup cooked plain rice into a soup plate or bowl and spoon the gumbo over it. Six servings.

Saturday

Pork Chops with Herbs and Wine

Pork Chops with Herbs and Wine
Mashed Squash
Tomato Aspic
Fruit Salad of Oranges, Grapefruit and Bananas

1 tablespoon crushed dried rosemary
2 teaspoons powdered sage
1-2 teaspoons grated lemon peel
1 garlic clove, mashed
salt (about 1 teaspoon)
freshly ground pepper
4 large lean pork chops, trim excess fat
water
½ cup dry white wine *or* ¼ cup dry vermouth and ¼ cup water

Mix the rosemary, sage, lemon peel, garlic, salt and pepper. Rub mixture into both sides of chops. Place chops into heavy frying pan. Add enough water to reach edge of chops. Cover and simmer over low heat about 45 minutes. When the water has evaporated, the chops will begin to brown. Turn over several times to insure even browning. Add wine and bring to boiling point. Cook about 1 minute. Serve the chops in heated serving dish and pour the sauce over top. Serves four.

To crush rosemary, place it between two sheets of waxed paper and roll with rolling pin or pound with the back of a plate or anything heavy. Crushed, rosemary will release its fragrance in cooking.

QUICK & EASY DINNERS FOR TWO

February

Sunday

Piquant Beef Stew

Piquant Beef Stew
Mashed Potatoes
Buttered Carrots
Avocado Vinaigrette
Chocolate Cake

1 pound chuck or round, in one piece
salt
freshly ground pepper
flour
3 tablespoons butter or salad oil
2 medium onions, thinly sliced
½ can fillet of anchovies, drained
6 black or green olives, pitted and coarsely chopped
½ cup Port wine
1 cup beef bouillon or water
¼ cup chopped parsley

Trim off all fat and gristle from the meat. Cut into 1½-inch cubes. Sprinkle with salt and pepper. Coat the meat with flour, shaking off excess. Heat the butter in a heavy saucepan and brown the meat over high heat, stirring constantly. Add the onions and cook for 2 minutes more, stirring continually. Add the anchovies, olives, the Port wine and bouillon. Check the seasoning; you may need a little pepper since anchovies and bouillon are salty. Mix well and bring to boil. Turn heat to very low and cover. Stir occasionally. Simmer covered for 45 minutes or until the meat is tender. Sprinkle with parsley before serving.

Monday

Bob Holleron's Crema Azteca Bean Soup

Bob Holleron's Crema Azteca Bean Soup
Chef Salad
Hot Garlic Bread
Cherries Jubilee

Put into blender:
3 cups cooked frijole beans
½ cup canned beef bouillon (or enough to make blender work easily)
Puree above
In large saucepan, heat blender mixture until hot. Add:
⅔ cup half and half
½ teaspoon salt
cracked pepper to taste
dash of Tabasco
1 teaspoon chili powder
⅔ teaspoon ground cumin

Cook for about 5 minutes or until thoroughly blended and hot. Before serving, stir in 1-2 jiggers of sherry. Serve topped with a little sour cream.

Tuesday

Leeks with Lemon Juice

Leeks with Lemon Juice
Broiled Ham Steak
Rice with Cheese Sauce
Brownies

1 bunch leeks (2-3 leeks)
2 tablespoons butter
2 tablespoons water
2 tablespoons fresh lemon juice
salt
freshly ground pepper
½ teaspoon cornstarch
1 tablespoon water

Trim and wash the leeks, leaving as much green as possible. Cut the leeks into 3-inch pieces. Wash again, making sure that every trace of sand is removed. Drain. Heat the butter in a deep frying pan. Add the leeks in one layer. Cook over medium heat, turning over once, for 2 minutes. Add the water, lemon juice, salt and pepper. Cover the frying pan and cook until the leeks are tender but not mushy. Blend the cornstarch with the water to a smooth paste. Add to the pan juices, mixing with a fork. Cook 1 or 2 minutes longer, or until the sauce has thickened. Transfer to a serving dish, and serve hot over toast or at room temperature as salad.

Wednesday

Belgian Pork Chops

Belgian Pork Chops
Red Cabbage
Boiled Potatoes
Coffee Sponge

4 thick, lean pork chops
salt
freshly ground pepper
2 tablespoons lard or bacon fat
2 medium onions, thinly sliced
1 tablespoon flour
2 cups dry red or white wine
½ teaspoon ground thyme
2 bay leaves
2 tablespoons minced parsley

The lard or bacon fat gives this dish a characteristic flavor, but any shortening may be used. Cut all excess fat off the pork chops. Rub salt and pepper into the meat on both sides. Heat the lard in a large frying pan and brown the chops over high heat on both sides. Transfer them to a casserole. Cook the onions in the frying pan juices until they are soft. Stir in the flour and wine. Cook, stirring constantly, until the sauce thickens. Stir in the thyme, bay leaves and parsley. Pour the sauce over the pork chops. Cook covered in a preheated oven 350° for 40 minutes. Check occasionally for moisture; if the sauce is too thick, add a tablespoon or two of water at a time. If too thin, cook uncovered to reduce. Check the seasoning before serving.
Note: The dish may also be made with beer. This will of course change the flavor but it is also very good and very Belgian.

Thursday

Margarethe Schanne's Hamburgers

Thick Potato Soup
Margarethe Schanne's Hamburgers
Tossed Green Salad
Broiled Grapefruit with Honey

6 tablespoons butter
4 small onions, thinly sliced
1 teaspoon sugar
1 pound ground steak, shaped into 4 patties
salt
freshly ground pepper
4 tablespoons brandy
toast

Heat 4 tablespoons of butter in a frying pan. Cook the onions, stirring constantly, for 2 minutes. Stir in the sugar and cook until the onions are soft and golden. Transfer the onions to a heated dish and keep hot over a low flame or a low oven. Sprinkle the meat on both sides with salt and pepper. Using the same frying pan, over high heat, brown the meat patties on both sides. Lower heat, add 4 tablespoons of brandy and flame. When the flames have died down, add the 2 remaining tablespoons of butter. When the butter has melted and is hot, add the remaining 2 tablespoons of brandy and flame again. Serve on hot plates, with onions piled on top of each patty, and cover with sauce. Serve toast on the side.

Friday

Coquilles St. Jacques

Coquilles St. Jacques
Rice Pilaff
Mixed Green Salad
Baked Apples

½ to ¾ pound fresh scallops
juice of 1 lemon
1 cup water
3 tablespoons butter
1 bay leaf
1 tablespoon flour
1 cup milk or light cream
2 egg yolks
⅓ cup grated Swiss cheese
2 tablespoons sherry
salt
freshly ground pepper
paprika

Wash and dry the scallops. If very large, cut into pieces. Sprinkle with lemon juice. Cook them in water with 1 tablespoon of butter and bay leaf for 5 minutes. Drain. Heat the remaining butter in a saucepan, stir in the flour, and cook 1 minute longer. Stir in the milk and cook, stirring constantly, until the sauce is smooth and thickened. Remove from the heat. Beat in the eggs and cheese. Cook over low heat 3 minutes longer. Add the scallops and the sherry. Season with a little salt and pepper. Pour into individual buttered ramekins or scalloped-shaped baking dishes. Sprinkle with paprika. Bake in a preheated oven 350° for 10-15 minutes or until golden brown on top.

Saturday

Finocchio Au Gratin

Lamb Chops
Finocchio Au Gratin
Yellow Risotto
Grapes in Sour Cream and Brown Sugar

2 medium heads finocchio
boiling water
salt
freshly ground pepper
⅓ cup butter, melted
½ cup freshly grated Parmesan cheese

Cut off the green tops and the "fingers" of the finocchi. Cut off hard base. Like cutting an apple, cut each finocchio into 4 parts. Put into a small saucepan. Add boiling water to cover. Cook covered for 3-4 minutes or until barely tender. Drain. Butter a shallow baking dish and place the finocchio pieces on it. Season with salt and pepper. Drizzle the butter and sprinkle the Parmesan cheese over the vegetable. Bake in a preheated hot 400°F oven for 5-10 minutes or until the top of the finocchio is bubbly and golden or broil at least 6 inches from heat. Serve immediately.

BUDGET DINNERS

February

Sunday

Belgian Red Cabbage and Apples

Smoked Boneless Butt
Belgian Red Cabbage and Apples
Hashed Potatoes
Lemon Chiffon Pie

2 tablespoons lard or bacon fat
6 slices bacon, minced
2 large onions, thinly sliced
1 firm head red cabbage, thinly sliced (about 8-10 cups)
4 tart cooking apples, peeled, cored and sliced
2 tablespoons sugar
¼ cup water
salt
freshly ground pepper
¼ teaspoon ground nutmeg

Combine the lard, minced bacon and onions in a heavy casserole. Cook over low heat, stirring frequently, until the onions are half soft. Do not brown them. Add the cabbage. Continue cooking, covered, over very low heat for about 15 minutes, *without stirring*. Check frequently for moisture; if the cabbage looks too dry, add a little water, 2 tablespoons at a time. Add the apples, sugar, water, salt and pepper to taste and nutmeg. Stir thoroughly to blend. Simmer covered over very low heat for 1½ hours. This can be made ahead of time and reheated. Good with pork and roast duck.

Monday

Lasagne Verdi Bolognese

Lasagne Verdi Bolognese
Tomato Aspic Salad
Vanilla Pudding

½ pound pork sausage links, parboiled and thinly sliced
1 pound ground chuck
1 medium onion, chopped
3 tablespoons tomato paste
salt
dash of ground nutmeg
dash of ground cloves
8 ounces spinach lasagne, cooked until tender but not mushy
Cream Sauce*
1 cup freshly grated Parmesan cheese

In a large frying pan, brown the sausage and remove to a plate. Drain off excess fat. Add beef to frying pan and cook, stirring with a fork, until beef is browned. Stir in onion, tomato paste, salt, spices and return sausages to frying pan. Into the bottom of a 13 × 9 × 2-inch buttered baking pan, pour a small amount of Cream Sauce*. Lay lasagne across bottom of pan, starting at middle and letting half extend over edge of pan; repeat on 3 remaining sides. Spread ½ of meat mixture on top. Add more sauce and sprinkle with ⅓ of the Parmesan cheese. Arrange another layer of lasagne and cover with remaining meat. Top with about ½ of remaining sauce and sprinkle with another ⅓ of the Parmesan. Fold overhanging lasagne from bottom layer over the top. Add remaining sauce and Parmesan. Bake in a prehearted 375° oven for 20-30 minutes or until golden and bubbly. Serves four to six.

Cream Sauce*: In the top of a double boiler, over boiling water, heat ½ cup butter. Stir in ½ cup flour, 1 teaspoon salt and ⅛ teaspoon freshly ground pepper. Gradually stir in 3½ cups milk and heat. Reduce heat to low and cook for 1 hour, stirring occasionally. Sauce should be of medium consistency. About 3½ cups.

Tuesday

Potato, Sausage and Cabbage Casserole

Potato, Sausage and Cabbage Casserole
Green Salad with Roquefort Dressing
Baked Apples with Cream

2 tablespoons bacon fat
1 medium cabbage, cut into 8 chunks and trimmed
6 medium potatoes, peeled and cut into ½-inch slices
salt
freshly ground pepper
about ½ cup boiling water
1 pound Polish or Italian sausage

Heat the bacon fat in a deep 9-inch frying pan. Add the cabbage and top with potatoes. Season with salt and pepper. Pour boiling water over the vegetables. Lay the sausage or sausages on top. Cover the frying pan very tightly. Over lowest possible heat, simmer for about 40 minutes or until potatoes are tender. Check occasionally for moisture; if necessary, add a little more hot water, 2 tablespoons at a time. At serving time, place potatoes in a heated serving dish and circle with cabbage chunks. Slice the sausage and top with vegetables. Makes four to six servings.

Wednesday

Hamburger Soufflé

Hamburger Soufflé
Molded Vegetable Salad
Canned Peaches and Cupcakes

4 tablespoons butter
3 tablespoons flour
1 cup beef bouillon (can be made with 1 bouillon cube)
3 tablespoons grated Parmesan or Swiss cheese
1½ teaspoons Worcestershire or soy sauce
freshly ground pepper
1 tablespoon grated onion
½ pound hamburger
4 or 5 eggs, separated
½ teaspoon cream of tartar (optional)

Heat 3 tablespoons of butter in a heavy saucepan and stir in flour. Over low heat, stirring constantly, cook for 1-2 minutes. Stir in the beef bouillon and cook until sauce has thickened. Stir in the cheese and Worcestershire sauce. Season with pepper. Remove from heat. Heat the remaining tablespoon butter in a small frying pan. Add onion and cook, stirring constantly, for 2-3 minutes or until onion is soft. Add the hamburger and cook over medium heat until browned. Add the meat to sauce and mix well. Stir in egg yolks, one at a time and blend thoroughly. Cool mixture. Beat egg whites until frothy. Add cream of tartar. Continue beating until stiff but not dry. Spoon a third of the egg whites into meat mixture and fold until blended. Add this mixture to remaining egg whites and fold. Spoon into a buttered 2-quart soufflé dish. Bake in preheated oven 350° F for 30 minutes or until firm. Serve immediately. Serves three to four.

Thursday

Chicken and Rice Pilaf

Chicken and Rice Pilaf
Coleslaw from Red Cabbage
Jellied Dark Sweet Cherries

½ cup butter or margarine
1 medium onion, minced
1 small garlic clove, minced
3 cups diced cooked or canned chicken
salt
freshly ground pepper
½ teaspoon thyme
1 cup uncooked rice
3 cups canned chicken consommé, or consommé made from powder or cubes
½ cup chopped walnuts or pignoli nuts

The virtues of this simple, pleasant dish are numerous. It is inexpensive, filling, easy and quick to make from ingredients that can be kept ready on the kitchen shelves. It can readily be doubled or tripled.

Heat the butter in a heavy casserole and cook the onion and garlic until they are soft and golden, but do not let them brown. Add the chicken and cook, stirring frequently, 3-4 minutes longer. Season with salt, pepper and thyme. Add the rice and consommé. Cover and simmer over low heat 20-25 minutes or until the rice is tender. Check the seasoning and stir in walnuts.
Note: For a change, use 2 cups consommé and 1 cup tomato juice.

Friday

Fried Rice

Chow Mein
Fried Rice
Carrot Salad
Chocolate Pudding

2 tablespoons salad oil
1 cup of thinly sliced single
or mixed celery,
green peppers, mushrooms
or cooked leftover vegetables
2 tablespoons soy sauce
4 cups cooked rice
1-2 eggs, well beaten
salt
freshly ground pepper

Heat the oil in a large frying pan. Add the vegetables. Over medium heat, cook the vegetables for about 3 minutes, or until very crisp. Stir in the soy sauce and add rice. Over low heat, stirring frequently, cook for 5 more minutes, or until the mixture is very hot. Stir in the eggs. Cook for 2-3 more minutes, or until the eggs are set. Season to taste and pepper. Serve with more soy sauce on the side. Makes four servings.

Saturday

Quick Applesauce Cream

Baked Chicken and Biscuits
Green Salad
Quick Applesauce Cream
Cookies

Combine equal parts of thick homemade or commercial applesauce with whipped cream or cold vanilla pudding. Serve in glass dish or individual sherbet dishes. Sprinkle with a little ground nutmeg, ginger or cinnamon, depending on taste. Serve immediately.

ENTERTAINING

February

Sunday **Tortino of Artichokes/Peas with Prosciutto**

Tortino of Artichokes
Peas with Prosciutto
Orange and Onion Salad
Brownies

juice of 1 lemon and
the squeezed lemon
6 medium artichokes
flour
1 cup olive oil
6 eggs
salt
freshly ground pepper
¼ cup light or heavy cream
⅛ teaspoon ground nutmeg

Fill a bowl with cold water. Add lemon juice and squeezed lemon. Remove the tough outer leaves of the artichokes until only tender leaves remain. Cut off the spiny part and all but ¼ inch of the stem. As you prepare each artichoke, drop into lemon water to prevent discoloring. Then cut each artichoke into quarters as you would an apple, and keep in lemon water. Core each quarter and cut into thin, approximately ⅛-inch slices. Drop slices immediately into lemon water to prevent darkening. When ready to use, drain and dry well on kitchen toweling. Coat the artichoke slices with flour and shake off excess. Heat olive oil in a deep frying pan and fry slices for 3 minutes or until tender and golden brown. Drain on paper towels. Place the fried artichokes in a shallow buttered baking dish. Beat together the eggs, salt, pepper, cream, and nutmeg. Pour mixture over the artichokes. Bake in a preheated oven 350° 15-20 minutes or until golden and puffy. Serve immediately. Serves six.

Peas with Prosciutto

4 tablespoons butter
4 tablespoons minced onion
1 cup diced Italian prosciutto,
smoked ham, Canadian
bacon, or lean bacon
4 pounds fresh peas, shelled,
or 3 10-ounce packages
frozen peas
½ cup chicken bouillon
salt
freshly ground pepper

Combine the butter, onion, and prosciutto in a heavy saucepan. Cook over medium heat, stirring constantly, for 5 minutes, or until the onion is tender. Add the peas and ⅓ cup of the bouillon. Season with salt and pepper. Cook, covered, over low heat for 10 minutes or until the peas are tender. If necessary to prevent scorching, add a little more bouillon, one or two tablespoons at a time. Serves six.

Monday

Ham Biscuits

Scalloped Oysters
Ham Biscuits
Brussels Sprouts with Buttered Crumbs
Pecan Pie

3 cups flour
1 teaspoon salt
6 teaspoons baking powder
6 tablespoons butter
½ cup milk
½ cup heavy cream
½ cup ground cooked ham

Sift the flour, salt, and baking powder into a bowl. Cut in the butter with two knives, a pastry blender or your fingers, rubbing the butter and flour together. Gradually stir in milk and cream, just enough to make a soft, nonsticky dough. Turn the dough out of the bowl onto a floured board and knead for 2-3 minutes. With a floured rolling pin roll the dough into a 10 × 18-inch rectangle to the thickness of ¼ inch. Spread ham over the dough. Fold one end over the middle. Fold the other end over the middle, making 3 layers of dough. Turn the open side toward yourself and roll out again. Repeat the folding process, ending with a ½-inch thick rectangle. Using a 1-to 1½-inch round cutter, cut out rounds and place them on a lightly greased baking sheet. Bake in a preheated 450° oven for 12-15 minutes or until risen and golden brown. Serve hot with butter. Makes about two dozen biscuits.

Tuesday

Fillet of Beef/Amber Onions

Fillet of Beef
Baked Stuffed Mushrooms
Amber Onions
Endive Salad with Avocado Dressing
Coffee Jelly with Whipped Cream

1 tenderloin of beef, weighing 6 to 8 pounds, tied but not larded
1 teaspoon salt
watercress

Preheat the oven to 425°. Wipe the beef with a paper towel, place on middle rack in shallow roasting pan and roast for 35 minutes. Remove and sprinkle with salt. Let stand for 10 minutes before carving. Place on a heated platter in overlapping slices and garnish with watercress. Serves six to eight.

Note: This produces a rare roast. For a medium-rare tenderloin, cook 5 minutes longer.

Amber Onions

8 large yellow onions
4 tablespoons melted butter
salt
¾ teaspoon paprika
⅓ cup tomato juice
⅓ cup honey

Peel the onions. Cut into halves crosswise. Place the halves side by side in a buttered baking dish. Blend together the butter, salt, paprika, tomato juice, and honey. Heat until well blended. Pour over onions. Cover the baking dish with lid or foil. Bake in a preheated 350° oven for 30–40 minutes or until the onions are tender. Baste occasionally with sauce. Serves six to eight.

Wednesday

Cream of Lettuce Soup

Cream of Lettuce Soup
Ham Slices in a Sherry-and-Raisin Sauce
Gratin Dauphinois
Broccoli Puree
Lemon Meringue Pie

2 tablespoons butter
1 large head Romaine lettuce, shredded
12 to 18 green onions, sliced
1½ quarts chicken bouillon
salt
freshly ground pepper
2 tablespoons cornstarch
2 tablespoons water
2 egg yolks
⅓ cup heavy cream
butter-fried croutons

Combine the butter, lettuce, and onions in a deep, heavy saucepan. Cook over medium heat, stirring occasionally, for 5 minutes or until lettuce is wilted. Add the bouillon and season with salt and pepper. Simmer, covered, over low heat for 15 minutes. Blend the cornstarch and water to a smooth paste and stir into the soup. Cook for 5 minutes longer. Puree the soup in a blender or strain through a food mill. Beat together the egg yolks and cream. Spoon a little of the hot soup on this mixture, and then stir this into the remaining soup. Heat through but do not boil. Serve hot with croutons. Serves four to six.

Thursday

Russian Braised Veal

Spinach Soufflé
Russian Braised Veal
Heart of Palms Salad
Chocolate Mousse
Almond Cookies

3 to 4 pounds boneless veal, in one piece
2 tablespoons butter
2 large onions, thinly sliced
2 medium carrots, shredded
1 celery stalk with leaves, chopped
¼ cup parsley heads, chopped
2 bay leaves
3 inches lemon peel, yellow part only, minced
1–2 tablespoons water
2 tablespoons salad oil
1 cup dry white wine
salt
freshly ground pepper
½ cup sour cream
1 teaspoon fresh lemon juice

Trim all fat and gristle from the meat. Tie it with string to hold it together during cooking. Heat the butter in a heavy 6-quart casserole or Dutch oven. Add the onions, carrots, celery, parsley, bay leaves, and lemon rind. Cook over medium heat, stirring constantly, about 2 minutes. Stir in the water, cover, and cook over low heat about 10 to 15 minutes, or until the vegetables are tender but not browned. Stir frequently. Heat the salad oil in a large, heavy frying pan. Add the veal. Over high heat, turning the meat frequently with two spoons (make no holes the juice could ooze from), brown the meat on all sides. This takes 5 to 10 minutes. Lay it on top of the vegetables in the casserole. Pour the wine over the meat. Season lightly with salt and pepper. Bring to a boil and immediately lower heat to simmer. Cover tightly. Simmer over very low heat about 1¼ to 1½ hours — until meat is tender but not mushy. Transfer the meat to a heated platter, cover loosely with foil, and keep it warm in a low oven. Remove as much fat as possible from the pan juices. Pour the casserole contents into a sieve over a bowl. With the back of a spoon, strain the vegetables through the sieve; extract all the juices. Again skim off any fat. Return the sauce to the casserole; cook over medium heat as long as necessary to reduce it to medium-sauce consistency. Remove from heat; stir in sour cream. Heat it through, but do not boil. Remove again from heat, check the seasonings, and stir in the lemon juice. Slice the meat; spoon a little sauce over the slices to keep them moist. Serve the rest in a gravy boat. Serves six.

Friday

Italian Baked Rice Timbale

Cold Celery Remoulade
Italian Baked Rice Timbale
Mushroom or Tomato Sauce
Grilled Tomatoes
Cheese Tray, Apples and Pears

For the Timbale:
2⅔ cups Carolina rice
6 cups boiling salted water
½ cup butter, at room temperature, cut into small pieces
½ cup grated Parmesan cheese
4 egg yolks, beaten
fine dry bread crumbs
butter

For the Filling:
2 tablespoons butter
¼ cup grated onion
1 garlic clove, mashed
½ pound lean veal, ground twice
½ pound lean pork, ground twice
½ pound ground chicken livers
⅓ cup minced pimiento
1½ cups cooked drained peas
4 tablespoons very thick tomato sauce flavored with basil
1 teaspoon sugar
½ teaspoon dried oregano or thyme
salt
freshly ground pepper

Cook rice in boiling salted water until tender but not mushy. Drain. Stir in ½ cup butter, Parmesan cheese, and beaten egg yolks. Mix throughly. Butter a 3-quart baking dish generously and coat thoroughly with fine dry bread crumbs. Spoon ⅔ cup of rice mixture into baking dish. Press the rice with the back of a spoon against bottom and sides of dish, leaving a well in middle. Spoon filling into well. Spoon remaining rice over the filling, covering thoroughly and completely. Sprinkle top with bread crumbs and dot with butter. Cook in preheated oven 350° for 1 hour, or until rice is well set. Serve from the dish or unmold on a warm platter. Cut into wedges and serve with tomato or mushroom sauce, if desired.

To make the filling: Heat butter in a frying pan and cook the onion and garlic for 3 minutes or until soft. Do not brown. Add the ground meats and chicken livers. Cook over medium heat, stirring frequently, for about 10 minutes. Add pimiento, peas, tomato sauce, sugar, oregano, and season with salt and pepper. Mix well. Lower the heat and cook for 10-15 more minutes, stirring frequently. Cool slightly before filling rice timbale. Serves six.

Saturday

Curry Party

Malay Curry*   Indian Pilau*
Mango Chutney   Lemon Chutney
Any Fresh Homemade Chutneys
Little Bowls with Chopped Salted Peanuts, Fried Plantain Rounds, Crumbled Crisp Bacon, Fried Chopped Eggplant and Finely Chopped Green (Spring) Onions
Cucumbers in Yogurt or Sour Cream Dressing
Caramel Custard or Bavarian Cream or Fresh Fruit Salad

**Recipe in book*

When planning a curry party for guests whose tastes she is not absolutely sure of, a hostess should prepare a mild curry. Guests can always sprinkle their own Tabasco on the curry for additional spice.

It is not necessary to have side dishes, although they add interest and show that the hostess fussed. The only essential accompaniments are some sort of rice, plain or fancy, and several chutneys; many of these can be purchased in gourmet stores. Cold cucumber in yogurt dressing is a good accompaniment providing a flavor contrast. It is simply made by peeling cucumbers, slicing very thin and mixing with yogurt or sour cream, not forgetting salt, pepper and perhaps a dash of cayenne or Tabasco. The dish should be chilled.

Curry needs a smooth, creamy dessert or a fresh fruit salad, again as a flavor and texture contrast.

To sum up: A Curry Party can be simple or complicated. There is no end to the authentic Indian dishes that can be added such as "dahls," "raitas," etc., all found in Indian cookbooks. However, the menu suggested above has proved satisfactory in the authors' experience.

Drinks: A well flavored imported beer is far the best choice for a curry dinner whose flavors are too overwhelming for wines. However, a dry champagne will suit, and if a wine must be served, make it a well-chilled rosé. It is a shame to serve fine wines with a curry dinner.

Malay Curry

This curry may look complicated — it isn't, only a bit lengthy. Like all curries, it can be made beforehand and heated up later. When made ahead of time, the meat should not be overcooked, since it has to cook again. A curry should not be a mush. This curry is different from the usual Indian curries as it is of Malay origin and somewhat adapted. Since the ingredients are freshly ground, no curry powder is used. The curry is spicy rather than hot though it can be made hot with the addition of Tabasco or chili peppers. The recipe can be doubled without losing its flavor as many recipes cooked in larger quantities so often do.

Step One: Make the spice mixture. This can be done with a mortar and pestle, but a blender is quicker. Blend to a paste, scraping down sides with a rubber spatula. Begin with one tablespoon oil and add more as needed. Into a blender put the following:

10 whole peppercorns
½ teaspoon ground cumin or cumin seeds
1 teaspoon caraway or fennel seeds
1 teaspoon coriander seeds or ½ teaspoon ground coriander
1 teaspoon ground turmeric
½ teaspoon ground nutmeg
grated rind of 1 large lemon
3 tablespoons minced fresh green ginger *or* 1 tablespoon ground ginger (the fresh ginger is infinitely better)
4 garlic cloves, chopped
6 cashews or 8 blanched almonds
1-2 tablespoons salad oil

Step Two:

4 pounds very lean beef, all fat removed and cut into 1½-inch cubes
4 tablespoons salad oil
6 whole cloves, crushed or ¾ teaspoon ground cloves
¾-inch cinnamon bark, finely crushed (put into a paper bag and pound with something heavy)
seeds from 5 whole cardamom pods
1 large onion, finely chopped

Step Three:

3 large tomatoes, peeled and coarsely chopped
¼ cup grated coconut, fresh or dry unsweetened
8 dried apricots, coarsely chopped
3 large hard pears, peeled, cored and coarsely chopped
2-3 cups coconut milk
salt
Tabasco or minced chili pepper to taste
juice of 1 lemon

Assembling the curry: Make sure that every trace of fat and gristle is removed from the beef. Heat oil in a heavy saucepan which is large enough to hold all the ingredients. Add the cloves, cinnamon bark, cardamom, and cook over medium heat, stirring constantly, for about 1 minute. Add the onion. Cook, stirring all the time, for 2–3 more minutes or until the onion is soft. Add the spice mixture. Cook, stirring steadily, for 2–3 minutes. Add the meat and the tomatoes. Cook over medium heat, stirring constantly, until the meat and tomatoes have been coated with spices and are browned. Add the grated coconut, apricots, pears and coconut milk, beginning with 2 cups. Mix well. Season with salt and Tabasco to taste. Bring to boil. Lower heat to very low and cover saucepan. Simmer for 45 minutes to 1 hour or until the meat is tender, stirring frequently. If too thick and in danger of scorching, add a little more coconut milk, ¼ cup at a time. Just before serving, stir in the lemon juice. Serves six.

Note: Go easy on the Tabasco and the chili pepper. One inch of seeded fresh hot chili, minced, is quite hot.

Indian Pilau

6 tablespoons butter
1 medium onion, finely chopped
1½ cups white rice
3 cups boiling chicken bouillon
1 teaspoon salt
freshly ground pepper
½ cup seedless or golden raisins, plumped in warm water 10 minutes and drained
½ cup slivered almonds

Heat 4 tablespoons of butter in a 2-quart ovenproof casserole and cook the onion until soft and golden. Add the rice, stirring constantly, for 3 minutes or until rice is opaque. Add the chicken bouillon, salt, pepper and raisins. Cover. Cook in a preheated 350° oven for 30 minutes or until the rice is soft and has absorbed the bouillon. While the rice is cooking, heat the remaining butter in a small frying pan and cook the almonds, stirring constantly, until they are golden. Sprinkle the almonds over the rice at serving time. Serves six.

MARCH

Is the family meal still with us? As if we didn't know it, surveys show that many family members breakfast and lunch separately, except possibly on Sundays. Now another survey proclaims that the family dinner is also on its way out, because of conflicting schedules of parents' and children's activities. A sad state of affairs, but not totally unavoidable, though the cook may have to make some compromises. He or she may have to admit, and be agreeable about it, that on some nights it is not possible for everybody to sit down together at dinner. The thing to do is to poll the family as to the nights when family dinner is possible, and make the schedule stick. How? By providing excellent dinners in a sunny mood, at a prettily set table. Why not cook favorite dishes for each member of the family in turn, as one does on birthdays, or make meals of favorite dishes? These aren't any more expensive or harder than ordinary meals. And if there were nothing to Mother's cooking, why would there be so many imitations of it?

MARCH

FAMILY FARE

	LUNCHES	DINNERS
Sunday	Broiled Grapefruit Cheese and Bacon Flan* Homemade Corn Muffins and Jam	Leg of Lamb White Beans Provencale* Orange and Onion Salad Apple Tart
Monday	Chive and Parsley Omelets French Fried Potatoes Pickled Beets Fresh Orange Jelly*	Chicken Breasts in Red Wine* Brown Rice Green Peas Cooked with Bacon Bits and Shredded Lettuce Custard
Tuesday	Chipped Beef on English Muffins Cucumber Salad Baked Pears*	Cassoulet* Sweet Pickle Relish Lettuce Wedges with Russian Dressing Fruit Compote of Dried Apricots and Prunes
Wednesday	Farina Cheese Soufflé* Green Beans Vinaigrette Applesauce and Cookies	Stuffed Pork Chops* Baked Acorn Squash with Pecans Green Peas Lemon Layer Cake with Vanilla Ice Cream
Thursday	Onion Soup* Grilled Cheese Sandwiches Fruit and Cookies	Ham Steaks with Almonds* Mashed Potatoes Green Beans Cheese Cake
Friday	Simple Cheese Skewers* Tossed Green Salad Chocolate Pudding	Sole Meuniére Buttered Broccoli Steamed Potatoes Sena's Lemon Tart*
Saturday	Caesar Salad with Croutons* Rice Pudding	Pork Chops in Orange Sauce* Mashed Sweet Potatoes Steamed Cabbage Fruit Yogurt and Cookies

QUICK & EASY Dinners For Two	BUDGET DINNERS	ENTERTAINING
Pan Broiled Minute Steaks with Fresh Squeezed Lemon Juice Melting Potatoes* Buttered Spinach Radishes Cold Lemon Soufflé	Marinated Chuck Steak* Roast Potatoes Buttered Green Beans Winter Fruit Compote and Cookies	Finnan Haddie Delmonico* Toast Points Marinated Mushrooms with Herbs Cold Coffee Soufflé
Sausages Cooked in Beer Creamed Cabbage* Baked Acorn Squash Tossed Green Salad Pears Cooked in Red Wine	Hot Consommé with Rice Cold Cuts Vegetable Aspic* Custard Pie	Cheese Soufflé Marinated Celery and Artichoke Hearts Garlic Melba Toast Ambrosia*
Roman Deviled Chicken* Mexican Rice Green Salad Sliced Oranges with Sherry	Stuffed Cabbage Leaves* Orange and Onion Salad Apple Pie	Rock Cornish Hens with Ginger Orange Sauce* Persian Rice Buttered Baby Carrots Vanilla-Poached Apples with Real Custard Sauce
Eggs Lucerne* Spoon Bread Stewed Okra and Tomatoes Carrot and Celery Sticks Applesauce	Chicken Marengo* Buttered Noodles Tossed Green Salad Ice Cream	Hot Borscht with Sour Cream Roast Duck Stuffed with Onions Eggplant and Bean Salad* Strawberry Bavarian
Hamburgers on Buns Piquant Mushrooms* Cheese and Crackers Frozen Raspberries and Cookies	Tongue with Raisin Sauce* Stuffed Onions French Fried Potatoes Maple Cake	American Bouillabaisse Hot Cornsticks or Muffins Belgian Endive, Watercress, and Shredded Red Beet Salad Ricotta Dessert*
Fish Fillets in White Wine Boiled Parsleyed Potatoes Curried Carrots* Baked Bananas and Cream	Tuna Pie* Orange and Onion Salad Baked Bananas	Cream of Mushroom Soup Roman Lamb Casserole with Artichokes* Barley Pilaf Tossed Green Salad Cold Orange Soufflé
Quick Shrimp Curry* Rice Orange and Onion Salad First Stewed Rhubarb of the Season	Hamburger Pie* Pickles Carrot and Celery Sticks Fruit Salad with Oranges, Grapefruit and Apples	Cold: Country Terrine* Watercress Greek Olives Radishes Tiny Pickles French Bread Hot: Beef Bourguignon Rice and Mushroom Casserole Salad of Belgian Endives, Watercress and Avocado Pieces Fresh Pineapple with Kirsch Almond Cookies

FAMILY FARE LUNCHES

March

Sunday

Cheese and Bacon Flan

Broiled Grapefruit
Cheese and Bacon Flan
Homemade Corn Muffins and Jam

1 pound bacon, cut into 1-inch pieces
4 medium leeks, thinly sliced
8 eggs
2 cups light cream or Half and Half
1 teaspoon salt
freshly ground pepper
½ teaspoon ground nutmeg
2 cups grated Swiss cheese

Cook the bacon in a frying pan until it is crisp. Remove with a slotted spoon to a paper towel and drain. Pour off all but 2 tablespoons of the bacon fat. Cook the leeks in the bacon fat, stirring frequently, until they are tender. Do not brown them. Beat together the eggs, cream, salt, pepper, nutmeg, and cheese. Reserve 3 tablespoons of bacon and 3 tablespoons of cheese. Combine eggs, leeks, the remaining bacon and the remaining cheese. Mix well. Pour the mixture into a buttered 2-quart baking dish. Sprinkle with the reserved bacon and cheese. Bake in a preheated oven 350° for 35-40 minutes or until a knife blade inserted into the edge of the flan comes out clean. Serve immediately. Serves four to six.

Note: Cut off all but 1 inch of the green tops of the leeks. Wash very well in cold water to remove sand; if necessary, soak for 15 minutes, changing the water once.

Monday

Fresh Orange Jelly

Chive and Parsley Omelets
French Fried Potatoes
Pickled Beets
Fresh Orange Jelly

2 packages unflavored gelatin
3 cups fresh orange juice
½ cup fresh lemon juice
⅔ cup sugar
2 tablespoons grated orange rind

Sprinkle the gelatin over ½ cup of the orange juice. Stir to mix. Combine remaining orange juice, lemon juice and sugar. Place over low heat and stir until sugar is dissolved. Stir in gelatin and have it dissolve completely. Remove from heat and stir in the orange rind. Pour into a serving dish and chill until set. Makes about four cups.

Tuesday

Baked Pears

Chipped Beef on English Muffins
Cucumber Salad
Baked Pears

6 large firm Bosc
or other winter pears
1 cup water
1½ cups light
or dark brown sugar
4 whole cloves
1 3-inch stick cinnamon
juice of 1 lemon
½ cup bitter orange
or ginger or lemon marmalade

Peel the pears, cut into halves and core. Place the pear halves into a buttered baking dish. Combine the water, sugar, cloves and cinnamon. Heat, and cook, stirring constantly, until the sugar has dissolved. Stir in lemon juice and marmalade. Simmer, covered, for 10 more minutes. Pour over the pears. Bake in a preheated oven 350° for 20 minutes, basting occasionally with the syrup. Serve warm. Six servings.

Wednesday

Farina Cheese Soufflé

Farina Cheese Soufflé
Green Beans Vinaigrette
Applesauce and Cookies

4 cups (1 quart) milk
2 tablespoons butter
⅔ cup farina
½ pound (2 cups) grated
 or shredded Swiss cheese
1 teaspoon salt
dash Tabasco
4 large eggs, separated

Heat the milk. Add butter and stir until melted. Gradually stir in the farina, stirring all the time to make sure it won't lump. Cook, stirring constantly, until thickened and smooth. Stir in the cheese, salt and Tabasco. Cook over low heat, stirring all the time, until the cheese has melted. Remove from the heat and cool. Beat in the egg yolks, one at a time, beating well after each addition. Beat the egg whites until stiff and fold into the first mixture. Pour into a generously buttered 2-quart baking dish. Bake in a preheated oven 350° for 40 minutes or until golden brown and puffy. Serve immediately. Makes four to six servings.

Thursday

Onion Soup

Onion Soup
Grilled Cheese Sandwiches
Fruit and Cookies

3 tablespoons butter
1 tablespoon oil
4 cups thinly sliced yellow onions
1 tablespoon sugar
2 tablespoons flour
7 cups beef bouillon
1 cup dry white wine
salt
freshly ground pepper
2 tablespoons brandy (optional)
grated Parmesan or Swiss cheese

Heat the butter and oil in a heavy saucepan. Add onions and cook over low heat, stirring constantly, until soft. Do not brown them. Stir the sugar and flour into the onions and cook, stirring all the time, for 5 more minutes. The onions should be golden brown. Add the bouillon and wine. Season with salt and pepper to taste. Simmer, covered for 20 minutes. Stir in the brandy just before serving. Pour into individual bowls and sprinkle with grated cheese. Makes four to six servings.

Friday

Simple Cheese Skewers

Simple Cheese Skewers
Tossed Green Salad
Chocolate Pudding

Swiss cheese, in hunk, not slices
stale bread, crusts trimmed off
butter

Cut the cheese and bread into matching square pieces. Each piece should be about ½ inch thick and 2 inches square. Thread alternate pieces of bread and cheese on the skewers, beginning and ending with bread. Metal knitting needles will do if there are no skewers. Melt enough butter in a heavy frying pan to the depth of ½ inch. Cook the skewers in the butter, turning frequently, until the cheese melts and the bread is golden.

Saturday

Caesar Salad with Croutons

Caesar Salad with Croutons
Rice Pudding

2 medium bunches Romaine lettuce
2 large garlic cloves
3 anchovies or 2-3 teaspoons
anchovy paste
1 tablespoon capers
1½ teaspoons dry mustard
1 teaspoon salt
freshly ground pepper
1 teaspoon Worcestershire sauce
3 tablespoons olive oil
1 tablespoon vinegar
juice of ½ lemon
3 tablespoons freshly grated
Parmesan cheese
1 egg yolk
1 cup croutons

Trim and wash Romaine lettuce and shake dry. Tear the leaves into largish pieces, removing the tough spines. In the bottom of a large salad bowl, mash the garlic cloves, anchovies and capers with a fork. Stir in the mustard, a little salt (the other ingredients are salty) pepper, and Worcestershire sauce. Mash all the ingredients together into a paste. Blend in the oil, vinegar and lemon juice. Add the lettuce, the Parmesan and the egg yolk. Toss well so that each leaf is coated with dressing. Sprinkle with croutons and toss some more. Serves six.

To prepare **Croutons,** trim the crust off fresh or dry white bread slices. Butter the bread, cut it into dice and brown in oven 375°. Or dice the bread and sauté in butter until an even brown.

FAMILY FARE DINNERS

March

Sunday

Leg of Lamb
White Beans Provençale
Orange and Onion Salad
Apple Tart

White Beans Provençal

1 pound dried white beans
3 tablespoons olive oil
1 garlic clove, minced
½ teaspoon dried thyme
1 teaspoon dried basil
2 cups Italian-type
 canned plum tomatoes
salt
freshly ground pepper
¼ cup minced parsley

Wash the beans in cold water and drain. Put them into a large, heavy saucepan and add enough cold water to cover and to reach 3 inches above them. Bring to boil. Cook for exactly 2 minutes at a full boil. Remove the saucepan from heat and cover. Let stand for 1 hour. Return to heat, bring to boil and lower heat to very low. Simmer, covered, until the beans are just tender. Cooking time depends on the beans. Test for doneness after 30 minutes and every 10 minutes thereafter until the beans are barely soft, not mushy. Drain the beans well. When ready to cook, heat the olive oil in a heavy saucepan. Add the garlic, thyme and basil. Cook, stirring all the time, for ½ minute; the garlic must not burn. Add the tomatoes, the beans and salt and pepper to taste. Mix gently. Simmer covered for about 15-25 minutes, but do not overcook. Sprinkle with the parsley before serving. Serves six.

Monday

Chicken Breasts in Red Wine

Chicken Breasts in Red Wine
Brown Rice
Green Peas Cooked with Bacon Bits and Shredded Lettuce
Custard

8 tablespoons butter, at room temperature
1 tablespoon minced chives
½ teaspoon dried basil
½ teaspoon dried tarragon
salt
freshly ground pepper
4 large whole chicken breasts, split into halves
2 cups dry red wine

Combine the butter, chives, basil, tarragon and mix well. Season with salt and pepper to taste. Remove any excess fat from the chicken breasts. With a very sharp knife, carefully loosen the skin from the flesh of the chicken breasts, to form pockets. Spread the herb butter inside these pockets. Place the chicken breasts in one or two layers in a baking dish. Pour enough red wine around them to reach halfway up the meat. Cover and refrigerate for 4 hours, turning over once. When ready to cook, preheat the oven to 400° for 15 minutes. The temperature is important, so make sure the oven registers correct temperatures. Uncover the chicken and cook for 30 minutes, basting two or three times with the pan liquid. Serve immediately. Four servings.

Tuesday

Cassoulet

Cassoulet
Sweet Pickle Relish
Lettuce Wedges with Russian Dressing
Fruit Compote of Dried Apricots and Prunes

½ pound seasoned sausage meat
3 tablespoons minced shallots or onion
1 garlic clove, minced
1 teaspoon crumbled dried rosemary
4 cups cooked white beans
4 tablespoons minced parsley
2 cups diced cooked lamb, all fat trimmed off
salt
freshly ground pepper
1½ cups beef bouillon
½ cup fresh white bread crumbs
2 tablespoons butter cut into small pieces

This simple cassoulet is made with leftover cooked lamb and cooked beans. If canned beans are used, drain them, place in a strainer and rinse under running cold water until water runs clear. Shape the sausage meat into 2-inch diameter flat patties. Place them in frying pan and brown on both sides over medium heat. Transfer patties to a plate and pour off all but 2 tablespoons of fat from frying pan. Cook the shallots, garlic and rosemary in fat 3-4 minutes, mixing well, or until shallots are soft. In a deep ovenproof dish, layer the ingredients as follows: half of the beans, half of the shallot mixture, 2 tablespoons of parsley, all the lamb, all the sausage patties, the remaining shallot mixture and the remaining beans. Sprinkle with remaining parsley. Add salt, pepper, and pour in bouillon; it should reach up to about 1 inch from top of layered ingredients. Sprinkle with crumbs and dot with butter. Bake uncovered in a preheated 350° oven for 1 to 1½ hours or until all the liquid is absorbed. Serves four to six.
Note: To make bread crumbs, put crustless slices of white bread into your blender and turn to high.

Wednesday

Stuffed Pork Chops

Stuffed Pork Chops
Baked Acorn Squash with Pecans
Green Peas
Lemon Layer Cake with Vanilla Ice Cream

6 1-inch thick pork chops, trimmed of excess fat
¾ cup fine dry bread crumbs
⅔ cup minced celery
⅔ cup minced peeled and cored apple
1 tablespoon minced shallots or green onions
1 tablespoon minced parsley
salt
¾ teaspoon dry mustard
3 tablespoons butter
1 tablespoon oil
¾ cup chicken bouillon

Using a sharp knife, make a 2-inch long opening in the pork chops by cutting from the fat side through almost to the bone. Mix together the bread crumbs, celery, apple, shallots, parsley, salt to taste and mustard. Dive the stuffing into 6 parts. Fill each chop with stuffing. Skewer the openings together so that the stuffing won't ooze out during cooking. Heat the butter and oil in a frying pan and brown the chops quickly on both sides. Transfer the chops to a shallow baking dish and place side by side in one layer. Pour the chicken bouillon over chops. Cover or tie foil over the dish. Bake in a preheated oven 350° for about 1 hour. Makes six servings.

Thursday

Ham Steaks with Almonds

Ham Steaks with Almonds
Mashed Potatoes
Green Beans
Cheese Cake

6 slices cooked ham, at least ½-inch thick
1 garlic clove
2 egg yolks, beaten
1½ to 2 cups slivered or chopped blanched almonds
6 tablespoons butter
1 cup heavy cream
1 teaspoon Dijon mustard or more to taste

Rub the ham slices on both sides with the garlic clove. Combine the egg yolks and almonds. Dip the ham slices in the egg mixture. With a spatula, tap the almonds to the meat so that they will stick. Heat 4 tablespoons of butter in a heavy frying pan and cook the ham slices until the almonds are golden brown on both sides. If necessary, add the remaining butter to the frying pan. Transfer the ham to a heated serving dish and keep hot. Stir the cream and mustard into the pan juices. Heat through but do not boil and pour the sauce over the fried ham slices. Makes six servings.

Friday

Sena's Lemon Tart

Sole Meuniére
Buttered Broccoli
Steamed Potatoes
Sena's Lemon Tart

For the pastry shell:
½ cup (1 stick) butter,
cut into pieces
1 cup flour
3 tablespoons confectioners' sugar
pinch of salt

For the filling:
4 eggs, separated
¾ cup + 4 tablespoons sugar
3 tablespoons fresh lemon juice

This tart should be made and eaten the same day as it will collapse the following day. But the shell can be made ahead and frozen after pre-baking for 12 minutes. **To make pastry:** Combine all ingredients in a bowl. Work them together with the fingers until there is a sticky ball. Using a 9-inch layer or cake pan with a removable bottom, put pastry ball into pan. With the heel of your hand, push pastry into pan until a shell is formed. Be sure to make pastry high and thick on the edges, so that the filling won't spill over. Place the pan in freezer and chill for 15 minutes or longer. When needed, bake shell in a preheated oven 425° for 12 minutes, or until lightly browned. Remove from the oven and cool. **To make the filling:** Combine egg yolks, ¾ cup of sugar and lemon juice in a heavy saucepan. Cook over medium heat, stirring constantly, until mixture is thickened. Remove from heat and cool. Beat 2 of the egg whites until stiff and fold into the egg mixture. Pour into baked pastry shell and smooth out top with a spatula. Beat remaining 2 egg whites with 4 tablespoons of sugar until very stiff and shiny. Spread them over top of pastry shell covering the filling completely. Bake in a preheated oven 350° for 10 minutes or until the meringue is golden. Makes one nine-inch tart.

Saturday

Pork Chops in Orange Sauce

Pork Chops in Orange Sauce
Mashed Sweet Potatoes
Steamed Cabbage
Fruit Yogurt and Cookies

6 pork chops
1 teaspoon salt
¼ cup flour
2 tablespoons salad oil
1 cup orange juice
1 tablespoon grated orange rind
1 teaspoon flour
freshly ground pepper

Trim any excess fat off the pork chops. Sprinkle with salt and coat on both sides with flour. Heat the oil in a large frying pan and brown pork chops on both sides. Pour off the fat from the frying pan. Add ½ cup of orange juice to the pork chops. Cover and simmer over low heat for 30 minutes. Transfer the cooked chops to a heated serving dish and keep warm in a very low oven. Stir the remaining ½ cup orange juice, the orange rind and flour into the pan juices, scraping up the brown bits at the bottom. Cook, stirring all the time, until the sauce has thickened. Check the seasoning and add salt and pepper to taste. Pour the sauce over the chops and serve immediately. Makes six servings.

QUICK & EASY DINNERS FOR TWO

March

Sunday

Melting Potatoes

Pan Broiled Minute Steaks with Fresh Squeezed Lemon Juice
Melting Potatoes
Buttered Spinach
Radishes
Cold Lemon Souffle

4 medium potatoes
2 tablespoons olive oil
1 garlic clove, minced
2 tablespoons minced parsley
  or fresh dill weed
½ cup chicken or beef bouillon
  (can be made with cube or instant powder)
salt
freshly ground pepper

Peel the potatoes and cut into ¼-inch dice. Wash and dry potatoes. Heat the oil in a heavy saucepan or casserole. Add the potatoes and stir constantly over low heat for 3-4 minutes or until half cooked. Add the garlic, parsley and bouillon. Season with a little salt (the bouillon is salty) and pepper. Cook covered over low heat until the potatoes are done, about 7-10 minutes. Stir frequently.

Note: Different kinds of potatoes absorb liquid differently. The finished dish should be soft and moist, not soupy. If the potatoes appear to scorch during cooking, add a little more bouillon. If the dish looks too liquid, cook without cover to allow evaporation.

Monday

Creamed Cabbage

Sausages Cooked in Beer
Creamed Cabbage
Baked Acorn Squash
Tossed Green Salad
Pears Cooked in Red Wine

½ small cabbage or about
3 cups shredded
½ cup heavy sweet or
dairy sour cream
1 teaspoon caraway seeds
salt
freshly ground pepper

Trim the cabbage and shred coarsely. Place it in a heavy saucepan. Add about ½ inch boiling water. Cook, shaking the pan frequently, until barely tender, about 3-4 minutes. Check for moisture; if necessary add a little more water, but not too much. The cooked cabbage should be dry. Stir in cream and caraway seeds. Season with salt and pepper. Cook over low heat until just heated through, but do not boil.

Tuesday

Roman Deviled Chicken

Roman Deviled Chicken
Mexican Rice
Green Salad
Sliced Oranges with Sherry

1 1½-pound broiler
olive oil
1 teaspoon crushed red pepper flakes
(or less, for a milder dish)
salt
about ¼ cup dry white wine

Split the chicken in half. Crush flat, bones and all, using a meat mallet, a rolling pin or a corked bottle filled with water. Brush both sides lavishly with olive oil. Sprinkle with red pepper flakes and a little salt. Preheat broiler. Broil about 4 inches away from heat, skin side down for about 15 minutes, brushing twice with more oil. Turn and broil 5-10 minutes longer, brushing twice with more oil. Transfer the chicken to a heated platter and keep hot. Place broiler pan with chicken juices over direct heat and stir in the wine. Bring to the boiling point and pour the sauce over the chicken.

Wednesday

Eggs Lucerne

Eggs Lucerne
Spoon Bread
Stewed Okra and Tomatoes
Carrot and Celery Sticks
Applesauce

½ pound Swiss Cheese, sliced
4 eggs
salt
freshly ground pepper
⅓ cup light or heavy cream
¼ cup grated Swiss cheese

Heavily butter the bottom of a shallow baking dish. Line with the sliced cheese. Break the eggs over the cheese. Season with salt and pepper. Pour the cream over the eggs. Sprinkle with grated cheese. Bake in a preheated moderate 350° oven for 10 minutes or until set.

Thursday

Piquant Mushrooms

Hamburgers on Buns
Piquant Mushrooms
Cheese and Crackers
Frozen Raspberries and Cookies

½ pound small whole mushrooms or large mushrooms, cut into halves or quarters
3 tablespoons butter
1 small onion, minced
1 tablespoon fresh lemon juice
1 tablespoon water or bouillon
salt
freshly ground pepper
1 egg yolk
2 tablespoons heavy cream
2 tablespoons minced parsley or dill weed

Trim the stems of the mushrooms. Wash the mushrooms very quickly under running cold water. Pat them dry with paper towel. If the mushrooms are large, cut them into halves or quarters. In a casserole that can go to the table heat the butter and cook the onion until soft and golden. Add the lemon juice, mushrooms and water. Cook covered over medium heat until the mushrooms are barely tender; shake the pan frequently to prevent sticking. Season with salt and pepper. Beat together the egg yolk and cream. Remove the mushrooms from the heat and stir in the egg mixture. Sprinkle with parsley and serve immediately, from the casserole.

Friday

Curried Carrots

Fish Fillets in White Wine
Boiled Parsleyed Potatoes
Curried Carrots
Baked Bananas and Cream

3 tablespoons butter
1 teaspoon curry powder
  or to taste
5 medium carrots,
  coarsely shredded
salt
freshly ground pepper
2 tablespoons hot water

Melt the butter in a saucepan which has a tight fitting lid. Stir in the curry powder. Cook over medium heat, stirring constantly, for about 2 minutes. Add the carrots and season very lightly with salt and pepper. Add the hot water. Cover tightly. Cook, shaking the saucepan frequently, for about 5 minutes or until just tender.

Saturday

Quick Shrimp Curry

Quick Shrimp Curry
Rice
Orange and Onion Salad
First Stewed Rhubarb
of the Season

2 tablespoons butter or
  salad oil
2 teaspoons curry powder
  or to taste
1 small onion, minced
¼ cup minced celery
1 hard apple or pear, cored,
  but not peeled, and cut into
  ½-inch pieces
⅔ cup hot water
salt
freshly ground pepper
½ to ¾ lb. shelled
  fresh shrimp, or
  shelled frozen shrimp, defrosted
½ cup heavy cream

Heat the butter in a heavy saucepan. Stir in the curry powder. Cook over medium heat, stirring constantly, for about 1 minute. Add the onion and celery. Cook, stirring all the time, for 2–3 minutes or until the onion is soft but not brown. Add the apple or pear and water. Mix well and season with salt and pepper to taste. Cook over low to medium heat, stirring frequently, for about 5 minutes. Add the shrimp and cream. Cook over low heat, stirring frequently, until the liquid in the pan is reduced to sauce consistency.

Note: The amounts of liquid used in this dish also depend on the size of the saucepan in which it is cooked. If your saucepan is small, add only ½ cup of water first, if it is large, add water if the mixture is scorching.

BUDGET DINNERS

March

Sunday **Marinated Chuck Steak**

Marinated Chuck Steak
Roast Potatoes
Buttered Green Beans
Winter Fruit Compote and Cookies

2 pounds chuck steak, 1-inch thick, well-trimmed
¼ cup chopped onion
2 tablespoons chopped celery leaves
5 crushed peppercorns
2 garlic cloves, crushed
2 tablespoons chopped parsley
½ cup dry red wine
1 tablespoon vinegar
¼ cup olive or salad oil
½ teaspoon salt
juice of 1 lemon

Place the meat in a non-metal bowl. Sprinkle with onion, celery, peppercorns, garlic and parsley. In a small saucepan, heat together the wine, vinegar, oil and salt. Bring to boil and pour over meat. Cover the bowl with plastic wrap or aluminum foil. Let stand in a cool place or refrigerator for 8 hours, turning every two hours and thoroughly moistening each side. When ready to broil, wipe the meat dry and place on broiler pan. Preheat broiler for 10 minutes, then put in broiler pan. Broil 2 inches from heat for 4 minutes on the first side. Turn and broil 2 minutes on the reverse side. This will produce rare meat. For medium rare, broil 1 minute longer on each side. Remove to carving platter. Squeeze the lemon juice over the meat. Carve very thin slices against the grain with a very sharp knife. Serves four.

Monday

Vegetable Aspic

Hot Consommé with Rice
Cold Cuts
Vegetable Aspic
Custard Pie

2 envelopes unflavored gelatin
¼ cup cold water
4 cups tomato juice
½ cup celery tops
1 medium onion, chopped
½ teaspoon dried thyme
salt
freshly ground pepper
1 cup sliced celery stalks, white part only
½ cup diced green pepper
½ cup sliced peeled and seeded cucumber

Sprinkle the gelatin over the water and stir to blend. In a medium saucepan, combine the tomato juice, celery tops, onion, thyme and salt and pepper to taste. Bring to boil. Reduce the heat and simmer over low heat without a cover for 30 minutes. Strain and stir in the gelatin, stirring until it is totally dissolved. Cool. Stir in the sliced celery, green pepper and cucumber. Pour into a 5-cup ring mold or pan which has been rinsed with cold water and chill until firm. To unmold, place for 1 second in a bowl of hot water and loosen edges with a knife. Four servings.

Tuesday

Stuffed Cabbage Leaves

Stuffed Cabbage Leaves
Orange and Onion Salad
Apple Pie

12 large cabbage leaves
1 cup cooked rice
1 pound mixed beef, pork and veal, or any two, ground together
1 medium onion, minced
1 egg
2 tablespoons minced parsley
salt
freshly ground pepper
2 tablespoons bacon fat
½ cup beef bouillon
tomato sauce (about 2 cups)

Place the cabbage leaves in a large bowl. Cover with boiling water and let stand for 5 minutes. Drain. Mix together the rice, meat, onion, egg, parsley and salt and pepper to taste. Divide the mixture evenly among the 12 leaves and place a little on each leaf. Roll up, tucking in sides and making neat packages. Tie each package with string. Heat the bacon fat in a large frying pan and brown cabbage rolls on all sides. Place them in a single layer in a rectangular baking dish. Rinse out the frying pan with bouillon and pour over the cabbage rolls. Cover tightly with foil. Bake in a preheated oven 350° for 1 hour. Serve with tomato sauce on the side.

Wednesday

Chicken Marengo

Chicken Marengo
Buttered Noodles
Tossed Green Salad
Ice Cream

2 2½-pound fryers, cut into serving pieces
½ cup flour
1 teaspoon salt
freshly ground pepper
4 tablespoons olive oil
6 tablespoons butter
1 cup dry white wine
2 garlic cloves, minced
2 cups canned tomatoes
½ to 1 pound mushrooms, sliced

Trim any excess fat from chicken. If desired skin, but remember that skinned pieces will cook quicker. Mix together the flour, salt and pepper. Coat the chicken pieces with mix on all sides and shake off excess flour. Heat the oil and 4 tablespoons of butter in a large, deep frying pan. Add the chicken pieces and brown them on all sides. Transfer the chicken to a large casserole which can go to the table. Stir wine into the frying pan. Cook over low heat, stirring constantly, until the sauce is thick and smooth. Add garlic and tomatoes and cook for 2-3 minutes longer. Pour sauce over the chicken. Bake covered for about 30-45 minutes or until the chicken is tender. Saute the mushrooms briefly in the remaining 2 tablespoons butter; they must retain their shape. Add them to the chicken 5 minutes before serving time to heat through. Serves four to six.

Thursday

Tongue with Raisin Sauce

Tongue with Raisin Sauce
Stuffed Onions
French Fried Potatoes
Maple Cake

1 fresh tongue, weighing about 4 pounds
1 onion stuck with 4 cloves
1 bay leaf
2 celery stalks with leaves
4 parsley sprigs
2 teaspoons salt
6 peppercorns

Put the tongue into a large kettle with water to cover. Add the onion, bay leaf, celery stalks, parsley, salt and peppercorns. Bring to boil. Reduce heat to very low, and simmer covered for 2½ to 3 hours or until tender. Remove the tongue from the broth. With a sharp knife, cut off the thick covering skin and gristly part at the root end. Slice the tongue and serve either warm or cold. Serves six.

Raisin Sauce: Mix together in a saucepan ½ cup brown sugar, ½ tablespoon dry mustard and ½ tablespoon cornstarch. Stir in 1½ cups water and stir until smooth. Stir in ½ cup Madeira, 3 tablespoons vinegar and 1 cup seedless raisins. Cook without a cover over medium heat, stirring all the time, until the sauce is thickened and syrupy. One and a half cups.

Friday

Tuna Pie

Tuna Pie
Orange and Onion Salad
Baked Bananas

plain pastry for a 2 crust pie,
 using 2½ cups flour
 and ¾ cup shortening
4 tablespoons butter
½ cup minced celery
¼ cup flour
1¾ cups milk
salt
Tabasco
1 teaspoon Worcestershire
 sauce
1 cup frozen peas, thawed
2 7-ounce cans tuna, drained and
 broken into bite-size pieces

Make the pastry and line a 9-inch pie pan with it. Chill. Heat butter in a frying pan and cook the celery for 7-10 minutes or until very soft but not browned. Stir in flour and cook 2 minutes longer. Stir in the milk. Cook, stirring constantly, until the sauce is smooth and thickened. Season with salt and Tabasco to taste and stir in Worcestershire sauce. Fold the peas and the tuna into sauce. Spoon into the pie shell. Cover with the top crust. Bake in a preheated oven 400° for 15 minutes, lower heat to 350° and bake for 25 minutes longer, or until the crust is golden. Serves four to six.

Saturday

Hamburger Pie

Hamburger Pie
Pickles
Carrot and Celery Sticks
Fruit Salad with Oranges,
 Grapefruit and Apples

2 pounds of lean ground beef
salt
freshly ground pepper
1 tablespoon Dijon mustard
1 large Spanish onion,
 thinly sliced
1 large green pepper,
 cut into strips
1 1-pound can peeled tomatoes,
 drained, juice reserved
4 tablespoons grated Cheddar or
 Parmesan cheese

Season the meat with salt and pepper to taste. Divide into 2 parts and put one part into a 9-inch round cake pan or casserole. Spread the meat with mustard. Top with onion slices and top these with pepper strips and half of the tomatoes. Cover with remaining meat. Spread the remaining tomatoes over the meat and sprinkle with 2 to 4 tablespoons of the reserved tomato juice. Sprinkle with the cheese. Bake in a preheated oven 350° for 30 minutes. Makes six servings.

ENTERTAINING

March

Sunday

Finnan Haddie Delmonico

Finnan Haddie Delmonico
Toast Points
Marinated Mushrooms with Herbs
Cold Coffee Soufflé

2 pounds smoked finnan haddie
milk
6 hard-cooked eggs, peeled and sliced
1 cup heavy cream
4 tablespoons butter
dash of Tabasco
¼ cup minced parsley

Place the fish in a buttered shallow baking pan. Add enough milk to cover the fish. Cover the dish with foil and tie with string. Place in a preheated oven 350°. Poach for 20 minutes or until the fish flakes easily. Pour off the milk, remove fish from pan, and cool enough to handle. Bone and flake the fish into largest possible pieces. Place the flaked fish in an ovenproof serving dish and arrange the sliced eggs on top. Keep warm in a low oven. Heat together the cream, butter, and Tabasco. Pour over the fish and eggs. Sprinkle with the parsley and serve crisp toast points on the side. Serves four to six.

Monday

Ambrosia

Cheese Soufflé
Marinated Celery and Artichoke Hearts
Garlic Melba Toast
Ambrosia

4 large navel oranges
1 small fresh pineapple
½ cup superfine sugar or sifted confectioners' sugar
1 cup fresh grated coconut
2 bananas

Peel the oranges, removing all yellow and white skins. Section carefully and put into a glass bowl. Peel the pineapple, making sure no eyes remain. Remove the hard core and dice. Add to the oranges. Mix together the sugar and coconut and sprinkle over the oranges and pineapple. Chill. Just before serving, slice the bananas and add them to the fruit bowl, mixing carefully. Serves five to six.

Note: To prepare fresh coconut: Using an ice pick, a skewer, or a knitting needle, pound holes in the coconut's eyes. Turn over a bowl and let the water (which is *not* the coconut milk) run out. Place the whole coconut into a baking pan and put it into a oven 350° for 20-30 minutes. Remove, cool, and break open with a mallet or a hammer. Remove the shell and with a sharp knife peel off the inner skin. Cut the white meat into pieces. Grate on a cheese grater or in a blender. Excess coconut can be frozen in small amounts for later use, such as in curry, cakes, or as dessert toppings.

Tuesday

Rock Cornish Hens with Ginger Orange Sauce

Rock Cornish Hens with Ginger Orange Sauce
Persian Rice
Buttered Baby Carrots
Vanilla-Poached Apples with Real Custard Sauce

6 Rock Cornish hens, split
salt
freshly ground pepper
6 tablespoons butter
2 tablespoons salad oil
¼ cup Grand Marnier or other orange liqueur
2 cans undiluted frozen orange juice
¾ cup ginger marmalade
3 tablespoons grated orange rind
watercress
mandarin orange sections

Wash and wipe the hens dry. Sprinkle with salt and pepper on both sides. Heat the butter and salad oil in a deep frying pan and brown the hens, one or two at one time, turning frequently. Place the hens in a baking dish in one or two layers. Heat the Grand Marnier and flame the hens. In a saucepan heat together the orange juice, ginger marmalade, and orange rind. Pour the sauce over the hens. Cover the baking dish tightly with a lid or tied-on foil. Bake in a preheated oven 350° for 30 minutes. Remove cover, cook for 10-15 minutes longer, basting frequently. Place on a heated serving platter and garnish with watercress and mandarin orange sections. Six servings.

Wednesday

Eggplant and Bean Salad

Hot Borscht with Sour Cream
Roast Duck Stuffed with Onions
Eggplant and Bean Salad
Strawberry Bavarian

2 large eggplants
2 large tomatoes
2 large garlic cloves
⅔ cup parsley sprigs
2 teaspoons dried basil leaves or
1 teaspoon dried oregano or thyme
½ cup olive oil
juice of 1 large lemon
salt
freshly ground pepper
2 cups drained canned cannelline
or white beans
2 tablespoons drained capers
salad greens

Prick the eggplants with a fork, place on a baking sheet, and cook in a 350° oven for 30-50 minutes or until they are soft. Cool the eggplants. Slit the skin open and remove the seeds with a spoon. Scrape the flesh into a bowl and throw the skins away. Mash the eggplants with a fork until they are mushy. Skin the tomatoes, squeeze out the seeds, and chop the pulp finely. Mince together on a chopping board the garlic, parsley, and basil. Add tomatoes and the garlic mixture to the eggplant and mix well. Combine the olive oil, lemon juice, salt, and pepper and stir into eggplant. Mix well. Rinse the canned beans under running cold water and shake dry; this eliminates the soupiness of canned beans. Add beans to the eggplant mixture, stir carefully with a fork, and check the seasoning. Stir in the capers and serve on a bed of salad greens. Serves four to six.

Thursday

Ricotta Dessert

American Bouillabaisse
Hot Cornsticks or Muffins
Belgian Endive, Watercress,and Shredded Red Beet Salad
Ricotta Dessert

1 cup mixed glacé fruit, cut
into very small dice
⅓ cup Kirsch or rum
2 pounds fresh ricotta cheese
(no substitutes)
4 tablespoons sugar, or to taste
¼ cup heavy cream
grated rind of 1 lemon
⅓ cup chopped bitter sweet chocolate
(do not use milk chocolate)

Soak the glacé fruit in Kirsch or rum for at least 2 hours. Strain the ricotta through a fine sieve to make it fluffy, or use a potato ricer. Stir in, one at a time and stirring well after each addition, the sugar, cream, lemon rind, the glacé fruit and its juice and chocolate. Pile into a glass serving dish. Cover with plastic or aluminum foil and chill before serving. Makes four to six servings.

Friday

Roman Lamb Casserole with Artichokes

Cream of Mushroom Soup
Roman Lamb Casserole with Artichokes
Barley Pilaf
Tossed Green Salad
Cold Orange Soufflé

juice of 1 lemon
4 large artichokes, sliced
2 tablespoons butter
2 tablespoons olive oil
3 pounds boneless lamb
1 large onion, minced
2 garlic cloves, minced
1 cup minced parsley
3 tablespoons flour
1½ cups beef bouillon
salt
freshly ground pepper

Slice artichokes and drop them into acidulated cold water to prevent them from darkening. At cooking time drain and dry the artichoke pieces on a paper towel. Cut off all fat, gristle, and connective tissue from meat. Cut into 1½-inch cubes. Wash and dry the meat thoroughly; if not totally dry, it will not brown. Heat butter and olive oil in a large frying pan and brown the lamb on all sides over high heat. Transfer the meat to a 3-quart casserole. In the same frying pan, and stirring constantly, cook the onion, garlic, and parsley until onion is tender. Stir in flour and cook, stirring constantly, for 1-2 minutes. Stir in the beef bouillon and season with a little salt and pepper to taste. Cook, stirring all the time, for about 3 more minutes or until sauce has thickened. Pour sauce over meat in the casserole. Bring to boil and, if too thick, add a little more beef bouillon. Lower the heat to low. Simmer covered for about 30 minutes or until meat is about ¾ done. Add artichokes and simmer 15 more minutes or until meat and artichokes are tender but not mushy. If the sauce is too thin, cook with a cover to reduce it. Serves four to six.

Note: After the meat has reached the boiling point, it may be cooked in a preheated medium oven (350°). If this is for a party with no fixed dining time, cook the dish in as slow an oven as desired, 300° or even 250°, and adjust cooking time accordingly.

Saturday

Buffet for Twenty

COLD:

Country Terrine*

Watercress **Greek Olives** **Radishes**

Tiny Pickles **French Bread**

HOT:

Beef Bourguignon†

Rice and Mushroom Casserole

Salad of Belgian Endives, Watercress and Avocado Pieces

Fresh Pineapple with Kirsch Almond Cookies

**Recipe in book*

† You will need 10 pounds of lean beef, such as round, to serve twenty because it cooks down. Even lean beef has to be trimmed of surprisingly much gristle and fat. Purchase 12 pounds to realize 10 pounds of serving beef. If the wine you are serving with the meal is not too expensive, use it for the Beef Bourguignon. Otherwise, use a good quality dry red wine, such as a generic Burgundy from California or Spain.

A buffet does not have to feature a dozen or so dishes. Of course, it can do so and that makes it one kind of buffet. But a buffet can also have the number of courses that would be served at a regular dinner, provided that all the courses can be eaten with a fork only. This is important because not all people who give parties for twenty can sit them down at a table; most likely, the guests will sit where they can and eat from their laps. If this is the case, the guests should be given large napkins to protect their clothing. These napkins can be old-fashioned white ones, but they can also be made from any pretty, inexpensive fabric and roughly hemmed.

The most practical way of serving a buffet is to place the cold foods at one end of the table and the hot ones at the other. Two sets of plates and silverware, napkins, salt and pepper occupy the space in the middle. The wine and wine glasses stand on another small table, and so does the dessert and its plates and whatever cookies are served with it.

By keeping the number of dishes down, the cooking can be much more careful. The whole buffet becomes much more manageable for the hostess who has to do everything herself than one that is a hodgepodge of various foods.

A meal for this many people should only have dishes that are sure to appeal to everybody. This, in a way, excludes surprises in the choice of the foods, but not surprises at how well and interestingly it has been prepared. Even the best-known dish can be made with any number of variations. Fish and seafood should never be the main dish; too many people do not care for them or are allergic, even to lobster.

The wine that goes well with the following menu is a good Burgundy from France, such as a Richebourg or an Aloxe-Corton or from California, a Robert Mondavi Pinot Noir or a Parducci Petite Sirah.

Country Terrine

2 tablespoons butter
1½ cups minced shallots
2½ teaspoons Spice Parisienne *or* ½ teaspoon each: ground allspice, ground mace, rosemary (crumbled) and dried thyme
1 teaspoon ground cardamom
½ pound cooked ham, cut into very small dice
1 pound boneless lean pork, ground twice
1 pound boneless lean veal, ground twice
1 pound fresh pork fat, ground twice
1 pound chicken livers, cut into fine strips with scissors
4 teaspoons salt
2 teaspoons freshly ground black pepper
¼ teaspoon cayenne pepper
3 eggs, slightly beaten
1 cup shelled pistachios, chopped (optional)
½ cup brandy
1 cup heavy cream
2 bay leaves
1 cup minced parsley

This is flavorful, but not too highly spiced. If you trust your butcher, you can ask him to grind the meats for you; generally, it is advisable to do it oneself.

Heat butter in frying pan. Add the shallots. Cook, stirring constantly, until shallots are soft. Stir in the Spice Parisienne and the cardamom. Cook for 1 more minute. Remove from heat and reserve. Combine all the other ingredients except the bay leaves and the parsley in a large bowl. Add the shallot mixture. Mix well, using a spoon and your hands. This will take a little time because the mixture is very stiff. Pack the mixture into a 3-quart ovenproof dish, preferably an oval one. A heavy casserole will do. Place the 2 bay leaves, one at each end, on the mixture. Tightly cover the dish. Set in a baking pan filled with 2 inches of water. Bake in a preheated 350° oven for 2½ hours. Uncover and bake 30 more minutes. As needed during baking time, add hot water to the baking pan to keep up the level. Remove the cooked terrine from the baking pan with the water. Cool it under a heavy weight by placing another heavy casserole on it, or food cans. Remove the weight when terrine is cold. Chill it for at least ¾ hours. There will be a lot of liquid fat around the meat which will solidify during chilling. Scrape off at serving time. Place terrine on a serving dish and sprinkle parsley over it. Garnish with more parsley sprigs, watercress, and olives. Serves twenty.

Note: The terrine will keep in the refrigerator for 1 week if it is uncut and in its fat and tightly covered. If only a part of the terrine is wanted for a serving, cut off what you need but leave the rest in its fat. Scrape off fat before serving cut portion.

APRIL

It's spring! It's asparagus time! The strawberries are coming! Is there a soul so dead as not to rejoice in treats that cost so little compared to the pleasure they give? I've always admired a friend who buys herself a pound or two of the first asparagus to feast on all by herself — her private celebration of the Rites of Spring. And I've always despised those who serve their guests a measly three or four spears of the most ambrosial of all vegetables. Peel your asparagus, friends, with a swivel vegetable parer up to the tip or down to the the stalk, as the case may be. This way, the whole asparagus can be eaten, though of course, you must break or cut off the woody stem base. Enjoy asparagus while it lasts. I like to make a whole meal of it, followed by a bit of cheese and a bowl of the fresh, new strawberries. Add a bottle of good, cool white wine, and I have heaven on earth.

APRIL

	FAMILY FARE	
	LUNCHES	**DINNERS**
Sunday	Waffles with Creamed Chicken* Pickled Peaches Baked Apples with Caramel Sauce	Pork Roast Piquant* Browned Potatoes Red Cabbage Lady Baltimore Cake
Monday	Croque Monsieur* Shredded Carrots with Mayonnaise Applesauce	Curried Lamb Meatballs with Bananas* Rice Avocado and Orange Salad Fresh Pineapple with Rum
Tuesday	Corned Beef Hash on English Muffins Coleslaw Mocha Mousse*	Vorschmack* Baked Potatoes Belgian Endive and Watercress Salad Pear Crunch Pie
Wednesday	Spinach Salad Bowl* French Bread Cheese	Swedish Pot Roast* Mashed Potatoes Peas and Onions Cauliflower Vinaigrette Orange Cake
Thursday	Eggs Baked in Bacon Rings* Waldorf Salad Brownies	Pasta Rustica* Sliced Ham and Cold Cuts French Bread Lemon Meringue Pie
Friday	Three Bean Rarebit* Carrot and Celery Sticks Orange, Grapefruit and Apple Fruit Salad	Fish Chowder* Corn Bread Spinach Salad Fudge Cake
Saturday	Lentil Soup* Egg Salad Sandwiches Fruit Salad	Roast Chicken Buttered Noodles Watercress Salad with Mustard Dressing 3-Minute Fudge Cake*

QUICK & EASY Dinners For Two	BUDGET DINNERS	ENTERTAINING
Marinated Lamb Chops* White Beans in Tomato Sauce Sauteed Broccoli Boston Cream Pie	Pork and Sausage Casserole* Boiled Potatoes Coleslaw Lemon Nutmeg Pie	Sausages Poached in Wine* Black Beans and Rum Sliced Avocados and Tomatoes with Hot Salad Dressing (Chili Peppers to Taste) Flambéed Bananas
Welsh Rarebit* Toast Buttered Whole Leaf Spinach Pickled Beets Grapefruit with Honey	Jambalaya* Cucumber Salad Coffee Ice Cream Topped with Chopped Peanuts	Spring Soup* Fillet of Sole in White Wine Sauce Watercress Salad Cream Cheese, Guava Shells, and Crackers
Pork Chops with Sautéed Apples Lima Beans in Cream* Home Fried Potatoes Lemon Pie	Shoulder Lamb Chops en Casserole* Spinach Salad Baked Stuffed Potatoes Cut Up Oranges, Grapefruits and Bananas	Roquefort Timbales/Sauce Aurore* Parslied Leg of Spring Lamb Sauteed Beets with Sour Cream Butter-Steamed New Potatoes Rum Chiffon Pie
Minute Steaks with Herb Butter Mashed Potatoes Dandelion Greens Grated Carrot Salad Sliced Oranges and Apples with Marsala or Sherry*	Eggs Divan* Mixed Green Salad Pears and Cheese	Broiled Grapefruit with Sherry Smoked Ham (Virginia, Kentucky, etc.) Potatoes with Leeks from Fribourg* Watercress Salad Apple Tart with Whipped Cream
Grilled Mustard Chicken Carrots and Shallots* French Fries Watercress and Mushroom Salad Fresh Pineapple	Sweet and Sour Beef* Boiled Potatoes Green Beans with Parsley Butter Chocolate Pudding	Hungarian Cream of Mushroom Soup* Stuffed Roast Chicken Gratin of Potatoes Buttered Peas and Tiny Onions Fruit Salad and Cookies
Fish Fillets Baked in Cream Egg and Lemon Rice* Broccoli Vinaigrette Pound Cake and Ice Cream	Broiled Fish Fillets with Lemon and Dill Baked Corn and Tomatoes* Orange Raisin Pie	Marinated Mushrooms and Pimento on Salad Greens Singapore Shrimp* Dry Rice Chutney Pears in Red Wine Cookies
Eggs in Mustard Sauce* Rice and Mushrooms Grilled Tomatoes Orange Bavarian	Glazed Pork Loin Browned Potatoes Glazed Carrots Sour Cream Apple Pie*	Pâté and Melba Toast Veal with Artichokes* Buttered Rice Salad and Cheeses Ice Cream Bombe

FAMILY FARE LUNCHES

April

Sunday **Waffles with Creamed Chicken**

Waffles with Creamed Chicken
Pickled Peaches
Baked Apples with Caramel Sauce

Waffles

2 cups flour
1 teaspoon baking powder
½ teaspoon baking soda
1 teaspoon salt
1½ cups buttermilk
3 eggs
½ cup melted butter

Sift directly into a bowl, the flour, baking powder, baking soda and salt. Quickly stir in the buttermilk, eggs and butter. Beat until smooth. Make the waffles the usual way in the waffle iron, keeping the ready waffles warm in a low oven. Makes eight double waffles.

Note: This batter may be used immediately or left standing for several hours. In this case, stir before using.

Creamed Chicken

4 whole chicken breasts
2 cups chicken bouillon
4 tablespoons butter
3 tablespoons flour
1 cup milk
salt
freshly ground pepper

Put chicken breasts into a heavy saucepan and add bouillon. Bring to boil, lower heat, cover and simmer for 30 minutes or until tender. Cool. Remove chicken breasts from broth. Save the broth. Cut all the meat off the bones, remove all skin and sinews and cut into ½-inch dice. Bring broth to boil and cook over high heat until it is reduced to about 1 cup. Heat butter in a saucepan and stir in flour. Cook, stirring constantly, for 2 minutes. Add the milk and broth all at once. Cook, stirring all the time, until the sauce is thickened and smooth. Season with salt and pepper. Add the diced chicken to the sauce. Cook over lowest possible heat, preferably over an asbestos plate or in the top of a double boiler over simmering water, for about 30 minutes, to blend the flavors of the chicken and the sauce. To serve, spoon the creamed chicken over the waffles. Makes about six cups.

Monday

Croque Monsieur

Croque Monsieur
Shredded Carrots with Mayonnaise
Applesauce

8 slices stale white bread
butter, softened
4 slices boiled ham
8 thin slices Swiss cheese
approximately 6 tablespoons butter
1 cup hot Medium White Sauce
paprika

Spread each slice of bread with butter. Make 4 sandwiches, using 2 slices of cheese and 1 slice of ham for each sandwich, placing ham between 2 slices of cheese. Cut each sandwich in half. Tie each sandwich half lightly with string or skewer it together. Heat 4 tablespoons of the butter in a frying pan. Cook the sandwiches in it until golden on both sides, turning once. Place 2 sandwich halves on a heated dinner plate, cover with some of the White Sauce and sprinkle with paprika. Serve immediately. Serves four.
Medium White Sauce Heat 2 tablespoons of butter in a saucepan. Stir in 2 tablespoons of flour. Stir in 1 cup of milk. Cook, stirring constantly, until the sauce is smooth and thickened. Stir in ¼ cup grated Swiss cheese and cook until the cheese has melted.

Tuesday

Mocha Mousse

Corned Beef Hash on English Muffins
Coleslaw
Mocha Mousse

1 cup strong coffee
3 squares unsweetened chocolate (2 ounces)
¾ cup sugar
pinch of salt
1 package unflavored gelatin
1 tablespoon rum
1 cup heavy cream

Combine the coffee and 2 of the chocolate squares in a heavy saucepan. Cook over very low heat, stirring constantly, until the chocolate has melted. Add the sugar, salt and gelatin. Cook until both are dissolved. Remove from heat and beat until smooth. Chill until the mixture begins to thicken. Stir in the rum. Beat the cream to whipped cream and fold into the chocolate mixture. Turn into a glass serving dish and chill or freeze until firm. Decorate with chocolate curls made by grating the remaining square of chocolate on the coarse side of a cheese grater. Makes four to six servings.

Wednesday

Spinach Salad Bowl

Spinach Salad Bowl
French Bread
Cheese

½ cup olive oil
¼ cup lemon juice
2 tablespoons wine vinegar
1 garlic clove, mashed
salt
freshly ground pepper
1 pound fresh young spinach
2 tablespoons grated
  Parmesan cheese
2 hard cooked eggs, chopped
6 bacon slices, fried
  crisp and crumbled
½ cup croutons

Combine the olive oil, lemon juice, vinegar, garlic clove and salt and pepper to taste. Mix well. Clean the spinach by pulling the leaves off the stems and washing them thoroughly in several waters. Tear the drained spinach leaves into bite size pieces with your fingers. Place them in a salad bowl. Add the dressing and the Parmesan cheese and toss. Add the eggs, the crumbled bacon and the croutons and toss once more. Makes six servings.

Thursday

Eggs Baked in Bacon Rings

Eggs Baked in Bacon Rings
Waldorf Salad
Brownies

2-3 bacon slices
1 tablespoon chili sauce
1 egg
2 teaspoons melted butter
salt
freshly ground pepper
buttered toast

Cook or broil the bacon until it is just beginning to get crisp; it should still be pliable. Grease the bottom of muffin pans or individual baking dishes. Line the sides with the bacon which must cover the sides of the dish completely to prevent the egg from oozing out during cooking. Pour the chili sauce into the muffin pan or baking dish. Drop the egg on top of the chili sauce. Drizzle the butter over the egg and sprinkle with salt and pepper. Bake in a preheated oven 325° for 10 minutes or until the egg is set. Turn out on buttered toast and serve immediately. Makes single individual serving.

Friday

Three Bean Rarebit

Three Bean Rarebit
Carrot and Celery Sticks
Orange, Grapefruit and Apple Fruit Salad

4 slices bacon
1 large onion, minced
1 1-pound can baked beans in tomato sauce
1 1-pound can red kidney beans, drained
1 1-pound can lima beans, drained
½ pound Cheddar cheese, cubed
½ cup light or dark brown sugar
⅓ cup tomato ketchup
1 tablespoon Worcestershire sauce
grated Parmesan cheese (optional)

Though we usually distrust dishes made almost exclusively from canned ingredients, this casserole is good, inexpensive, easy and filling. What more can anybody want? Cook the bacon in a large deep frying pan until it is crisp. Drain and crumble. Cook the onion in the bacon fat until it begins to turn brown. Remove from heat and stir in beans, cheese cubes, brown sugar, ketchup and Worcestershire sauce. Spoon the mixture into a buttered baking dish. Sprinkle with Parmesan cheese. Bake in a preheated oven 350° for about 30 minutes. Makes six servings.

Saturday

Lentil Soup

Lentil Soup
Egg Salad Sandwiches
Fruit Salad

2 cups dried lentils
2 quarts cold water
¼ pound bacon, in one piece
1 large onion, finely chopped
1 large carrot, finely chopped
1 celery stalk, finely chopped
2 tablespoons bacon fat
½ cup minced onion
2 tablespoons flour
2 tablespoons vinegar
salt
freshly ground pepper

Wash lentils under running cold water. Pour 2 quarts of water into a large kettle and bring to boil. Add the lentils, bacon, onion, carrot and celery. Cover partially and simmer over low heat for 30 minutes. Heat bacon fat in a large heavy frying pan. Add minced onion and cook, stirring constantly, until golden brown. Stir in flour and cook, stirring all the time, until golden brown. Ladle about ½ cup of lentil soup into the frying pan and stir thoroughly until mixture is smooth and thickened. Stir in vinegar. Turn whole contents of frying pan into the lentil soup, scraping the bottom with a rubber spatula. Season with salt and pepper. Stir thoroughly. Simmer over low heat covered for 30 more minutes or until lentils are tender but not mushy. Before serving, cut bacon into ½-inch dice and return to soup. Serves six.

Note: The soup may be made more substantial with the addition of sliced frankfurters. Add them 15 minutes before the soup is finished.

FAMILY FARE DINNERS

April

Sunday

Pork Roast Piquant

Pork Roast Piquant
Browned Potatoes
Red Cabbage
Lady Baltimore Cake

¼ cup Dijon mustard
1 tablespoon freshly grated or drained bottled horseradish
1 teaspoon anchovy paste
1 tablespoon sugar
1 pork loin, weighing about 3-4 pounds
⅔ cup fine dry bread crumbs
2 cups boiling dry white wine or water

Blend the mustard, horseradish, anchovy paste and sugar to a smooth paste. Trim excess fat off the meat. With a pastry brush, spread the meat on all sides with mustard mixture. Place on a rack in a baking pan. Cover the top and sides with bread crumbs. Roast 35 - 40 minutes to the pound in a preheated oven 325°. After 45 minutes of roasting time, pour 1 cup of boiling wine into the pan, around the meat. Be careful that the wine or water does not touch the meat. When the liquid has evaporated, pour the remaining wine into the pan, around the meat. Slice the meat and place it in overlapping slices on a heated platter. Keep warm. Skim the fat off the pan juices. Bring them to boil and reduce to about ½ cup. Spoon this gravy over the meat slices.

Monday

Curried Lamb Meatballs with Bananas

Curried Lamb Meatballs with Bananas
Rice
Avocado and Orange Salad
Fresh Pineapple with Rum

1½ pounds ground lamb
1 egg
3 tablespoons fine dry bread crumbs
1 teaspoon salt
½ teaspoon ground cumin
½ teaspoon ground cinnamon
2 tablespoons salad oil
½ cup minced onion
1 garlic clove, minced
1 teaspoon curry powder or to taste
1 cup chicken bouillon
1 apple, peeled, cored and diced
1 tablespoon apricot jam
2 bananas, peeled and sliced
2 tablespoons butter

Mix together the lamb, egg, crumbs, salt, cumin and cinnamon and shape into small balls. Heat oil in a frying pan. Cook the lamb balls until lightly browned. Add the onion and garlic and cook, stirring constantly, until soft. Stir in the curry powder and cook for 3 minutes longer. Curry powders vary greatly in intensity of flavor. A true India curry powder will be quite a lot hotter than a domestic curry powder. Add chicken bouillon, the apple and the jam. Cover and simmer for 30 minutes. After 15 or 20 minutes cooking time, remove the cover to reduce the sauce. Just before serving, peel and slice bananas. Sauté them quickly in the butter until golden. Garnish the meatballs with the sautéed bananas. Serves six.

Tuesday

Vorschmack

Vorschmack
Baked Potatoes
Belgian Endive and Watercress Salad
Pear Crunch Pie

2 tablespoons butter
¼ cup minced onion
1 cup mushrooms, chopped
1 cup any leftover meat, trimmed free of fat and diced
1 cup diced ham
1 cup diced cooked chicken
1 cup diced boiled potatoes
1 dill pickle, diced
½ cup black or green olives, stoned and chopped
1 teaspoon salt
freshly ground pepper
1½ cups sour cream
2 hard-cooked eggs, chopped
2-3 tomatoes, sliced
¼ cup grated Parmesan or Swiss cheese

Heat butter in a frying pan and cook the onion until soft. Add mushrooms and cook, stirring constantly, for 3 minutes. Turn the mixture into a bowl and add the meat, ham, chicken, potatoes, pickle and olives. Season with salt and pepper. Turn into a buttered baking dish. Spoon sour cream over the mixture. Cover with chopped eggs. Place the tomato slices around the edges. Sprinkle with cheese. Bake in a preheated oven 350° for 20 minutes or until thoroughly heated through. Makes four to five servings.

Wednesday

Swedish Pot Roast

Swedish Pot Roast
Mashed Potatoes
Peas and Onions
Cauliflower Vinaigrette
Orange Cake

4 pounds beef chuck or round
2 teaspoons salt
1 teaspoon allspice
½ teaspoon freshly ground pepper
3 tablespoons butter
3 tablespoons brandy or whiskey
⅓ cup hot beef bouillon
2 medium onions, sliced
3 minced anchovy fillets or 1 teaspoon anchovy paste
2 bay leaves
2 tablespoons white or cider vinegar
2 tablespoons molasses or dark syrup
1 cup heavy cream, whipped

The anchovies give it a subtle flavor, not at all fishy. Trim all excess fat and gristle off meat; you'll be surprised how much this will amount to. Rub meat with salt, allspice and pepper. Heat butter in a heavy casserole or kettle which is large enough to hold the meat. Brown meat over high heat. Pour brandy over the hot meat and flame. When the flame has died down, add the remaining ingredients except the whipped cream. Simmer covered over very low heat for 2 hours or until meat is tender. Check occasionally for moisture; if necessary, add a few tablespoons of hot bouillon or water. Transfer the cooked meat to a heated platter and keep hot. To make gravy, remove the bay leaves and skim off fat. Put the vegetables and the pan juices into a blender and puree. Return to the pan and heat through. Check the seasonings. Fold in the whipped cream and heat for 15 seconds. Remove from heat. Slice the meat and arrange it in overlapping slices on a heated platter. Spoon a little gravy over the slices and serve the rest of gravy separately. Serves six.

Thursday

Pasta Rustica

Pasta Rustica
Sliced Ham and Cold Cuts
French Bread
Lemon Meringue Pie

1 cup parsley sprigs
2 garlic cloves
1 large onion
¾ cup olive oil
1 large leek, chopped or 3 spring onions, white and green parts, chopped
2 medium carrots, chopped
1 teaspoon dried basil
3 tomatoes, peeled and chopped
2 cups beef bouillon
3 cups shredded cabbage
2 zucchini, chopped
salt
freshly ground pepper
2 cups cooked drained white or kidney beans
½ to 1 pound elbow macaroni, cooked (quantity depends on thickness of soup wanted)
½ cup freshly grated Parmesan cheese

On a chopping board, mince together the parsley, garlic and onion. Heat the olive oil in a large kettle. Add the parsley mixture, leek, carrots and basil. Cook over medium heat, stirring constantly, for about 7 minutes. Do not brown. Add the tomatoes, bouillon, cabbage and zucchini and season with salt and pepper. Cook covered over low heat until the vegetables are almost tender. Add the beans and cook for 5 minutes longer. Add the cooked elbow macaroni and toss with Parmesan. Heat through but do not boil. Serve with additional grated Parmesan. Six servings.

Friday

Fish Chowder

Fish Chowder
Corn Bread
Spinach Salad
Fudge Cake

½ pound salt pork
6 large onions, thinly sliced
6 large potatoes, peeled and cut into ½-inch dice
2 pounds fresh cod or haddock or any firm white fish
6 cups milk, heated
1 tablespoon Worcestershire sauce
salt
freshly ground pepper

Pour boiling water over the salt pork and let stand for 5 minutes to remove excessive salt. Drain and cut into ¼-inch dice. Put salt pork into a large, heavy frying pan. Cook, stirring constantly, until crisp and golden brown. Remove with a slotted spoon and drain on paper. Reserve. Cook the onions in pork fat until golden brown. Keep them in the frying pan. Put the potatoes in a large, heavy saucepan. Add just enough water to cover. Cook potatoes for 5 minutes or until they are half tender. Skin the fish and cut into 2-inch pieces. Remove any bones. Place the fish on the potatoes. With a slotted spoon remove onions from frying pan and put on top of fish. Pour any remaining fat from the frying pan and rinse out with 2 cups of the milk. To the fish and potatoes, add the remaining 4 cups of milk, the Worcestershire sauce, and salt and pepper to taste. Simmer covered over lowest possible heat (preferably over an asbestos plate) for 1 hour, or until the potatoes are cooked and the fish flakes. Sprinkle the reserved pork fat bits on top of the chowder before serving in heated bowls. Serves six.

Saturday

3-Minute Fudge Cake

Roast Chicken
Buttered Noodles
Watercress Salad with Mustard Dressing
3-Minute Fudge Cake

2 eggs
1½ cups firmly packed dark brown sugar
2 squares (2 ounces) unsweetened chocolate, melted
2 cups sifted cake flour
1 teaspoon baking soda
½ teaspoon salt
¼ cup vinegar (not wine vinegar)
¾ cup milk
1 teaspoon vanilla extract
½ cup butter, softened

A fine, medium-rich cake which first appeared, many years ago, on the Arm & Hammer Baking Soda package. People still write for it. Have all the ingredients at room temperature. In a deep bowl, and preferably using an electric beater at high speed, beat together for 1 minute the eggs, brown sugar and chocolate, or beat energetically by hand for 3 minutes. Sift together the flour, baking soda and salt. Combine the vinegar, milk and vanilla extract. Add the flour, ½ of the milk, and butter to the chocolate mixture. Beat for 1 minute with electric beater at high speed, or 3 minutes by hand. Add the remaining liquid and beat again for 1 minute, as above. Butter and flour two 8-inch layer pans or a 13 × 9 × 2-inch pan. Pour batter into pans. Bake in a preheated 350° oven for 35–45 minutes or until the cake tests clean. Cool and frost any desired way.

QUICK & EASY DINNERS FOR TWO

April

Sunday

Marinated Lamb Chops

Marinated Lamb Chops
White Beans in Tomato Sauce
Sauteed Broccoli
Boston Cream Pie

⅔ cup dry white wine
1 tablespoon fresh or dried rosemary
1 small garlic clove, chopped
2 lamb chops, excess fat trimmed, about 1-inch thick

Combine the wine, rosemary and garlic in a bowl. Add the lamb chops. Let stand at room temperature 15 minutes, turning once. Remove the lamb chops from the marinade and wipe off the rosemary and garlic. Broil about 4 inches from the heat, allowing 3 minutes to each side, or to taste.

Monday

Welsh Rarebit

Welsh Rarebit
Toast
Buttered Whole Leaf Spinach
Pickled Beets
Grapefruit with Honey

2 tablespoons butter
½ teaspoon salt
1 teaspoon dry mustard
¼ teaspoon freshly ground pepper
3 cups grated or slivered sharp Cheddar cheese
¾ cup beer or ale
1 egg, well beaten
toast, hot rice or hot noodles

Melt the butter in a heavy saucepan. Add the salt, mustard, pepper and cheese. Cook over very low heat, stirring constantly, until the cheese has melted, but is not stringy. Stir in the beer or ale. Just before serving, quickly stir in the egg. Pour over toast, hot rice or hot noodles.

Tuesday

Lima Beans in Cream

Pork Chops with Sautéed Apples
Lima Beans in Cream
Home Fried Potatoes
Lemon Pie

1 package frozen lima beans
½ cup heavy cream
salt
freshly ground pepper
pinch of ground thyme

Cook the lima beans according to directions in as little water as possible; they should be dry. When they are cooked, add the cream, salt, pepper and thyme. Bring to the boiling point once. Serve very hot.

Wednesday

Sliced Oranges and Apples with Marsala or Sherry

Minute Steaks with Herb Butter
Mashed Potatoes
Dandelion Greens
Grated Carrot Salad
Sliced Oranges and Apples with Marsala or Sherry

1 large or 2 small seedless oranges
1 large Red Delicious apple
sugar
½ cup Marsala or sherry

With a sharp knife, peel the oranges so that they are free of all yellow and white peel. Slice into thin, round slices. Core but do not peel the apple. Cut it into thin slices. Make alternate layers of orange and apple slices in a glass dish, sprinkling each layer with a little sugar and Marsala or sherry. Chill for several hours before serving.

Thursday

Carrots and Shallots

Grilled Mustard Chicken
Carrots and Shallots
French Fries
Watercress and Mushroom Salad
Fresh Pineapple

5 medium carrots, thinly sliced
5 medium shallots
1 large beef bouillon cube
salt
freshly ground pepper

Put the carrots and the shallots into a saucepan. Add enough water to come one third of the way up to the carrots. Crumble in the bouillon cube. Season with salt and pepper. Cover tightly and cook 5–7 minutes or until the carrots are just tender.

Friday

Egg and Lemon Rice

Fish Fillets Baked in Cream
Egg and Lemon Rice
Broccoli Vinaigrette
Pound Cake and Ice Cream

1 large egg
juice of ½ lemon
¼ cup minced parsley
⅓ cup freshly grated
Parmesan cheese
1 cup rice
salt
freshly ground pepper

Beat together the egg, lemon juice, parsley and Parmesan cheese. Cook the rice in boiling salted water until just tender. Drain well and turn immediately into a very well heated serving dish or back into the pot. Stir the egg mixture into the hot rice and mix well. Check the seasoning and serve immediately.

Saturday

Eggs in Mustard Sauce

Eggs in Mustard Sauce
Rice and Mushrooms
Grilled Tomatoes
Orange Bavarian

2 tablespoons butter
2 tablespoons flour
1 cup well flavored beef bouillon
2 tablespoons Dijon
mustard or to taste
juice of ½ lemon
salt
freshly ground pepper
1 egg yolk
4 hard-cooked eggs,
shelled and quartered

This sauce, like all flour sauces, should be cooked at least 10 minutes over direct heat to get rid of the raw-flour taste, or 20 and more in double boiler over hot water. Heat the butter in the top of a double boiler, but set on direct heat. Stir in the flour and cook, stirring constantly, for 2 minutes. Gradually stir in the bouillon and cook until the sauce is smooth and thickened. Set the double boiler top over the bottom filled with simmering water. Cover and cook, stirring frequently, for about 20 minutes. Stir in the mustard and the lemon juice. Season lightly with salt and pepper. Remove from the heat and stir in the egg yolk. Add the quartered eggs. Stirring them gently with a fork, cook only until heated through. Serve immediately.

BUDGET DINNERS

April

Sunday

Pork and Sausage Casserole

Pork and Sausage Casserole
Boiled Potatoes
Coleslaw
Lemon Nutmeg Pie

2 tablespoons butter
1 tablespoon salad oil
2 pounds lean boneless pork, trimmed of excess fat and cut into 1½-inch pieces
1 pound smoked sausage, cut into 1-inch pieces
1 cup minced onion
1 garlic clove, minced
1 bottle dark beer
1 cup canned tomatoes
2 tablespoons minced parsley
2 bay leaves
salt
freshly ground pepper
2 1-pound cans pinto beans
1 tablespoon flour mixed to a paste with 1 tablespoon soft butter

Heat the butter and oil in a large, deep frying pan. Cook the pork and sausage until browned. Transfer the meats to a deep 4-quart casserole. In the same frying pan, cook the onion and garlic, stirring constantly, until soft. Add the beer, tomatoes, parsley, and bay leaves. Season with salt and pepper and mix well. Simmer uncovered for 5 minutes. Pour the canned beans into a strainer and rinse briefly under running cold water. Drain well and place the beans on top of meats in the casserole. Pour the sauce over meat and beans. Cover and bake in a preheated oven 350° for 45 minutes to 1 hour. If too thin, stir in the butter and flour mixture during the last 10 minutes of cooking. Serves six.

Monday

Jambalaya

Jambalaya
Cucumber Salad
Coffee Ice Cream Topped with Chopped Peanuts

3 tablespoons bacon fat
2 small onions, minced
½ medium green pepper, minced
2 celery stalks, minced
2 tablespoons chopped parsley
1 tablespoon flour
2 cups canned tomatoes
1 cup chicken bouillon
salt
1 teaspoon dried red pepperflakes or to taste
1½ pounds raw shrimp, peeled or 1 pound frozen peeled shrimp
2 cups cooked rice
½ cup cooked ham, diced small

In some areas, it is more economical to use packed raw frozen shrimp. If so, follow general cooking directions, but cook for a shorter time than specified because the directions frequently make for a mushy cooked shrimp. Heat bacon fat in a large, heavy saucepan and cook the onions, pepper, celery and parsley until soft. Stir in the flour. Cook, stirring constantly, for 1 more minute. Stir in the tomatoes, bouillon, salt to taste and red pepperflakes. Bring to boil. Reduce heat and simmer covered for about 30 minutes. Add the shrimp. Cook until just pink and tender, or for about 3-5 minutes depending on the size of the shrimp. Do not overcook. Stir in the rice and the ham and cook for about 3 minutes longer, or until thoroughly heated through. Serves four to six.

Tuesday

Shoulder Lamb Chops en Casserole

Shoulder Lamb Chops en Casserole
Spinach Salad
Baked Stuffed Potatoes
Cut Up Oranges, Grapefruits and Bananas

4 large potatoes, peeled and cut into ½-inch slices
6 shoulder lamb chops, well trimmed
salt
freshly ground pepper
2 garlic cloves, minced
1 tablespoon crumbled dried rosemary
2 large sweet or Bermuda onions, thinly sliced
1 cup dry white wine
1 cup chicken bouillon
2 tablespoons minced parsley

Into the bottom of a buttered 4-quart casserole, place a layer using half the sliced potatoes. Top the potatoes with 3 of the lamb chops. Sprinkle the meat with salt and pepper, 1 of the garlic cloves and half of the rosemary. Top with the onion slices and top these with the remaining 3 chops. Cover the meat with the remaining potatoes. Sprinkle with a little more salt and pepper, and the remaining garlic and rosemary. Pour the wine and bouillon over meat and potatoes. Bake in a preheated oven 325° for 1 hour. Sprinkle with the parsley before serving. Four to six servings.

Wednesday

Eggs Divan

Eggs Divan
Mixed Green Salad
Pears and Cheese

2 bunches fresh broccoli
8 hard-cooked eggs, halved
4 tablespoons butter
2 tablespoons grated onion
4 tablespoons flour
2 teaspoons dry mustard
3 cups milk
salt
freshly ground pepper
1 cup fine dry bread crumbs
½ cup grated Parmesan cheese

Trim the broccoli, cutting off tough stalk ends and peeling the stems. Cook in boiling salted water until not quite tender. Drain. Place the broccoli side by side in a buttered 9 × 12-inch rectangular baking dish or casserole. Top with the egg halves. Heat the butter in a saucepan. Stir in the grated onion, flour and mustard. Cook, stirring constantly, for 2-3 minutes. Stir in the milk and cook, stirring constantly, until the sauce is smooth and thick. Season with salt and pepper. Pour the sauce over the broccoli and eggs. Sprinkle with bread crumbs and Parmesan cheese. Bake in a preheated 400° oven for 20 minutes or until golden and bubbly. Four to six servings.

Thursday

Sweet and Sour Beef

Sweet and Sour Beef
Boiled Potatoes
Green Beans with Parsley Butter
Chocolate Pudding

2½ pounds stewing beef, well-trimmed and cut into 1½-inch pieces
½ cup flour
2 teaspoons salt
freshly ground pepper
3 tablespoons butter
2 tablespoons salad oil
1 cup chili sauce
½ cup light or dark brown sugar
½ cup red wine or cider vinegar
2 tablespoons Worcestershire sauce
2 cups beef bouillon
1 large onion, thinly sliced
4 medium or large carrots, sliced
4 tablespoons minced parsley

Cut off all fat and gristle from the beef or you'll have a greasy dish. You'll be surprised how much waste there is. Coat meat with flour, salt and pepper and shake off excess flour. Heat butter and oil in a large, deep frying pan. Over high heat, cook meat, in small amounts at a time, until browned on all sides. Transfer to a Dutch oven or large heavy casserole. In a saucepan, combine the chili sauce, sugar, vinegar, Worcestershire sauce and beef bouillon. Bring to boil and pour over meat. Check the seasoning; if necessary, add a little more salt and pepper. Cover and simmer for 1 hour or until the meat is almost tender. Add the onion and carrots and cook for 15 minutes longer, or until meat and vegetables are tender. Sprinkle with the parsley before serving. Makes four to six servings.

Friday

Baked Corn and Tomatoes

Broiled Fish Fillets with Lemon and Dill
Baked Corn and Tomatoes
Orange Raisin Pie

2 tablespoons butter
1 tablespoon salad oil
1 medium onion, chopped
1 green pepper, chopped
3 cups canned plum tomatoes
salt
freshly ground pepper
1 tablespoon sugar (optional)
dash of Tabasco
3 10-ounce packages frozen corn niblets
2 tablespoons minced parsley

Heat the butter and oil in a large, deep frying pan. Add the onion and pepper. Cook, stirring frequently, for 7 minutes or until the vegetables are soft. Add the tomatoes, the salt, pepper, sugar and Tabasco. Simmer uncovered over low heat, stirring frequently, for 20 minutes or until thickened. Place the corn in a buttered 2-quart baking dish. Pour the tomato sauce over the corn. Bake covered in a preheated oven 350° for 25-30 minutes. Sprinkle with the parsley before serving. Makes four to six servings.

Saturday

Sour Cream Apple Pie

Glazed Pork Loin
Browned Potatoes
Glazed Carrots
Sour Cream Apple Pie

1 unbaked 9-inch pie shall
¼ cup chopped toasted almonds
2 tablespoons + ⅓ cup flour
¾ cup sugar
1½ teaspoons ground cinnamon
½ teaspoon ground mace
1 egg
1 cup sour cream
6 firm apples, peeled, cored and thinly sliced
⅓ cup light or dark brown sugar
¼ cup butter, at room temperature

Bake the pie shell in a preheated oven 400° for 10 minutes. Remove pie shell to cool, but leave oven on. Sprinkle almonds on the bottom of the pie shell. Into a large bowl, sift together 2 tablespoons of the flour, sugar, cinnamon and mace. Stir in the egg and sour cream. Stir until smooth. Fold the apple slices into the mixture. Spoon into the pie shell. Bake for 15 minutes. Reduce oven heat to 350° and bake for 30 minutes. While the pie is baking, stir together into a paste the remaining ⅓ cup flour, brown sugar and butter. Spread over the top of the pie. Return oven to 400° and bake for another 10 minutes. Cool before serving. One nine-inch pie.

ENTERTAINING

April

Sunday

Sausages Poached in Wine

Sausages Poached in Wine
Black Beans and Rum
Sliced Avocados and Tomatoes with Hot Salad Dressing (Chili Peppers to Taste)
Flambéed Bananas

12 Bratwurst or veal sausages
4 tablespoons butter
¼ cup minced onion
3 tablespoons flour
⅛ teaspoon ground marjoram
2½ cups dry white wine

Prick the sausage skins with a fork so they will not split in cooking. Put 1 tablespoon of butter into a deep frying pan and brown the sausages on all sides. Remove to platter lined with absorbent paper and keep warm in low oven. Pour off any excess fat from the frying pan. Add the remaining butter and scrape off all the brown bits at the bottom. Heat the butter and cook the onion until tender but not browned. Stir in the flour. Cook, stirring constantly, for 2-3 minutes. Add the marjoram and wine. Cook over low heat, stirring very frequently, for 5 minutes, or until sauce is smooth and thickened. Return sausages to the sauce. Cook, covered, over low heat for 15 minutes or until sausages are cooked through *thoroughly;* cooking time depends on their size. Turn into heated serving dish and serve hot. Serves six.

Monday

Spring Soup

Spring Soup
Fillet of Sole in White Wine Sauce
Watercress Salad
Cream Cheese, Guava Shells, and Crackers

2 pounds fresh peas, shelled; reserve pods
4 cups chicken bouillon
3 tablespoons butter
4 tablespoons flour
1 teaspoon sugar
4 cups milk
salt
freshly ground pepper
1 tablespoon minced fresh mint

Wash and drain the pea pods. Put pods and peas in a deep saucepan and add the chicken bouillon. Cook over medium heat for about 10 minutes. Remove and discard pods. Cook the peas until soft. Put peas and cooking liquid in blender. Add butter, flour, and sugar. Blend until smooth. If too thick to blend, use some of the milk to make blending possible. Pour into large saucepan. Add the milk. Cook, stirring constantly, until the soup is smooth and slightly thickened. Season with salt and pepper. Sprinkle with minced mint and serve either hot or cold, depending on the weather. Serves six.

Tuesday

Roquefort Timbales/Sauce Aurore

Roquefort Timbales/ Sauce Aurore
Parslied Leg of Spring Lamb
Sautéed Beets with Sour Cream
Butter-Steamed New Potatoes
Rum Chiffon Pie

1 3-ounce package Roquefort or blue cheese
1 3-ounce package cream cheese
6 tablespoons sour cream
4 eggs
2 tablespoons chopped chives
1 tablespoon chopped parsley
½ teaspoon white pepper
½ teaspoon paprika
Sauce Aurore

This is a first course that can be served at the table or in the living room between cocktails and dinner. Put all ingredients in blender and blend until very smooth. Generously butter 6 or 8 straight-sided individual baking dishes and fill each ½ full with the mixture. Set dishes in a baking pan with 2 inches of hot water. Cover whole pan with a large sheet of foil. Bake in a preheated oven 350° for 20 minutes or until firm. Remove from oven, take baking dishes from the hot water, and let stand for 5 minutes. Run a knife around inside edge of each dish and unmold on a small butter plate. Pour Sauce Aurore *around,* not over, each timbale. Serves six to eight.

Sauce Aurore

3 tablespoons butter
3 tablespoons flour
1½ cups hot milk
1½ cups hot light cream
1 to 2 teaspoons tomato paste
salt
freshly ground pepper
1 to 2 tablespoons minced mixed fresh herbs (such as chives, parsley, and dill)

Heat butter in a heavy saucepan. Stir in flour and cook, stirring constantly, for 2 minutes. Add milk and cream. Cook, stirring constantly, until sauce is smooth and thickened. Stir in enough tomato paste for desired color and season with salt and pepper. Reduce heat to lowest possible (use an asbestos plate) and simmer, covered, for 20 minutes to remove raw flour taste. Stir frequently and if necessary for the proper consistency either simmer without a cover or add a few spoonfuls of milk. Stir in the herbs just before serving.

Wednesday

Potatoes with Leeks from Fribourg

Broiled Grapefruit with Sherry
Smoked Ham (Virginia, Kentucky, etc.)
Potatoes with Leeks from Fribourg
Watercress Salad
Apple Tart with Whipped Cream

2½ to 3 pounds potatoes, peeled
2 tablespoons butter
3 large leeks, white part only, thinly sliced and well washed
2 cups grated Swiss cheese
3 eggs, well beaten
1⅓ cups milk
1 teaspoon salt
½ teaspoon ground nutmeg or to taste
½ cup grated Parmesan cheese

Cook the potatoes in boiling salt water until tender but still firm. Drain and dry with paper towels. Cool and slice the potatoes into ⅛-inch slices. Heat the butter in a frying pan and cook the leeks, stirring constantly, until golden. Thoroughly butter a 2-quart casserole or baking dish. Make alternate layers with the ingredients, beginning with a layer of potatoes, one of leeks, one of cheese and repeat, ending with potatoes. Beat together the eggs, milk, salt, and nutmeg. Pour the mixture over the potatoes. Sprinkle with grated Parmesan cheese. Cook in a preheated oven 350° for 20 to 30 minutes or until eggs are set and the top golden brown. Six servings.

Thursday

Hungarian Cream of Mushroom Soup

Hungarian Cream of Mushroom Soup
Stuffed Roast Chicken
Gratin of Potatoes
Buttered Peas and Tiny Onions
Fruit Salad and Cookies

2 tablespoons lard or butter
1 pound mushrooms, thinly sliced
1 tablespoon sweet paprika
2 tablespoons flour
2 tablespoons minced parsley
6 cups chicken or beef bouillon
4 tablespoons heavy cream
2 egg yolks
1 cup sour cream

Heat lard or butter in a heavy soup kettle or large casserole. Cook mushrooms stirring constantly, for 4 minutes or until they are beginning to get soft. Stir in paprika and cook for about 2 minutes longer. Stir in the flour and parsley. Add the bouillon and heavy cream. Simmer, covered, over low heat for about 45 minutes. Beat together the egg yolks and sour cream. Remove the soup from heat, take a couple of spoons of soup and stir into the egg-cream mixture. Then stir the egg-cream mixture into soup, a little at a time, stirring well after each addition. Return to low heat for just long enough to heat the soup through without boiling. Serves four to six.

Friday

Singapore Shrimp

Marinated Mushrooms and Pimento on Salad Greens
Singapore Shrimp
Dry Rice
Chutney
Pears in Red Wine
Cookies

3 pounds raw medium shrimp
4 tablespoons butter
2 tablespoons curry powder or more to taste
¼ cup minced onion
1 cup minced carrots
1 cup minced celery
1 cup chopped mushrooms
1 cup skinned, chopped tomatoes
salt
freshly ground pepper
½ cup water
1 cup dry white wine

Shell and devein shrimp; wash, drain, and reserve. Heat butter in a large casserole. Stir in curry powder. Cook over medium heat, stirring constantly, for about 2 minutes. Add the onion, carrots, celery, mushrooms, and tomatoes. Stir thoroughly. Season with salt and pepper and stir in the water and wine. Cook, covered, over low heat for about 20 minutes. Strain through a sieve or puree in the blender. Return the sauce to the casserole and add the shrimp.

Before cooking the shrimp, check the seasoning and the consistency of the sauce. If too thick, add a little more wine or water, and if too thin, cook without a cover. Cook, covered, for 5 to 10 minutes, depending on size. Serves six.

Saturday

A Cooperative French Dinner Party for Eight

Pâté and Melba Toast
Veal with Artichokes*
Buttered Rice
Salad and Cheeses
Ice Cream Bombe
**Recipe in book*

Making a French dinner party into a cooperative effort takes the burden off the hostess and gives each guest the opportunity to show off his or her culinary abilities. Planned for eight people, we suggest the hostess supply the main dish, rice, wine and such extras as a crusty loaf of French bread and espresso coffee.

Pick your guests for their interest in food; this provides built-in conversation and compatability. Tell your guest what the main course will be and be definite as to what they should do as their share of the meal since the meal must have a continuity of taste and texture. For instance, your first course provider and your "dessert guest" can be told your suggestions as to what their pâté and their bombe should be. Since this is a seated, semiformal dinner, treat it as if you had prepared the whole — that is, have the guests bring their food early enough for you to have time to plan for its proper serving. Serve the salad as a separate course with the cheese.

Have plenty of wine, for nothing keeps a dinner, as well as the evening, going than a generous amount of wine. We have found that the majority of people who like French dinners can drink about half a bottle of wine each during a meal. For practical purposes, it is better to have an ample supply of good, though not overly expensive wine than a few sips of rare vintages. Keep these for a few kindred souls at a special occasion, such as a wine tasting.

Wines

Grande Marque Red, Maucaillou or any other good red Bordeaux; Robert Mondavi Cabernet Sauvignon, Heitz Cabernet Sauvignon, BV Cabernet Sauvignon (California)

Veal with Artichokes

2 10-ounce packages frozen artichoke hearts
2 cups dry white wine
4 pounds boneless veal, trimmed of fat and gristle, and cut into 1½-inch cubes
4 cups chicken bouillon
1 tablespoon salt
3 celery stalks
3 parsley sprigs
2 tablespoons fresh chopped dill weed
½ cup butter
½ cup minced onion
½ cup flour
2 cups heavy cream
salt
freshly ground pepper
3 egg yolks
juice of 1 lemon

For Garnish:

½ pound mushroom caps, sautéed briefly in ¼ cup butter. They must still be firm
4 tablespoons minced parsley

Cook the artichoke hearts until barely tender; usual cooking directions make for too soft an artichoke heart. Drain. Place into bowl and cover with wine. Marinate at room temperature for 2 hours. Combine the veal, chicken bouillon, salt, celery stalks, parsley and dill in a heavy saucepan. Bring to a boil. Reduce heat to very low and skim carefully. Cover and simmer for 30-45 minutes or until tender, but still firm. Drain the veal and reserve the broth. Place veal in a bowl and add about ½ cup of the broth to keep it moist. Cover and place in a low oven to keep the veal hot. Over high heat, reduce the remaining broth to about 2 cups. Reserve. Heat butter in a heavy saucepan or in the top of a double boiler. Cook the onion, stirring constantly, until soft and golden but not browned. Stir in flour and cook until golden and bubbly. Stir in the reduced broth and cream, and cook sauce over low heat, stirring constantly, until thick and smooth. Season with salt and pepper. Keep the sauce hot over low heat, on asbestos plate, to prevent scorching, or over hot water. Drain the artichoke hearts and reserve. Beat the egg yolks into the wine in which the artichoke hearts were marinated and stir in lemon juice. Stir this mixture into the sauce, and cook, stirring constantly, over low heat for 5 minutes or until everything is thoroughly heated through. To serve, place the hot veal in the center of a deep ovenproof serving dish. Arrange artichokes and mushroom caps around the edges. Pour about half of sauce over the veal and sprinkle with parsley. Serve the remaining sauce in a sauceboat. Serves eight.

This dish can be prepared ahead of time. Refrigerate covered with foil. To ready for serving, place covered into a preheated 350° oven. Heat for 45 minutes or until barely bubbling.

Important: If the dish is to be reheated, cook the artichokes and the veal until almost, but not quite tender, since the reheating will cook it further.

MAY

Somewhere, perhaps, there is a cook who must cook every day and finds this a wonderful challenge. I am not such a cook; I am one that gets bored and feels guilty about it. But there are ways of dissipating the tedium of all too familiar dishes, for example, by learning many different ways of preparing them. The possibilities of such simple food as ground meat or potatoes are truly surprising. Though there is the danger of making exotic dishes that nobody in the family will want to eat, it is great fun to come up with something new and lovely. It's also fun to work out meals or dishes that stay within a very definite, limiting expense; I keep whatever money has thus been saved for special treats. As I've found out during some forty-odd years of cooking; the situation in the kitchen is the same as in other parts of life — you've got to make your own fun.

MAY

	FAMILY FARE	
	LUNCHES	**DINNERS**
Sunday	Sliced Oranges Oeufs a la Matelote* Jelly Doughnuts	Roast Beef Asparagus with Brown Butter Steamed New Potatoes and Chives Rhubarb and Strawberry Pie*
Monday	Hamburger Corn Skillet Bake* Rice Chocolate Pound Cake	Baked Fish with Green Herbs* Boiled New Potatoes Orange and Onion Salad Chocolate Cream Pots
Tuesday	Bacon and Egg Casserole with Potatoes* Tomato Salad Stewed Rhubarb and Cookies	Veal Ragout* Fine Noodles Buttered Asparagus Lemon Sherbet with Strawberries
Wednesday	Frankfurters Potato Stew* Green Salad Melon with Lime Wedges	Flank Steak Orientale Sautéed Zucchini Baked Potatoes Molded Cream Ring with Strawberries*
Thursday	Cheese Pudding* Watercress and Mushroom Salad French Pastries	Sauerbraten Hamburgers* Buttered Noodles Peas and Carrots with Scallions Fruit Salad
Friday	Pasta e Fagioli Soup* Sliced Tomatoes Ice Cream	Chicken with White Wine* Green Rice Glazed Carrots Baked Bananas with Rum
Saturday	Bacon and Egg Sandwiches Carrot Sticks Coffee Apple Cake*	Picadillo* Rice Guacamole Blueberry or Apple Turnovers

QUICK & EASY Dinner For Two	BUDGET DINNERS	ENTERTAINING
Lobster with Whiskey* Green Rice Sliced Tomatoes Old Fashioned Strawberry Shortcake	Creamed Chicken Mr. K's Pilaff* Chopped Buttered Broccoli Raspberry Sherbet and Lemon Cookies	Ham and Spinach Roulade* Artichoke Hearts with Lemon Dressing and Fresh Herbs Spiced Baked Rhubarb Sugar Cookies
Flemish Asparagus* Cold Roast Beef Potato Salad Radish Salad Stewed Rhubarb	Baked Asparagus Casserole* Tomato Aspic Vanilla Ice Cream and Strawberries	Buckwheat Blini* Red or Black Caviar Sour Cream Chopped Hard-Cooked Egg Whites Sieved Hard-Cooked Egg Yolks Minced Parsley Lemon Wedges Shoestring Beet Salad Meringues with Lemon Filling
Veal Kidneys Liegeoise* Parsleyed Potatoes Green Peas Cooked with Lettuce Cucumber Salad Strawberry Ice Cream	Beef and Cheese Tortillas* Avocado and Onion Salad Custard	Stuffed Mushrooms Shrimp Puffs Baked Chicken with Wine and Herbs Rice Tian* Strawberries with Pureed Raspberry Sauce
Crostini Alla Mozzarella* White Bean and Tomato Salad with Prosciutto or Ham Strawberry Pie	Baked Spareribs Scalloped Potatoes with Sour Cream* Green Peas Fresh Fruits	White Bean Salad with Hunks of Italian Imported Tuna Fish Pork Chops in Rosemary- Flavored Cream Sauce Boiled Potatoes Roman-Style Broccoli or Cauliflower* Fresh Ginger-Flavored Applesauce
Fried Chicken French Fried Potatoes Zucchini Salad* Cheese Cake	Oxtail Stew* Poppyseed Noodles Green Salad Saltines with Cream Cheese and Jelly	Ham Horns with Asparagus* Deviled Grilled Chicken Mixed Green Bean and Potato Salad Hot Chocolate Souffle
Shrimp Creole Rice Pilaff Green Beans Amandine Fresh Fruit Salad with Zabaglione*	Chili Baked Fish* Green Beans Corn Crisps Rhurbarb Compote or Pie	Fresh Pea Soup Danish Curried Fillets of Flounder* Boiled Potatoes Pickled Cucumbers* Fresh Pineapple with Kirsch Cookies
Asparagus and Eggs* Buttered Noodles Creamed Mushrooms Cheese and Fruit	Farfalle* Steamed Zucchini Fruit Salad	Asparagus with Flemish Egg and Lemon Sauce* Cold Lobster Mayonnaise Watercress Strawberries Romanoff* Wines: Chilled Gewuerztraminer from Wente (California) or Hugel or Kitterle (Alsace)

FAMILY FARE LUNCHES

May

Sunday

Oeufs a la Matelote

Sliced Oranges
Oeufs a la Matelote
Jelly Doughnuts

1 cup dry red wine
1 cup chicken bouillon
2 chopped shallots or
  1 small onion, chopped
1 bay leaf
¼ teaspoon dried thyme
2 parsley sprigs
salt
freshly ground pepper
6 eggs
1 tablespoon flour
1 tablespoon butter
6 rounds of white bread,
  fried in butter

Combine the wine, bouillon, shallots, bay leaf, thyme, parsley sprigs and salt and pepper to taste in a wide, shallow saucepan. Bring to boil, lower the heat, cover and simmer for 5 minutes. Lower the heat for a barely simmering liquid and poach the eggs, one or two at a time. When the eggs are poached, transfer them with a slotted spoon to a heated serving dish, cover and keep warm in a low oven. Over high heat, cook the liquid in the saucepan down to about 1 cup. Keep hot over low heat. Knead the flour and butter to a paste. Beat small amounts of this paste gradually into the hot liquid. Cook, stirring all the time, until the sauce is smooth and thickened. Place each poached egg on a round of fried bread. Spoon a little sauce over each egg. Serve immediately. Serves four to six.

Monday

Hamburger Corn Skillet Bake

Hamburger Corn Skillet Bake
Rice
Chocolate Pound Cake

1 pound ground beef
1 cup fresh white bread crumbs
salt
freshly ground pepper
2 tablespoons butter
2 cups whole kernel corn, drained (about 1 12-ounce can)
1 medium onion, thinly sliced
2 cups tomatoes, drained (1 1-pound can)
1 green pepper, seeded and chopped

Mix together the meat, bread crumbs and the salt and pepper. Heat the butter in a large, deep frying pan and cook the meat until it browns, stirring frequently to break up lumps. Add the corn, onion, tomatoes and pepper. Check the seasoning. Simmer, covered, for 25 minutes. Serve from skillet over hot boiled rice. Makes four to six servings.

Tuesday

Bacon and Egg Casserole with Potatoes

Bacon and Egg Casserole With Potatoes
Tomato Salad
Stewed Rhubarb and Cookies

1 tablespoon butter
6 slices lean bacon, chopped
6 medium boiled potatoes, sliced
6 hard-cooked eggs, sliced
salt
freshly ground pepper
¼ cup minced parsley
1 cup sour cream

Heat the butter and cook the bacon until it is crisp. Drain the bacon and reserve the fat. Into a buttered 1½-quart baking dish put alternate layers of potatoes, eggs, and bacon, beginning and ending with potatoes. Season with salt and pepper and sprinkle with parsley. Stir the reserved bacon fat into sour cream and spoon over mixture. Cover and bake in a preheated 350° oven for about 15 minutes. Uncover and bake for 5 minutes longer. Makes four to six servings.

Wednesday

Potato Stew

Frankfurters
Potato Stew
Green Salad
Melon with Lime Wedges

½ pound bacon diced
1 large onion, minced
3 pounds potatoes, peeled and cut into 1½-inch cubes
1 cup chicken bouillon
salt
freshly ground pepper
1 tablespoon dried rosemary, crumbled
1 bay leaf
3 tablespoons white vinegar
¼ cup minced parsley

Over very low heat in a large, heavy saucepan, cook the bacon and onion until the onion is soft. Do not let it brown. Pour off any excess fat except for 2 tablespoons. Add the potatoes, chicken bouillon, salt and pepper to taste, rosemary and bay leaf. Simmer, covered, over low heat for 20 minutes or until the potatoes are tender. Stir occasionally and check for moisture; if necessary, add a little more bouillon, ¼ cup at a time. The dish should be moist, but not soupy. Stir in vinegar and parsley and cook for 1-2 minutes longer. Serve very hot. Six servings.

Thursday

Cheese Pudding

Cheese Pudding
Watercress and Mushroom Salad
French Pastries

2 cups milk
2 cups stale bread cubes
1 teaspoon salt
½ teaspoon dry mustard
freshly ground pepper
2 cups (½ pound) grated mild Cheddar or Swiss cheese
4 eggs, separated

Scald the milk. Add the bread cubes, salt, mustard, pepper and cheese. Cook over low heat, stirring constantly, until the cheese is melted. Beat the egg yolks thoroughly in a large bowl. Slowly pour the cheese mixture into the egg yolks. Stir until well mixed. Cool. Beat the egg whites until stiff and fold into the cheese mixture. Pour into a buttered 1½-quart baking dish. Bake in a preheated 350° oven for 40 minutes or until set, golden and puffy. Makes four to six servings.

Friday

Pasta e Fagioli Soup

Pasta e Fagioli Soup
Sliced Tomatoes
Ice Cream

½ pound dried pinto, navy or kidney beans
1 cup tomato sauce
6 cups hot beef bouillon or water
2 tablespoons bacon fat or lard
½ cup chopped blanched salt pork or bacon
1 medium onion, minced
1 garlic clove, minced
1 tablespoon flour
½ pound ditalini, small elbow noodles or other small pasta
½ cup minced parsley
freshly grated Parmesan cheese

This is the thick soup known colloquially as "pasta fazool". Soak the beans in water overnight or pour 1 quart boiling water over them and let stand for 1 hour. Cook beans over medium heat, using the water in which they soaked, until half tender. Add the tomato sauce and the bouillon. For a thinner or thicker soup simply increase or decrease the amount of bouillon. Keep warm over low heat. While the beans are cooking, heat together the bacon fat, salt pork, onion and garlic in a deep frying pan. Cook, stirring constantly, until onion is soft. Stir in flour and about 1 cup of the bean liquid. Cook, stirring all the time, for about 2 minutes. Add the mixture to the beans. Simmer over low heat, covered, until the beans are almost done. Add ditalini or other pasta and cook until tender. Sprinkle with parsley and serve with plenty of grated Parmesan cheese. Serves six.

Saturday

Coffee Apple Cake

Bacon and Egg Sandwiches
Carrot Sticks
Coffee Apple Cake

½ cup butter
½ cup sugar
½ cup light brown sugar
1 egg
1¾ cups flour
1 teaspoon ground cinnamon
½ teaspoon ground nutmeg
½ teaspoon baking soda
pinch of salt
½ cup cold coffee
1 cup peeled and diced apples

Cream the butter with both the sugar and the brown sugar until light and soft. Beat in the egg. Sift together the flour, cinnamon, the nutmeg, baking soda and salt. Beat the flour mixture and the coffee alternately into the batter, beginning and ending with flour. Fold in the apples. Turn into a buttered 9-inch square pan. Bake in a preheated 350° moderate oven for about 40 minutes or until the cake tests clean. Makes one nine-inch square cake.

FAMILY FARE DINNERS

May

Sunday

Roast Beef
Asparagus with Brown Butter
Steamed New Potatoes and Chives
Rhubarb and Strawberry Pie

Rhubarb and Strawberry Pie

For the Pastry:

¾ cup vegetable shortening
4 tablespoons butter, at room temperature
2½ cups flour
1 teaspoon salt
3–4 tablespoons ice water

With an electric mixer or fingers, and working quickly, blend vegetable shortening and butter to a paste. Put flour and salt into a bowl. With a pastry blender or fingers, cut the shortening into the flour until it is the size of small peas. Add 3 tablespoons of ice water, stir and blend until dough clears the side of bowl and still feels a little moist; if necessary, stir in remaining tablespoon of ice water. The dough should gather into a ball without crumbling. Cover in plastic wrap and refrigerate for 1 hour. Divide dough into halves. Take 1 half and roll it out between sheets of waxed paper to fit a 9-inch pie pan. Ease this half loosely into pie pan, but press down so that no air is left between dough and pan to form blisters while baking. Refrigerate or freeze for 1 hour. At baking time, fill shell with raw rice or beans. This keeps it from baking unevenly. Bake pie shell in a preheated 425° oven for 10 minutes. Remove the rice or beans a few minutes before the baking period is over. Cool. Roll out remaining half of the pie dough between sheets of waxed paper to 10 inches. Refrigerate in the waxed paper until ready to use.

For the Filling:

¼ cup ground almonds
2 cups rhubarb, cut into 1-inch pieces
2 cups sliced strawberries
1½ cups sugar
⅓ cup flour
pinch of salt
2 tablespoons butter, cut into small pieces
milk

Sprinkle grated almonds over bottom of baked pie shell. In a bowl, mix together the rhubarb, strawberries, sugar, flour and salt. Spoon into pie shell. Dot with butter. Top with the rolled-out pastry, sealing the edges tightly by pressing with a fork. To allow the steam to escape during baking, prick with a fork in several places. Brush with milk. Bake in a preheated 350° oven for 45 minutes. One nine-inch pie.

Monday

Baked Fish with Green Herbs

Baked Fish with Green Herbs
Boiled New Potatoes
Orange and Onion Salad
Chocolate Cream Pots

2½ pounds fish fillets (if frozen, thaw and dry)
salt
freshly ground pepper
½ cup minced parsley
lemon wedges
¼ cup minced chives or spring onion tops
1 tablespoon dried basil
juice of 1 lemon
½ cup fine dry bread crumbs
⅔ cup olive oil

Spread the fish in one or two layers in an oiled shallow baking dish. Season each layer with salt, pepper, parsley, chives and basil. Sprinkle lemon juice over the fish. Top with a layer of bread crumbs. Drizzle the olive oil over the crumbs and the fish. Bake uncovered in a preheated 375° oven for 20-25 minutes or until the fish flakes and the top is crisp. Serve hot or cold (but not chilled) with lemon wedges. Makes four to six servings.

Tuesday

Veal Ragout

Veal Ragout
Fine Noodles
Buttered Asparagus
Lemon Sherbet with Strawberries

3 tablespoons flour
1 teaspoon salt
½ teaspoon paprika
2½ pounds stewing veal, cut into 1-inch pieces
6 tablespoons butter
2 tablespoons salad oil
16 small white onions, peeled
½ cup chicken bouillon
½ pound mushrooms, sliced
2 tablespoons flour
1 cup light cream or milk
1 cup sour cream
6 large mushroom caps sautéed in 2 tablespoons butter
2 tablespoons minced parsley

Combine the flour, salt and paprika and dredge veal. Heat 2 tablespoons of butter and the oil in a large frying pan. Over high heat, quickly brown veal, transfer meat to a casserole that can go to the table. In the same frying pan, brown the onions and add to veal. Pour chicken bouillon into frying pan. Scrape up all the brown bits from the bottom and bring to boil. Pour over veal and onions. Add remaining 4 tablespoons of flour to frying pan and use to cook the mushrooms over medium heat, stirring constantly, until golden but still firm. Stir the flour into mushrooms and cook for 1 minute longer. Stir in cream or milk. Cook, stirring con tantly, until sauce is thickened. Spoon over veal and onions. Cover and bake in a preheated 325° oven for about 30 minutes. Stir in sour cream and bake for 30 more minutes or until meat and onions are soft. Garnish with mushroom caps and sprinkle with parsley. Serves four to five.

Note: The ragout can be prepared ahead of time up to the point where the sour cream is stirred in. When doing so, cool and freeze. Thaw before finishing the dish.

Wednesday

Molded Cream Ring with Strawberries

Flank Steak Orientale
Sautéed Zucchini
Baked Potatoes
Molded Cream Ring with Strawberries

3 eggs, separated
½ cup sugar
1 teaspoon vanilla extract
2 tablespoons unflavored gelatin
¼ cup milk
2 cups heavy cream, whipped
2 pints strawberries, washed, hulled and sugared (cut into halves if very large)

Beat the egg yolks with the sugar and vanilla extract until they are very thick and lemon colored. Sprinkle gelatin over milk and stir. Dissolve the gelatin over hot water and stir into egg mixture. Fold in the heavy cream. Beat the egg whites until very stiff and fold into egg mixture. Rinse a 1½ - 2-quart mold with cold water. Sprinkle inside with sugar. Spoon in the cream. Chill until set. Unmold on a large platter and fill the ring with strawberries. Makes six servings.

Note: The pudding may also be chilled in a glass or other serving dish and served with the strawberries on the side.

Thursday

Sauerbraten Hamburgers

Sauerbraten Hamburgers
Buttered Noodles
Peas and Carrots with Scallions
Fruit Salad

2 pounds lean ground beef
2 tablespoons grated onion
salt
freshly ground pepper
¼ cup fine dry bread crumbs
⅓ cup light cream or milk
1 teaspoon grated lemon rind
1 tablespoon butter
1¼ cups beef gravy (10¾-ounce can) or undiluted beef bouillon
3 tablespoons wine vinegar
½ teaspoon ground ginger
¼ cup light or dark brown sugar
¼ cup seedless raisins, plumped in lukewarm water
⅛ teaspoon ground cloves

Combine the meat, onion, salt and pepper, bread crumbs, milk and grated lemon rind. Mix well and shape into 6 large patties. Heat butter in a large frying pan and quickly brown patties on both sides. Do not cook them through as they will have to be cooked again later. Transfer the patties to a heated serving dish and keep warm. Put all remaining ingredients into frying pan. Bring to a boil, reduce heat to low and simmer, covered, for 10 minutes. If too thick, stir in a little water, 2 tablespoons at a time. Add the patties and cook 5-7 minutes longer. Turn twice and baste with the sauce. Serve in a heated deep serving dish. Four to six servings.

Friday

Chicken with White Wine

Chicken with White Wine
Green Rice
Glazed Carrots
Baked Bananas with Rum

½ cup butter, at room temperature
1 garlic clove, mashed
¼ cup minced parsley
½ teaspoon dried thyme
salt
freshly ground pepper
2 3-pound fryers, cut into pieces (no backs)
2 carrots, chopped
½ cup chopped onion
2 bay leaves
4 slices bacon, cut into ¼-inch pieces
1 cup dry white wine

Combine the butter, garlic, parsley and thyme to a paste. Season this paste with salt and pepper. Cut all excess fat from chicken. Spread the butter paste on the chicken pieces. Place carrot, onion and bay leaves on the bottom of a baking dish large enough to take all the chicken pieces in one layer. Put the chicken pieces, skin side down, on the vegetables in one layer. Sprinkle the bacon over the chicken pieces. Add the wine. Cover with a lid or tie on aluminum foil. Bake in a preheated 400° oven for about 45-50 minutes. Serves four to six.

Note: The chicken pieces may be skinned. If skinned, reduce cooking time 5-10 minutes.

Saturday

Picadillo

Picadillo
Rice
Guacamole
Blueberry or Apple Turnovers

2 tablespoons salad oil
1 large onion, thinly sliced
3 garlic cloves, minced
1½ pounds lean ground beef
salt
freshly ground pepper
½ cup dry red or white wine
3 large tomatoes, peeled and chopped
½ cup seedless raisins, plumped in lukewarm water and drained
½ cup pimiento-stuffed olives, cut into quarters
2 green peppers, seeded and cut into strips

Heat oil in a heavy saucepan and cook the onion and garlic until soft. Add the meat and salt and pepper to taste. Cook, stirring constantly with a fork to prevent lumping, for 3 minutes or until the meat is browning. Add the wine, tomatoes, raisins and olives. Simmer, covered, for 15 minutes. Add the pepper strips and cook for 2 minutes longer; the strips should remain crisp. Check the seasoning. If too acid, stir in ½ teaspoon sugar. Makes four to six servings.

QUICK & EASY DINNERS FOR TWO

May

Sunday

Lobster with Whiskey

Lobster with Whiskey
Green Rice
Sliced Tomatoes
Old Fashioned Strawberry Shortcake

2 large lobster tails (if frozen, thawed)
2 tablespoons butter
¼ cup scotch
½ cup heavy cream
1 teaspoon paprika
½ teaspoon Worcestershire sauce
salt
Tabasco
1 tablespoon lemon juice

Remove the meat from the tail. Cut it into even slices. Heat butter in a frying pan. Over medium heat and stirring constantly cook the lobster meat for about 4-5 minutes. Pour the scotch over the lobster and flame. When the flame has died down, transfer the lobster meat to a heated plate and keep warm. Add the cream, paprika, Worcestershire sauce, salt, and a little Tabasco to the frying pan. Bring to boil and cook for 1 minute. Return the lobster meat to the frying pan and heat through thoroughly. Remove from heat and stir in lemon juice. Serve immediately very hot.

Monday

Flemish Asparagus

Flemish Asparagus
Cold Roast Beef
Potato Salad
Radish Salad
Stewed Rhubarb

1 pound asparagus
2 hard-cooked eggs
½ cup butter, melted
salt
freshly ground pepper
1 teaspoon fresh lemon juice
2 tablespoons minced parsley

Trim and peel the asparagus stems. Cook in boiling salt water until tender but still firm. Drain and place on a paper towel to absorb surplus moisture. While asparagus is cooking, mash the eggs in a small bowl and stir in the butter, salt, freshly ground pepper, lemon juice and parsley. Serve immediately.

Tuesday

Veal Kidneys Liegeoise

Veal Kidneys Liegeoise
Parsleyed Potatoes
Green Peas Cooked with Lettuce
Cucumber Salad
Strawberry Ice Cream

2 tablespoons butter
2 veal kidneys, trimmed and split into halves
1 tablespoon juniper berries, crushed
1 tablespoon Holland-type gin, akvavit, Kirsch or brandy
1 tablespoon water
salt
freshly ground pepper
buttered hot toast

Preheat the oven to 400°. Using a shallow baking dish, appropriate for table use, heat the butter on top of the stove and quickly brown the kidneys on all sides. This should not take more than 2 minutes. Transfer kidneys to the hot oven. Cook for five minutes. Turn and cook for 3 minutes longer. Add the juniper berries, gin, water and salt and pepper to taste. Cook 3 minutes longer. Put the buttered hot toast on hot plates and pour the kidneys over toast.

Note: To trim the kidneys, remove all the fat and white membrane. It is important that the kidneys should not be overcooked or they will be tough. Cooking time may have to be adjusted depending on the size of the kidneys, which, when ready should be a faint pink inside.

Wednesday

Crostini Alla Mozzarella

Crostini Alla Mozzarella
White Bean and Tomato Salad with Prosciutto or Ham
Strawberry Pie

½ loaf of long Italian or French bread
8 ounces Mozzarella cheese
⅔ cup butter
4 anchovy fillets *or* 1 teaspoon anchovy paste

Remove the crust from the bread and cut off heel. Cut the bread into slices which are ⅓-inch thick. Cut mozzarella in the same size and thickness as the bread. Place alternate layers of bread and mozzarella on a skewer, beginning and ending with bread. Or use two skewers. Bake in a preheated 450° oven just long enough for the cheese to melt and the bread to brown slightly. Keep hot. Melt the butter in a small plan. Cut the anchovy fillets into small pieces and simmer in the butter for 3 minutes. Or, stir the anchovy paste into the butter and simmer for 3 minutes. Place the bread and cheese skewer in a hot serving dish and cover with anchovy butter. Serve as hot as possible on hot plates. Remove the skewer at the table.

Thursday

Zucchini Salad

Fried Chicken
French Fried Potatoes
Zucchini Salad
Cheese Cake

2-3 medium zucchini
White Wine Dressing

Wash but do not trim the zucchini. The watery zucchini must be drained. Cook in boiling salted water to cover for 5-7 minutes or until just tender. Cooking time depends on size of the vegetable and may be tested by poking with a skewer or poultry pin. Trim and slice into ½-inch slices. Place zucchini in a strainer over a bowl. Refrigerate for 10-15 minutes or until drained. Toss with White Wine Dressing or any French dressing.

White Wine Dressing
½ cup dry white wine
¼ cup olive oil
1 tablespoon vinegar or lemon juice
2 tablespoons minced onion
1 small garlic clove, minced (optional)
salt
freshly ground pepper

Combine all the ingredients and blend thoroughly.

Note: This dressing is very good with any vegetable or potato salad. Vegetables that do not need to be drained for long, like zucchini, should be tossed with the dressing while still hot, obviously after draining.

Friday

Zabaglione

Shrimp Creole
Rice Pilaff
Green Beans Amandine
Fresh Fruit Salad with Zabaglione

4 egg yolks
¾ cup sugar
¾ cup Marsala or dry sherry

Combine the ingredients in the top of a double boiler, *over* simmering, not boiling, water. Beat constantly with a wire whisk or an egg beater until the mixture puffs up and gets very thick. This will take about 5-7 minutes. Serve immediately with crisp cookies.

Saturday

Asparagus and Eggs

Asparagus and Eggs
Buttered Noodles
Creamed Mushrooms
Cheese and Fruit

1 pound asparagus
½ cup butter
4 eggs
salt
freshly ground pepper
¼ cup freshly grated Parmesan cheese

Trim and peel the asparagus. Cook in boiling salted water until barely tender. Drain and place on paper towel to absorb surplus moisture. Place on two individual hot dinner plates and keep hot. While the asparagus is cooking heat the butter in a frying pan and fry the eggs in the usual way. Season the eggs with salt and pepper. Gently put 2 fried eggs on top of each asparagus serving. Sprinkle with grated Parmesan and serve hot.

BUDGET DINNERS

May

Sunday

Mr. K's Pilaff

Creamed Chicken
Mr. K's Pilaff
Chopped Buttered Broccoli
Raspberry Sherbet and Lemon Cookies

½ cup butter
½ cup thin vermicelli noodles
2 cups long grained rice
salt
4 cups + 2 tablespoons water, chicken or beef bouillon

Heat the butter in a large, heavy saucepan. Crumble the vermicelli into small pieces and brown them in the butter. Do not overbrown. Add the rice. Cook, stirring constantly, for 3-4 minutes or until opaque. Season with salt. Pour in the water and bring to boil Reduce heat to very low. Simmer, covered, for 20 minutes. Turn off heat and let stand until all the moisture is absorbed. To hasten this, you may put a folded clean kitchen towel over the pilaff, and cover the pot once more. Makes four servings.

Monday

Baked Asparagus Casserole

Baked Asparagus Casserole
Tomato Aspic
Vanilla Ice Cream and Strawberries

2 pounds asparagus
4 tablespoons butter
4 tablespoons flour
2 cups milk
2 teaspoons Dijon mustard
salt
8 slices buttered toast
8 thin slices cooked ham
8 hard-cooked or deviled eggs, halved
1 cup grated Cheddar cheese
freshly ground pepper

Trim and peel the asparagus. Cook in boiling salted water until almost tender. Drain and dry on paper towel. Heat the butter in a saucepan. Stir in flour and cook stirring constantly, until barely golden. Stir in the milk and cook, stirring all the time, until thick and smooth. Stir in Dijon mustard. Season with very little salt (the deviled eggs may be and the cheese will be salted) and pepper. Spread the toast side by side on the bottom of a buttered rectangular or square baking dish. Place one slice of ham on each slice of toast, and top with a few asparagus spears and 2 egg halves. Pour the cream sauce over the foods. Sprinkle with cheese. Cook for 20-30 minutes in a preheated oven 350° or until brown and bubbly. Serves four to six.

Tuesday

Beef and Cheese Tortillas

Beef and Cheese Tortillas
Avocado and Onion Salad
Custard

1 tablespoon salad oil
1 medium onion, minced
2 pounds ground lean beef
salt
1 tablespoon hot dried or canned chili peppers, or to taste
2 7-ounce cans tomato sauce
16-18 packaged corn tortillas
2 ripe avocados
½ cup strong coffee
3 cups grated Monterey Jack or Cheddar cheese

Heat the oil in a large frying pan and cook the onion until soft. Add the meat. Cook, stirring constantly with a fork, until meat is browned. Pour off any excess fat. Stir in salt, chili peppers and 1 can tomato sauce. Simmer, stirring frequently, for 10 minutes. Soften the tortillas in hot oil according to package directions. Drain and dry on paper towel. Peel and slice avocados lengthways; there should be one slice for each tortilla. Place 1 slice of avocado and about 3-4 tablespoons meat sauce on each tortilla. Roll up and place, seam side down, in 2 buttered 10 × 12-inch baking dishes. Place any leftover meat sauce around the tortillas. Mix remaining can of tomato sauce with coffee and pour over tortillas. Sprinkle with cheese. Cover tightly with foil, tying it with string. Bake in a preheated oven 350° for 30 minutes. Serves six.

Wednesday

Scalloped Potatoes with Sour Cream

Baked Spareribs
Scalloped Potatoes with Sour Cream
Green Peas
Fresh Fruit

4 very large potatoes
1 cup sour cream
2 eggs
2 tablespoons milk
salt
freshly ground pepper
3 tablespoons minced chives or green onion tops
1 cup grated Cheddar cheese

Cook the potatoes in their skins until barely tender. Cool slightly. Peel and slice the potatoes. Place the sliced potatoes into a buttered shallow 2-quart baking dish. Beat together the sour cream, eggs, milk, salt and pepper and the chives. Pour over the potatoes and sprinkle with cheese. Bake in a preheated oven 350° for 30 minutes or until golden and bubbly. Makes four to six servings.

Thursday

Oxtail Stew

Oxtail Stew
Poppyseed Noodles
Green Salad
Saltines with Cream Cheese and Jelly

3 tablespoons butter
salad oil
6 pounds oxtails, well-trimmed, cut into joints
salt
freshly ground pepper
2 medium onions, minced
2 garlic cloves, minced
1½ cups dry red wine
3 cups beef bouillon
1 carrot, sliced
2 bay leaves
1 teaspoon dried thyme
4 parsley sprigs
6-inch piece fresh orange peel
beurre manie made with 1 tablespoon butter and 2 tablespoons flour
2 tablespoons minced parsley

Heat butter and 1 tablespoon oil in a large, deep frying pan and brown the oxtail joints on all sides, small amounts at a time. Transfer browned joints to a deep 4-quart casserole. Sprinkle with salt and pepper. Pour off all fat from frying pan. Add 2-3 more tablespoons oil and cook onions and garlic until browned. Add the vegetables to meat in the casserole. Pour off any excess fat. Rinse the frying pan with wine, scraping up all brown bits at the bottom. Add beef bouillon, carrot, bay leaves, thyme, parsley sprigs and orange peel. Bring quickly to boil and pour over meat. Cover and place in a preheated 325° oven. Cook for 1¾ hours or until meat is tender. Remove from oven. When cool enough to handle, take out meat with a slotted spoon and put into a bowl. Strain the sauce. Refrigerate the sauce until the fat can be easily removed. Put the sauce back into the casserole and reheat. If it is too thin, stir in the beurre manie and stir until smooth and thickened. Put oxtail joints back into sauce and heat through. Sprinkle with parsley before serving. Serves four to six.

Friday

Chili Baked Fish

Chili Baked Fish
Green Beans
Corn Crisps
Rhubarb Compote or Pie

3 tablespoons salad oil
1 medium onion, minced
½ green pepper, minced
3 canned green chiles, seeded and chopped or to taste
3 cups canned plum tomatoes with juice, or fresh tomatoes, peeled
2 garlic cloves, mashed
salt
freshly ground pepper
2 10-ounce packages frozen corn, thawed and drained or
2 cups fresh or canned corn kernels, drained
2 pounds swordfish, cod or any firm fish steaks
1 tablespoon butter, cut into pieces
juice of 1 lemon
2 tablespoons minced parsley
2 tablespoons minced chives

In a large deep frying pan, heat the oil and cook the onion and pepper until soft. Stir in the chilis, tomatoes (break up with a fork), garlic and salt and pepper. Simmer uncovered for 15 minutes. Stir in corn and simmer for 5 minutes longer or until thickened. Spoon into a large shallow baking dish. Arrange fish steaks on top of the sauce. Dot with butter and sprinkle with lemon juice. Cover and bake in a preheated oven 400° for 20 minutes or until the fish flakes. Sprinkle with chives and parsley before serving. Four to five servings.

Saturday

Farfalle

Farfalle
Steamed Zucchini
Fruit Salad

1 pound farfalle (bow macaroni)
4 tablespoons butter
2 medium onions, thinly sliced
1 garlic clove, minced
1½ pounds lean ground beef
salt
freshly ground pepper
4 tablespoons minced parsley
1 (1-pound) can tomatoes
1 cup beef bouillon
1 green pepper cut into strips
¼ pound mushrooms, thinly sliced
1 tablespoon dried basil
½ cup freshly grated Parmesan cheese
2 tablespoons butter, cut into pieces

Cook farfalle in about 6 quarts boiling salted water until almost tender. Drain well. Rinse quickly in colander under running hot water. Repeat. Heat butter in a large frying pan and cook the onion and garlic, stirring all the time, for 3-4 minutes or until soft. Add the beef and cook, stirring with a fork, until just browned. Pour off excess fat. Stir in the salt and pepper and 2 tablespoons of parsley. Add tomatoes and bouillon. Cook, stirring frequently, until thickened. Add pepper strips and mushrooms and turn over in sauce. Stir in basil. In a deep greased 4-quart casserole, spread half of the farfalle over bottom. Sprinkle with a little salt and pepper and half of the grated cheese. Pour meat sauce over farfalle and top with remaining farfalle. Dot with butter and sprinkle with remaining cheese and parsley. Bake in a preheated oven 350° for 20 minutes or until browned and bubbly. Serves six.

ENTERTAINING

May

Sunday

Ham and Spinach Roulade

Ham and Spinach Roulade
Artichoke Hearts with Lemon Dressing and Fresh Herbs
Spiced Baked Rhubarb
Sugar Cookies

4 tablespoons butter
8 tablespoons flour
2 cups milk
salt
freshly ground pepper
5 eggs, separated
3 tablespoons Ham and Spinach Filling
sautéed mushroom caps

Grease a 10 × 15-inch jelly-roll pan with vegetable shortening. Line the pan with a piece of waxed paper long enough to extend over the ends of the pan by about 2 inches. Grease the waxed paper generously with vegetable shortening.

Heat the butter in a saucepan, add flour, and cook, stirring constantly, for 3 minutes or until golden. Add milk, all at once. Cook, stirring constantly, until sauce is smooth and thick. Season with salt and pepper. Remove from heat and stir in the egg yolks, one at a time, beating well after each addition. Beat egg whites until stiff, but not dry, with a pinch of salt. Fold whites carefully into yolk mixture. Spread the batter evenly on the waxed paper-lined pan, making sure there are no holes or thin spots. Bake in a preheated 375° oven for 15-20 minutes or until golden and firm like a jelly-roll cake. Spread a long clean kitchen cloth over the kitchen counter. Sprinkle with flour. Turn the jelly-roll pan upside down on the cloth so that the waxed side of the roll is on top. Remove from pan. Cool for 5 minutes. Carefully peel off waxed paper. Cut off crisp edges if you like. Roll up the roulade while still warm by rolling cake and towel from the narrow end. Cool and unroll. Place the roll on an ovenproof platter and spread with the Ham and Spinach Filling. Roll up again and reheat in a preheated 325° oven for 15 minutes. Spoon the remaining filling over the top. Garnish with sautéed mushroom caps. Serves six.

Ham and Spinach Filling

2 tablespoons butter
1 tablespoon salad oil
4 minced shallots or ⅓ cup minced onion
1 10-ounce package frozen chopped spinach, cooked, drained, and squeezed dry
1 cup minced ham
1 tablespoon Dijon mustard
1 teaspoon paprika
½ teaspoon ground nutmeg
6 ounces cream cheese, softened, cut into pieces
1 cup sour cream

Heat butter and oil in a heavy saucepan and cook shallots or onion until soft but not browned. Stir in spinach, ham, Dijon mustard, paprika, and nutmeg. Mix well. Add cream cheese and sour cream and mix again. Cook over low heat, stirring constantly, until the mixture is well blended. Cool and reserve 3 tablespoons of the filling; spoon it later over the top of the roulade.

Monday

Buckwheat Blini

Buckwheat Blini
Red or Black Caviar
Sour Cream
Chopped Hard-Cooked Egg Whites
Sieved Hard-Cooked Egg Yolks
Minced Parsley
Lemon Wedges
Shoestring Beet Salad
Meringues with Lemon Filling

1 cup milk
½ package yeast (½ teaspoon)
2 eggs, separated
½ teaspoon salt
1 teaspoon sugar
2 tablespoons melted butter
1½ cups white flour
½ cup buckwheat flour

These pancakes can be cooked in the dining room in an electric frying pan. They could also be served at an informal kitchen party, where the guests finish their drinks in the kitchen while you make the pancakes on the stove. Scald milk and cool to lukewarm. Dissolve yeast in the milk. In a large bowl beat together the egg yolks, salt, sugar, and melted butter. Stir in yeast. Beat in white flour and buckwheat flour, a little at a time, beating until smooth. Cover the bowl with plastic wrap. Set in a warm place, such as near a heating register or on a rack placed on an electric hot tray turned on to warm or set in a pan of warm water, changing the water to keep it warm. The dough will rise to double its bulk in about 1 hour and 15 minutes. Beat the egg whites until stiff with a pinch of salt. Fold into the dough. Lightly grease a skillet or griddle. Drop batter on it by small spoonfuls — no more than a tablespoon to one blini. It will rise rather than spread. Brown on both sides. Stack the ready blinis on a plate and keep them warm in a very slow 200° oven until they are all cooked. Makes about 30 blinis.

Tuesday

Rice Tian

Stuffed Mushrooms
Shrimp Puffs
Baked Chicken with Wine and Herbs
Rice Tian
Strawberries with Pureed Raspberry Sauce (use frozen raspberries)

1 pound zucchini
2 large onions
2 tablespoons butter
1 tablespoon olive oil
1¼ cups Uncle Ben's rice
3¼ cups chicken bouillon
salt
freshly ground pepper
1 cup grated Parmesan cheese

Trim but do not peel the zucchini. Wash and dry. Cut zucchini and onions into small dice, but keep them separate. Heat the butter and oil in a frying pan and cook the zucchini for 2-3 minutes, stirring constantly. The zucchini should be well coated with the fat. Transfer zucchini to a 16-inch baking dish that is 2 inches deep. Cook onions in the same frying pan until soft. If necessary, add a little more butter. Add rice and cook, stirring constantly, for about 3 minutes. Transfer the rice to baking dish and mix with zucchini. Pour chicken bouillon over the rice. Season lightly with salt since the bouillon and cheese are on the salty side, but season liberally with pepper. Stir in the Parmesan cheese. Cook uncovered in a 300° oven for about 40 minutes. A thin crust should form to give a crunchy effect and all liquid should be absorbed. Makes six servings.

Wednesday

Roman-Style Broccoli or Cauliflower

White Bean Salad with Hunks of Italian Imported Tuna Fish
Pork Chops in Rosemary-Flavored Cream Sauce
Boiled Potatoes
Roman-Style Broccoli or Cauliflower
Fresh Ginger-Flavored Applesauce

1 large bunch broccoli or
  1 large head cauliflower
⅓ cup olive oil
2 garlic cloves
salt
freshly ground pepper
1½ to 2 cups dry white wine

Trim and wash the vegetable and cut into small flowerets. Throw away the thick stems. Heat olive oil in a large frying pan and cook garlic cloves until browned; remove them and throw away the garlic. Add the vegetable, salt, and pepper. Cook over medium heat, stirring constantly, for 5 minutes. Add 1 cup of wine. Cover, reduce heat to low, and cook for 5-10 more minutes or until just tender but still crisp. Stir frequently. Check for moisture; if the vegetables look dry, add a little more of the remaining wine. The end result should be a moist but not soupy dish. Makes four servings.

Thursday

Ham Horns with Asparagus

Ham Horns with Asparagus
Deviled Grilled Chicken
Mixed Green Bean and Potato Salad
Hot Chocolate Soufflé

12 large slices boiled ham
24 cooked asparagus spears
¾ cup mayonnaise
Boston lettuce
2 hard-cooked eggs, sliced
parsley
additional mayonnaise

Trim the fat off the ham and trim the slices to an even, identical size. On each ham slice place 2 asparagus spears and 1 tablespoon mayonnaise. Roll up the ham into the shape of a horn or cornucopia. Line a serving dish with Boston lettuce leaves. Place the ham horns on it in a circle. Garnish with the sliced eggs, parsley sprigs, and dabs of mayonnaise. Makes six servings.

Friday

Danish Curried Fillets of Flounder/ Pickled Cucumbers

Fresh Pea Soup
Danish Curried Fillets of Flounder
Boiled Potatoes
Pickled Cucumbers
Fresh Pineapple with Kirsch
Cookies

4 tablespoons butter
2 tablespoons grated onion
½ teaspoon salt
¼ teaspoon freshly ground pepper
2 teaspoons mild curry powder
1 cup dry white wine
2 pounds fillets of flounder or other white fish
2 tablespoons flour
½ cup heavy cream
4 tablespoons grated Parmesan cheese

Heat 2 tablespoons of butter in a frying pan. Stir in the grated onion, ½ teaspoon salt, ¼ teaspoon pepper, and curry powder. Cook over low heat, stirring constantly, for about 3 minutes. Stir in wine and bring to boil. Lower the heat. Poach fish fillets, a few at a time, in mixture. Transfer the poached fish to a well-buttered shallow baking dish. Reserve the frying pan liquid. Heat remaining butter in another frying pan and stir in flour. Gradually stir in cream and the liquid from the first frying pan in which the fish were poached. Cook over low heat, stirring constantly, for 5 minutes, or until sauce is thick and smooth. Pour this sauce over fish and sprinkle with Parmesan cheese. Cover and cook in a preheated 350° oven for about 10 minutes. Uncover and cook for 5 minutes longer or until lightly browned. Serves four to six.

Pickled Cucumbers

3 large cucumbers
1 tablespoon salt
¾ cup cider or white vinegar (do not use wine vinegar)
1 tablespoon sugar or to taste
¼ teaspoon white pepper
2 tablespoons minced parsley or fresh dill weed

Scrub cucumbers free of any waxy coating. Wash and dry. Score them lengthwise with the tines of a fork. Slice as thinly as possible, preferably with a vegetable slicer. The slices should be transparent. Place them in a deep bowl and sprinkle with salt. Cover cucumbers with a plate and weigh it down with something heavy, such as a large can of fruit or coffee. Let stand at room temperature for 1-2 hours. Drain thoroughly and squeeze out any remaining liquid. Combine the vinegar, sugar, and pepper. Pour over cucumbers. Check the seasoning. Chill cucumbers thoroughly. At serving time drain and sprinkle with parsley or dill. Serves six.

Saturday

Asparagus Party

Asparagus with Flemish Egg and Lemon Sauce*
Cold Lobster Mayonnaise
Watercress
Strawberries Romanoff*
Wines: Chilled Gewuerztraminer from Wente (California) or Hugel or Kitterle (Alsace)

For this party, the stress is on asparagus, not the usual 5-6 stalk serving, but plenty of it, enough to make it the main dish of the meal. This means ½ to ¾ pounds for each person, which sounds like a lot, but is not after peeling and trimming every bit of the stem which is hard. Asparagus, in cooking, retains much of the water in which it is cooked, so that it has to be drained thoroughly. The way to do this is to place the cooked asparagus on clean dish towels, which work better than paper towels in absorbing the moisture. It is also a good idea to tie the peeled and trimmed asparagus with soft string into fist-thick bundles before cooking it; that way it is easier to fish out of the boiling water. Lay the tied bundles on the dish towels, pat them dry with other towels, and untie the strings. Then serve the asparagus on heated plates if it is to be eaten hot. The sauce can be served from a sauceboat which is passed around or individual portions of sauce can be put into little bowls or midget white soufflé dishes, so that each diner can dunk his own asparagus.

What follows such an asparagus feast is not really that important. The course should not be bulky, but rather choice, such as a little lobster mayonnaise, or some pâté de foie gras or even good prosciutto ham.

Wines

A spicy, cold white wine goes well with this meal, such as a Wente California Gewuerztraminer, or a Hugel or Kitterle Gewuerztraminer, both from Alsace. They are medium priced wines.

Strawberries Romanoff

3 pints strawberries
grated rind of large orange
juice of large orange
¼ cup Curacao, Grand
Marnier, Triple Sec,
or Cognac
sugar to taste
2 cups heavy cream
2 tablespoons sugar

Wash strawberries very quickly under running cold water and shake dry. Stem the berries. Reserve 6 perfect ones. Put the others in a bowl. Gently stir in the orange rind and juice, the Curaçao and sugar to taste. Refrigerate for 2 hours. Whip the cream until stiff with 2 tablespoons sugar. Spoon a layer of cream into a glass serving dish. Top with a layer of strawberries and some juice. Repeat the layering of strawberries and cream and finish with a layer of cream. Decorate with the reserved strawberries. Refrigerate for 15 minutes before serving. Serves six.

Note: The dessert tends to separate. In practice, assemble the dessert just before starting to serve the meal.

Asparagus with Flemish Egg and Lemon Sauce

6 hard-cooked eggs,
shelled
1½ cups butter, melted
and hot
2 tablespoons fresh
lemon juice
salt
freshly ground pepper
¼ cup minced parsley

This sauce can be increased and decreased at will. The basic quantities for each person are: 1 hard-cooked egg, ¼ cup butter, melted, 1½ teaspoons fresh lemon juice, salt, freshly ground pepper and 2 teaspoons minced parsley. This quantity of sauce is sufficient for ½ pound cooked asparagus. The egg fragments should be the size of large peas or small limas. Crush the eggs with a fork in small saucepan. Pour butter over the eggs and mix well. Stir in the lemon juice, salt, pepper, and parsley. Heat through over very low heat, stirring constantly. Do not let the sauce boil. Serves six.

JUNE

This is the month to learn to eat well and healthfully with all the lovely vegetables of the season. Marvelous main dishes can be made with them, with the addition of eggs, pasta, rice, legumes or whatever shreds of meat are left over from a rare roast, not to speak of a little ground meat. At last we have discovered what the people of the Mediterranean and of the Far East have known all along — that you don't have to eat meat constantly to keep up your health and your working capacity. A point to be remembered is that when a number of vegetables are to be combined into a dish, they will be more flavorful if cooked separately in a little butter or oil before being put together. Don't overcook, or even cook them through, since they will be cooked some more in their final togetherness.

JUNE

	FAMILY FARE	
	LUNCHES	**DINNERS**
Sunday	Chicken Hash* Corn Bread Strawberries in Liqueur or Orange Juice	Veal Paprika* Buttered Egg Noodles with Poppy Seeds Green Pepper Salad Miniature Pancakes Filled with Apricot Jam
Monday	Tuna Fish Salad and Peanut Butter and Bacon Sandwiches Sliced Fresh Pineapple Orange Wafers*	Minted Fresh Pea Soup Persian Stuffed Roast Chicken* Zucchini Cooked with Tomatoes Strawberry Ice Cream
Tuesday	German Potato Soup with Cucumbers* Hard-Cooked Eggs in Mayonnaise Green Salad Sliced Mangoes with Lime Juice	Corn Beef Hash* Hot Potato Salad Dressed with French Dressing Watercress and Grapefruit Salad Blueberry Pie
Wednesday	Sloppy Joes with Homemade Chili Sauce* Ice Cream and Cookies	Broiled Flank Steak with Herb Butter Scalloped Potatoes Buttered Asparagus Mango Mousse with Orange Rum Sauce*
Thursday	Minced Chicken and Vegetable Sandwiches* Sliced Cantaloupe and Toll House Cookies	Oven-Barbecued Spareribs* Baked Potatoes and Sour Cream Mixed Green Salad with Avocado Blueberries with Orange Juice and Sugar
Friday	Italian Tuna Fish Omelet* Italian Bread Assorted Cheeses Fruit	Fried Fillets of Sole Cucumber and Sour Cream Sauce for Fried Fish* Steamed New Potatoes Cantaloupe Halves Filled with Vanilla Ice Cream and Blueberries
Saturday	Scrambled Eggs Paul Reboux* Strawberries with Brown Sugar and Cream Sponge Cake	Lamb Roasted with Herbs and White Wine New Potatoes Green Peas and Shallots Coeur a la Crème*

QUICK & EASY Dinners For Two	BUDGET DINNERS	ENTERTAINING
Chicken Breasts with Cognac and Cream* Spaetzle Buttered Asparagus Rhubarb Pie and Cream	Barbecued Sweet and Sour Chicken* Pilaff with Mushrooms Zucchini and Eggplant Casserole Fresh Fruit	Palace Court Salad with Green Goddess Dressing* Potato Rolls Raspberries and Cream Cookies
Spaghetti with Pizzaiola Sauce* Hard-Cooked Eggs with Caper Mayonnaise Red Radishes Celery Sticks Carrot Sticks Melon	Pot Roast Candied Tomatoes* Mashed Potatoes Chocolate Whip	Crab Soup* Cheese Straws Mixed Vegetable Risotto with Parmesan Cheese Rhubarb Shortcake
Consommé with Fresh Mushrooms* Calf's Liver and Bacon Boiled Potatoes Green Salad Apple Compote with Fresh Blueberries	Chicken Pojarski* Boiled Potatoes Baked Carrots Fresh Strawberries	Veal Braised in Wine with Tomatoes and Onions Green Noodles Petis Pois a la Française Chocolate Cream*
Cheese and Ham Cake* Fresh Corn Pudding Stewed Fresh Tomatoes Strawberries Marinated in Orange Juice Cookies	Cheese Puff* Asparagus Vinaigrette Biscuits Strawberry Pie	Asparagus Vinaigrette Greek Beef and Onion Stew* Parslied New Potatoes Strawberry Shortcake Made with Biscuit Dough
Rice Pilaff with Chicken Pieces Peas in Cream Watercress with Lemon French Dressing Peaches in Red Wine*	Chicken Livers and Grapes* Buttered Rice Fresh Peas Fruit and Cookies	Saffron Rice with Mushrooms Chicken Breasts in Cream Sauce* Peas Cooked with Lettuce and Shredded Prosciutto Strawberries Romanoff
Crab Meat Supreme* Popovers Mushroom, Bacon, Spinach and Tomato Salad Chocolate Cake	Scallop Casserole* Green Beans Sliced Cucumbers and Celery Strawberries	Bow Noodles with Three Cheeses* Chicken Marengo Fresh or Frozen Buttered Lima Beans Chocolate Mousse
Chinese Steak* Fried Rice Mixed Green Salad Strawberries, Blueberries and Melon Melange	Hamburger Rolls Spinach Tart* Tomato Salad Strawberry Ice Cream	Country Ham* Turkey Tossed Green Salad Potato Salad Jellied Cucumber Salad Watermelon Pickles Corn Bread Barbecued Limas* Deviled Eggs Birthday Cake

FAMILY FARE LUNCHES

June

Sunday

Chicken Hash

Chicken Hash
Corn Bread
Strawberries in Liqueur or Orange Juice

4 tablespoons butter
2 tablespoons salad oil
1 cup minced onion
½ cup minced green pepper
½ pound mushrooms, thinly sliced
¼ cup flour
1 cup chicken bouillon
1 cup light cream or Half and Half
4 cups finely diced leftover roast or boiled chicken
salt
dash of Tabasco
paprika

Heat butter and oil in a large deep frying pan. Add onion and pepper. Cook, stirring constantly, for 5 minutes or until vegetables are soft, but not brown. Add mushrooms. Cook, stirring frequently, over low to medium heat for 8-10 minutes or until all pan liquid evaporates. Do not brown mushrooms. Stir in flour and cook 1 minute longer. Add chicken bouillon and cream. Cook, stirring constantly, until sauce is smooth and thickened. Reduce to low heat. Add chicken to sauce, mix well and season with salt and Tabasco. Cook 5 minutes or until chicken is heated through. Sprinkle with paprika before serving. Six servings.
Note: For a more liquid hash, stir in an extra ¼ to ⅓ cup cream. This dish can also be made with leftover turkey.

Monday

Orange Wafers

Tuna Fish Salad and Peanut Butter and Bacon Sandwiches
Sliced Fresh Pineapple
Orange Wafers

1 cup butter
½ cup light or dark brown sugar, firmly packed
½ cup sugar
1 egg
1½ cups flour
¼ teaspoon baking soda
¼ teaspoon salt
2 tablespoons orange juice
2 tablespoons grated orange rind

Cream butter with brown sugar and sugar until light and soft. Beat in egg. Sift flour with soda and salt. Stir in the flour, orange juice and rind. Let the dough stand at room temperature for 10 minutes. Drop by teaspoonfuls on greased and floured baking sheets, leaving 2 inches between cookies. Bake in a preheated 350° oven for 8-10 minutes. Cool on racks. Makes about 60 small cookies.

Tuesday

German Potato Soup with Cucumbers

German Potato Soup with Cucumbers
Hard-Cooked Eggs in Mayonnaise
Green Salad
Sliced Mangoes with Lime Juice

2 large cucumbers
8 medium potatoes (about 2 pounds) peeled and diced into ½-inch cubes
4 cups chicken bouillon or water
salt
freshly ground pepper
1½ cups milk
1 cup heavy cream
1 tablespoon grated onion
1 tablespoon minced fresh dill weed or more to taste

Peel the cucumber and trim off ends. Cut them first into halves lengthwise, and then again, lengthwise, each half into two pieces. Scoop out seeds with a spoon, cut into ½-inch dice and reserve. Put the potatoes and the chicken bouillon into a large heavy saucepan. Bring to boil. Reduce heat to low and season with salt and pepper. Cook until potatoes are soft and easy to mash. Drain potatoes through a sieve or a food mill into a large bowl. With a large spoon, force potatoes through sieve or food mill to puree. Do not use a blender because mixture will be too slick. Return potatoes and their cooking liquid to saucepan. Bring to boil and reduce heat to low. Stir in milk, cream and grated onion. Add cucumber and simmer uncovered for 10 minutes or until tender but not mushy. Check the seasoning and stir in dill weed. Four to six servings.

Wednesday

Sloppy Joes with Homemade Chili Sauce

Sloppy Joes with Homemade Chili Sauce
Ice Cream and Cookies

2 tablespoons salad oil
1 pound lean ground beef
2 tablespoons grated onion
1 10-ounce can undiluted tomato soup
½ cup chili sauce
1 tablespoon Dijon or other prepared mustard
salt
freshly ground pepper
6 split and toasted hamburger buns

Heat oil in a large frying pan and cook meat, stirring constantly with a fork to prevent lumping, until browned. Pour off any excess fat. Add onion, tomato soup, chili sauce and mustard. Taste and if necessary, season with salt and pepper. Simmer uncovered over low heat for 10 minutes, or until thickened. Stir occasionally. Serve on hamburger buns. Serves six.

Chili Sauce

2 tablespoons salad oil
2 tablespoons flour
2-3 teaspoons chili powder, or to taste
1 cup (1 8-ounce can) prepared tomato sauce
2 tablespoons grated onion
1 garlic clove, mashed
1 tablespoon vinegar
1½ cups beef bouillon
salt
freshly ground pepper

Heat oil in a heavy saucepan. Stir in flour and cook, stirring constantly, until golden brown. Stir in all the remaining ingredients. Simmer over low heat, stirring constantly, for about 15 minutes. Store in sterilized jars for several months, or keep covered in refrigerator for 2-3 weeks. About two cups.

Thursday

Minced Chicken and Vegetable Sandwiches

Minced Chicken and Vegetable Sandwiches
Sliced Cantaloupe and Toll House Cookies

1 whole large chicken breast, poached
4 small carrots, peeled and chopped
4 celery stalks, chopped
2 green peppers, seeded and chopped
4 radishes
2 3-ounce packages cream cheese, cut into pieces
1 tablespoon minced chives or green onion tops
2 tablespoons minced parsley
salt
½ teaspoon paprika
mayonnaise
whole wheat or cracked wheat bread for sandwiches

Bone and skin the chicken breast and cut into pieces. Combine the chicken, carrots, celery stalks, green peppers and radishes in a bowl and mix. Force the mixture through the large blade of meat grinder. Return to bowl and add cream cheese, chives and parsley. Season with salt and paprika. Mix well and blend in enough mayonnaise to make mixture easy to spread on sliced whole wheat or cracked wheat bread. Makes about four cups.

Friday

Italian Tuna Fish Omelet

Italian Tuna Fish Omelet
Italian Bread
Assorted Cheeses
Fruit

4 eggs, beaten
¼ teaspoon pepper
1 tablespoon minced parsley
½ teaspoon dried parsley
or any other herb
1 medium (7-ounce) can tuna
fish, drained and chopped fine
salt
3 tablespoons olive oil

It is better to make 2 Tuna Fish Omelets than doubling the ingredients for a large one. Combine the eggs, pepper, parsley and tuna fish. Taste for seasoning; if necessary, add a little salt. Mix well. Heat oil in a large, heavy frying pan. Pour in the egg mixture. Cook over low heat for 7 minutes, or until set at the bottom. Turn over and cook about 5 minutes longer or until set. Makes three servings.

Saturday

Scrambled Eggs Paul Reboux

Scrambled Eggs Paul Reboux
Strawberries with Brown Sugar and Cream
Sponge Cake

10 eggs
grated rind of 1 orange
1 teaspoon salt
½ teaspoon freshly ground
pepper
3 tablespoons heavy cream
3 tablespoons dry sherry
6 tablespoons butter
hot buttered toast

Paul Reboux was a noted French gastronome, with many excellent and original ideas on food.

Beat the eggs lightly with a fork. Add the orange rind, salt, pepper, cream and sherry. Beat only to blend. Heat butter in a heavy frying pan. Add the eggs. Cook over very low heat, stirring constantly, until the eggs are softly scrambled but still moist. Serve immediately on hot buttered toast. Makes four servings.

FAMILY FARE DINNERS

June

Sunday

Veal Paprika

Veal Paprika
Buttered Egg Noodles with Poppy Seeds
Green Pepper Salad
Miniature Pancakes Filled with Apricot Jam

2 pounds veal cutlets, thinly sliced
2 tablespoons butter
1 garlic clove, mashed
1-2 tablespoons sweet paprika
1 cup chicken bouillon or water
salt
freshly ground pepper
1 cup heavy cream

Place the cutlets between two sheets of waxed paper. Pound as thin as possible with a meat mallet or a bottle. Dry on paper towel. Heat butter in a large deep frying pan. Stir in the garlic and paprika. Cook, stirring constantly, for about 2 minutes. Add veal and cook 2 minutes on each side. Reduce heat to low and add the bouillon, salt and pepper. Simmer, covered, for 10 minutes. Add the cream. Cook uncovered for 5-10 more minutes, basting the meat frequently. Serves four to five.

Note: This makes for a thin sauce. If a thicker sauce is wanted, blend the cream with 1-2 tablespoons of flour.

Monday

Persian Stuffed Roast Chicken

Minted Fresh Pea Soup
Persian Stuffed Roast Chicken
Zucchini Cooked with Tomatoes
Strawberry Ice Cream

1 4-pound roasting chicken, washed and dried
2 tablespoons butter
1 chicken liver, minced
1 cup cooked white or brown rice
¼ cup seedless raisins, plumped in lukewarm water and drained
½ cup pine nuts
grated rind of 1 lemon
salt
freshly ground pepper
salad oil
juice of 2 large lemons

Remove any fat from chicken. Mince, and put into bird's cavity. Heat butter and cook, stirring constantly, the chicken liver for 2 minutes. Add the rice, raisins and pine nuts and lemon rind. Cook for 3 more minutes. Season with salt and pepper. Cool mixture. Stuff the chicken and sew up vent. With a pastry brush, coat chicken on all sides with salad oi. Place on rack in a baking pan. Cook in a preheated 300° oven for 2 hours or until juices from the thickest part of the leg run clear when pricked with a skewer. Baste chicken every 15 minutes with the lemon juice and pan juices for the first 1½ hours, then baste every 7-8 minutes. When cooked, turn the chicken on its breast so that the juices can seep into it and let stand for 5 minutes before carving. Serves four to six.

Tuesday

Corned Beef Hash

Corn Beef Hash
Hot Potato Salad Dressed with French Dressing
Watercress and Grapefruit Salad
Blueberry Pie

½ pound corned beef, cooked
2 medium boiled potatoes
1 small onion, minced
¼ teaspoon salt
freshly ground pepper
⅛ teaspoon ground allspice
2 tablespoons butter
water

Buy the corned beef at a delicatessen, but unsliced, in one piece. Chop the corned beef coarsely. Peel the potatoes and chop them coarsely. Combine the beef, the potatoes, and the onion in a bowl and season with the salt, pepper and allspice. Heat the butter in a frying pan. Add the hash. Press it down with a spatula or the back of a spoon. Cook over low heat for about 3 minutes. Stir the hash with a fork and press it down again. Continue cooking it over low heat until the bottom of the hash is crusty. If it looks too dry, sprinkle a tablespoon or two of water over it. With a pancake turner fold the hash over as you do with an omelet. Slide it on a heated platter, crusty side up. Serve immediately, with chili sauce. Serves two.

Wednesday

Mango Mousse with Orange Rum Sauce

Broiled Flank Steak with Herb Butter
Scalloped Potatoes
Buttered Asparagus
Mango Mousse with Orange Rum Sauce

2 large ripe mangoes
juice of 1 lime
sugar to taste
1 cup heavy cream, whipped
orange slices
Orange Rum Sauce

Peel the mangoes and cut off flesh. Scrape any remaining flesh from the pit with a sharp knife. Cut the big pieces into 2-inch cubes and put all the mango flesh into blender top. Add the lime juice and sugar to taste; the mixture should be on the tart side. Puree and taste again; if necessary, add more lime juice and sugar. Fold whipped cream into mango puree. Pour into a 3-cup mold rinsed in water and freeze overnight. Unmold at serving time and let stand 10 minutes at room temperature. Garnish with orange slices and serve with the sauce drizzled over the mousse. Serves six.

Note: To unmold, fill sink with hot water and dip mold in so that the water comes half way up mold. Count to 7 and turn mousse onto a serving dish.

Orange Rum Sauce

1 cup sugar
¼ cup dark or golden rum
2 tablespoons butter
⅓ cup orange juice
grated rind of 1 orange

Combine all the ingredients in a heavy saucepan. Cook over medium heat, stirring constantly, until the sugar is dissolved and the sauce well blended. Serve warm or cold. About ⅔ cup.

Thursday

Oven-Barbecued Spareribs

Oven-Barbecued Spareribs
Baked Potatoes and Sour Cream
Mixed Green Salad with Avocado
Blueberries with Orange Juice and Sugar

1 cup Homemade Chili Sauce
1 cup minced onion
½ cup cider vinegar
2 tablespoons sugar
2 tablespoons Worcestershire sauce
2 teaspoons Dijon mustard
½ teaspoon Tabasco
juice of 1 orange
4 pounds spareribs, in 3 pieces, trimmed of excess fat
salt
freshly ground pepper
3 lemons, cut into ¼-inch slices, seeds removed

Combine the chili sauce, onion, cider vinegar, sugar, Worcestershire sauce, mustard, Tabasco and orange juice in a saucepan. Bring to boil, stirring constantly with a wooden spoon. Reduce heat and simmer for 5-10 minutes, stirring occasionally. Lay the spareribs on a rack in a large roasting pan, flesh side up. Sprinkle with a little salt and pepper. With a pastry brush, coat the meat with about ½ cup of the basting sauce. Top the meat with lemon slices. Roast in a preheated 400° oven for about 1 to1½ hours, brushing the meat every 20 minutes with the remaining sauce. The ribs are done when the meat is tender to the touch of a knife. Four to six servings.

Friday

Cucumber and Sour Cream Sauce for Fried Fish

Fried Fillets of Sole
Cucumber and Sour Cream Sauce for Fried Fish
Steamed New Potatoes
Cantaloupe Halves Filled with Vanilla Ice Cream and Blueberries

2 large cucumbers
3 teaspoons salt
1 medium onion, grated
1 cup sour cream
dash of Tabasco
2 tablespoons minced fresh dill weed or parsley

Peel the cucumbers and shred on a cheese shredder into a bowl. Stir in the salt and mix well. Let stand for 30 minutes. Put the cucumbers into a strainer and run cold water over them to remove excess salt. Drain thoroughly. Then, with the hands, squeeze out as much water as possible. Finally, dry the cucumbers with paper towel. Combine the cucumbers, onion, sour cream and Tabasco to taste. Mix well. Stir in dill weed. Chill for 10 minutes before serving in a bowl or sauce boat. Makes about 1½ cups.

Saturday

Coeur a la Crème

Lamb Roasted with Herbs and White Wine
New Potatoes
Green Peas and Shallots
Coeur a la Crème

1 pound creamy cottage cheese
1 pound cream cheese
pinch of salt
2 cups heavy cream
1 tablespoon Kirsch or brandy
1 quart strawberries or raspberries
sugar
heavy cream

Strain cottage cheese and cream cheese through a strainer or beat until softened with an electric beater. Both must be smooth and fluffy. Beat in the salt, heavy cream and Kirsch. Beat until well blended. Line the traditional heart shaped wicker or metal molds with moistened cheese cloth, or line any mold with a perforated bottom or clean, new brown ceramic flower pots with moistened cheese cloth. Turn the mixture into the molds. Cover with plastic or aluminum foil to prevent absorption of foreign odors. Set on plates to catch excess moisture which will drain off. Refrigerate overnight. Unmold on a platter. Surround with berries and serve sugar and additional heavy cream, unwhipped, on the side. Makes six servings.

QUICK & EASY DINNERS FOR TWO

June

Sunday

Chicken Breasts with Cognac and Cream

Chicken Breasts with Cognac and Cream
Spaetzle
Buttered Asparagus
Rhubarb Pie and Cream

2 small chicken breasts, split into halves
salt
freshly ground pepper
flour
¼ cup butter
⅓ cup cognac
1 cup heavy cream
4 large mushroom caps, sautéed in butter (optional)

Remove the skins and fat from the chicken breasts. Bone them, or at least remove the larger bones. Sprinkle with salt and pepper and coat with flour. Shake off excess flour. Heat butter in a frying pan and cook the chicken breasts for 2-3 minutes, turning once, or until golden brown on each side. Sprinkle with cognac and flame. When the flames have died down, add cream. Lower the heat to very low, cover, and cook for 10-15 minutes or until tender. Serve with a mushroom cap on each piece of chicken.

Monday

Tomato Sauce Pizzaiola

Spaghetti with Pizzaiola Sauce
Hard-Cooked Eggs with Caper Mayonnaise
Red Radishes
Celery Sticks
Carrot Sticks
Melon

¼ cup olive oil
1 small onion, minced
1 garlic clove, minced
1 to 1½ pounds fresh tomatoes, peeled, seeded and chopped small
salt
freshly ground pepper
2 tablespoons fresh chopped basil or 1 teaspoon dried basil
¼ cup minced parsley

This sauce is different from the long-simmered tomato sauces. It is cooked very quickly, over high heat, so that the tomatoes keep their fresh taste. Good for pasta, steak and chicken. Heat olive oil in a heavy saucepan. Add all the other ingredients. Cook over high heat, stirring constantly, for 7-8 minutes or until the tomatoes are just soft. Makes about 1½ cups.

Tuesday

Consommé with Fresh Mushrooms

Consommé with Fresh Mushrooms
Calf's Liver and Bacon
Boiled Potatoes
Green Salad
Apple Compote with Fresh Blueberries

3 cups beef consommé
¼ pound fresh mushrooms, thinly sliced
salt
freshly ground pepper
½ cup dry sherry

Heat the beef consommé to boil in a heavy saucepan. Add mushrooms. Simmer, covered, over low heat 5-10 minutes or until the mushrooms are tender. Season with salt and pepper. Remove from heat and stir in sherry. Serve very hot.

Wednesday

Cheese and Ham Cake

Cheese and Ham Cake
Fresh Corn Pudding
Stewed Fresh Tomatoes
Strawberries Marinated in Orange Juice
Cookies

3 tablespoons butter
2 eggs, separated
½ cup grated Parmesan cheese
1 cup finely diced cooked ham
1 teaspoon mustard
freshly ground pepper

Cream butter until soft. Stir in egg yolks. Beat until mixture is fluffy and well blended. Stir in the Parmesan, ham, mustard and pepper. Beat the egg whites until stiff and fold into the cheese mixture. Pour into a well-buttered 8-inch pie pan. Bake in a preheated 350° oven until fluffy and golden brown on top.

Thursday

Peaches in Red Wine

Rice Pilaff with Chicken Pieces
Peas in Cream
Watercress with Lemon French Dressing
Peaches in Red Wine

4 ripe but unblemished peaches
sugar
dry red wine

A good dry red wine, such as a Pinot Noir or a Bordeaux wine, should be used for this excellent simple dessert. Dip the peaches in boiling water and peel. Cut into thin slices. Place the sliced peaches in a deep serving dish. Sprinkle with sugar to taste. Add enough dry red wine to cover the fruit. Chill thoroughly before serving. (This can be done in the freezer or the freezing compartment of the refrigerator).

Friday

Crab Meat Supreme

Crab Meat Supreme
Popovers
Mushroom, Bacon, Spinach and Tomato Salad
Chocolate Cake

½ pound cooked crab meat picked over and flaked
2 tablespoons butter
1 tablespoon flour
⅔ cup light cream or milk
salt
freshly ground pepper
1 egg yolk, beaten
¼ cup dry white wine
¼ cup grated Swiss cheese

Make sure that there are no hard membranes left in the crab meat. Heat butter and cook the flour for 1 minute. Add cream and cook, stirring constantly, until smooth and thickened. Season with salt and pepper. Stir 2 tablespoons of the sauce into egg yolk and mix well. Stir this egg yolk mixture into remaining sauce and mix well. Cook over low heat, stirring constantly, for 2 minutes. Stir in wine and 2 tablespoons of cheese. Stir until cheese is melted. Pour into a buttered 4 cup baking dish. Sprinkle with remaining cheese. Bake in a preheated 400° oven for 5 minutes or until the top is golden brown.

Saturday

Chinese Steak

Chinese Steak
Fried Rice
Mixed Green Salad
Strawberries, Blueberries and Melon Melange

1 pound any steak
1 tablespoon soy sauce
1 small onion
¼ pound mushrooms
1 celery stalk, white part only
2 tablespoons salad oil
salt
freshly ground pepper

Remove all fat and bone from the meat. Cut meat into 1½-inch cubes. Place meat cubes in a bowl and sprinkle with soy sauce. Slice the onion, mushrooms and celery stalk very thinly. Heat oil in a deep frying pan or a wok. Add steak. Over high heat, stirring constantly, cook meat for 2 minutes. It should be only half done. Transfer the meat with a slotted spoon to a heated plate and keep hot. Add the onion, mushrooms and celery stalk to the frying pan. If necessary, add ½ to 1 tablespoon more oil. Over moderate heat, and stirring constantly, cook the vegetables for 3-4 minutes or until barely tender. Return meat to frying pan and mix. Turn the heat back to high and cook the steak and vegetables for another 2-3 minutes. Season with salt and pepper.

BUDGET DINNERS

June

Sunday

Barbecued Sweet and Sour Chicken

Barbecued Sweet and Sour Chicken
Pilaff with Mushrooms
Zucchini and Eggplant Casserole
Fresh Fruit

½ cup fresh lemon juice
½ cup honey
3 tablespoons Dijon mustard
½ cup dry white wine
2 tablespoons white vinegar
2 tablespoons Worcestershire sauce
1 teaspoon salt
dash Tabasco
4 chicken legs
4 chicken thighs

Combine all the ingredients except chicken in a saucepan. Bring to boil. Place chicken in a large, flat dish and pour the marinade over the pieces. Let stand at least 3 hours in a cool place or in the refrigerator, turning over several times. Drain and reserve marinade. Broil over low coals, turning often and basting with the marinade. Makes four servings.

Monday

Candied Tomatoes

Pot Roast
Candied Tomatoes
Mashed Potatoes
Chocolate Whip

6 cups canned drained tomatoes or 6 fresh peeled and chopped tomatoes
6 tablespoons minced onion
salt
freshly ground pepper
8 tablespoons light or dark brown sugar
½ cup fine dry bread crumbs
⅓ cup butter

Place the tomatoes, onion, salt, pepper and sugar in a large saucepan. Cook uncovered over medium heat until almost dry. Pour into a shallow baking dish. Top with the crumbs and dot with butter. Bake in a preheated 350° oven for 15 minutes. Makes four servings.

Tuesday

Chicken Pojarski

Chicken Pojarski
Boiled Potatoes
Baked Carrots
Fresh Strawberries

3 large chicken breasts, skinned and boned
1 teaspoon ground nutmeg
salt
½ tablespoon melted butter
flour
1 egg
2 tablespoons dry sherry
1 tablespoon oil
2 cups fine dry bread crumbs

For the Sauce:
2 tablespoons butter
2 tablespoons flour
1 cup chicken bouillon
½ cup heavy cream
salt
1 teaspoon paprika
2 teaspoons brandy

Chop or grind chicken meat very fine. Put into a bowl and mix with nutmeg, salt and half of the melted butter. Chill. Have ready 3 shallow bowls. Place flour in one bowl; egg, beaten with sherry and oil in the second; and bread crumbs in the third. With floured hands, shape the chilled chicken mixture into balls the size of pullet eggs. Then press flat into cutlet shapes. Dip cutlets first into flour, then into egg mixture and finally into bread crumbs. Shake off excessive crumbs. Heat remaining butter in a heavy frying pan and cook chicken cutlets for 4 minutes, turn and cook for 4 minutes longer, or until golden brown. To make the sauce, melt butter in a saucepan. Stir in flour and cook for about 2 minutes. Stir in bouillon and cream. Cook, stirring constantly, for 3-5 minutes, or until thick and smooth. Do not undercook or the flour in the sauce will taste raw. Stir in the salt, paprika and brandy. Serve in a sauceboat. Serves four.

Wednesday

Cheese Puff

Cheese Puff
Asparagus Vinaigrette
Biscuits
Strawberry Pie

3 tablespoons butter
2 cups chopped cooked ham
2 tablespoons minced chives or green onion tops
1½ cups milk
1 tablespoon butter
1 cup fresh white bread crumbs
1 cup coarsely grated sharp Cheddar cheese
3 eggs, separated
salt
freshly ground pepper

Heat butter in a frying pan and cook ham and chives, stirring frequently, for about 5 minutes. Spread half of the ham over the bottom of a buttered 2-quart baking dish. Heat milk with butter until butter is melted. Remove from heat and stir in bread crumbs, cheese, and egg yolks. Salt and pepper to taste. Let stand for 15 minutes. Beat the egg whites with a pinch of salt until stiff but not dry. Fold into the egg mixture. Pour over ham. Bake in a preheated 350° oven for 30-35 minutes or until firm and puffy. Makes three to four servings.

Thursday

Chicken Livers and Grapes

Chicken Livers and Grapes
Buttered Rice
Fresh Peas
Fruit and Cookies

1½ pounds chicken livers
flour
4 tablespoons butter
2 tablespoons minced onion
salt
freshly ground pepper
½ teaspoon ground ginger
1 teaspoon soy sauce
½ cup dry white wine
¼ cup chicken bouillon
½ cup heavy cream
2 cups seedless grapes, halved
2 tablespoons minced parsley

Dust the chicken livers lightly with flour. Heat butter in a large frying pan and cook the onion and livers for 5-7 minutes, turning frequently. Season lightly with salt and pepper and add ginger, soy sauce, wine and bouillon. Reduce heat. Cover and cook for 5 minutes longer. Stir in cream and grapes and heat through. Sprinkle with parsley before serving. Makes four to six servings.

Friday

Scallop Casserole

Scallop Casserole
Green Beans
Sliced Cucumbers and Celery
Strawberries

4 tablespoons butter
2 tablespoons minced shallots or onions
½ cup minced celery
salt
freshly ground pepper
2 teaspoons crumbled rosemary
2 cups sour cream
2 pounds scallops (if large, cut into halves)
¼ cup dry white wine
½ cup fresh white bread crumbs

Heat butter in a large frying pan and cook shallots and celery, stirring constantly, for 5 minutes. Season with salt and pepper, add rosemary and ½ cup of sour cream. Simmer, stirring constantly, for 3 minutes. Add scallops and mix well. Turn scallops into a 2-quart shallow baking dish. Rinse out the frying pan with wine. Add remaining sour cream to the wine and heat through. Pour over scallops. Sprinkle with bread crumbs. Bake in a preheated 350° oven for 15-20 minutes or until golden and bubbly. Four to six servings.

Saturday

Spinach Tart

Hamburger Rolls
Spinach Tart
Tomato Salad
Strawberry Ice Cream

2 pounds fresh spinach or 3 10-ounce packages frozen spinach, thawed
4 tablespoons butter
2 tablespoons minced shallots or onions
1 garlic clove, minced
3 eggs
½ pound farmer's cheese or large curd cottage cheese
½ cup heavy cream
salt
freshly ground pepper
½ cup freshly grated Parmesan cheese

Cook spinach in the water clinging to the leaves after it has been washed. Drain dry by pressing the spinach against the sides of a strainer. Heat butter in a frying pan and cook the shallots and garlic for 2-3 minutes or until soft. Put the spinach into a large bowl. Mix in the shallots, eggs, farmer's cheese, cream, salt and pepper. Blend thoroughly. Spread in a buttered shallow ½-quart baking dish. Sprinkle with Parmesan. Bake in a preheated 375° oven for 15-20 minutes. Four servings.

ENTERTAINING

June

Sunday

Palace Court Salad with Green Goddess Dressing

Palace Court Salad with Green Goddess Dressing
Potato Rolls
Raspberries and Cream
Cookies

shredded Boston or other tender lettuce
6 canned artichoke bottoms, drained and dried
1 pound large lump crab meat
2 hard-cooked egg yolks, sieved
18 green asparagus tips, cooked
salt
freshly ground pepper
Green Goddess Dressing

On 6 salad plates arrange beds of shredded lettuce. Place 1 artichoke bottom on each plate. Fill each artichoke bottom with crab meat and sprinkle some of the egg yolk over the crab meat. Garnish with the asparagus tips. Sprinkle with salt and pepper and cover with Green Goddess Dressing. Serves six.

Green Goddess Dressing

1 cup mayonnaise
½ cup sour cream
1 garlic clove, minced
3 anchovy fillets or 2 teaspoons anchovy paste or to taste
3 tablespoons chopped chives
¼ cup chopped parsley
1 tablespoon lemon juice
1 tablespoon tarragon vinegar
½ teaspoon salt
1 teaspoon freshly ground pepper

Place all ingredients in a blender and blend until smooth. Makes 1½ cups of dressing.

Monday

Crab Soup

Crab Soup
Cheese Straws
Mixed Vegetable Risotto with Parmesan Cheese
Rhubarb Shortcake

6 hard-cooked eggs
4 tablespoons butter, at room temperature
grated rind of 1 lemon
3 teaspoons Worcestershire sauce
4 tablespoons flour
6 to 7 cups milk, heated
2 pounds cooked and flaked crab meat
2 cups light cream
1 cup dry sherry
salt
paprika

In a large saucepan mash the hard-cooked eggs to a paste, using a fork. Mash in the butter, lemon rind, Worcestershire sauce, and flour. Stir 6 cups of hot milk gradually into the mixture; add remaining cup if you like a thinner soup. Add the crab meat. Cook over low heat, stirring constantly, for 5 to 10 minutes, or until heated through thoroughly. Add the cream and sherry. Heat through but do not boil. Season with salt and sprinkle with paprika. Serve very hot, with Cheese Straws. Makes six servings.

Tuesday

Chocolate Cream

Veal Braised in Wine with Tomatoes and Onions
Green Noodles
Petits Pois a la Française
Chocolate Cream

8 ounces German sweet chocolate, broken up
4 tablespoons butter
2 tablespoons light corn syrup
2 teaspoons instant coffee
3 tablespoons light or heavy cream
4 tablespoons fresh strained orange juice
2 eggs, separated
3 tablespoons Cointreau or other orange liqueur
⅓ cup heavy cream, whipped

In a heavy saucepan combine chocolate, butter, corn syrup, and coffee. Stir over low heat until chocolate and butter are melted and well mixed. Stir in cream and orange juice. Remove from heat and beat in 2 egg yolks, beating until slightly thickened and creamy. Stir in the Cointreau or other orange liqueur. Cool. Beat egg whites until stiff with a pinch of salt. Fold into the chocolate mixture. Spoon into individual little soufflé or other dessert dishes. Refrigerate thoroughly. Before serving, top each helping with a little whipped cream. Serves four to six.

Wednesday

Greek Beef and Onion Stew

Asparagus Vinaigrette
Greek Beef and Onion Stew
Parslied New Potatoes
Strawberry Shortcake Made with Biscuit Dough

2½ to 3 pounds lean round steak
4 tablespoons butter
3 tablespoons tomato paste
1 large garlic clove, minced
salt
freshly ground pepper
dry white wine
beef bouillon or water
2 pounds small white onions, peeled
¾ teaspoon ground cinnamon

Trim the meat free of all excess fat and gristle. Cut into 1-inch cubes. Heat butter in a large casserole. Over high heat, brown the meat. Lower the heat to medium and add tomato paste, garlic, salt, pepper, and equal quantities of dry white wine and bouillon in just sufficient quantity to cover the meat. The quantity depends on the size and shape of the casserole. Bring to boil and reduce heat to very low. Simmer, covered, stirring occasionally, for about 45 minutes. Add onions, cinnamon and mix well. Continue to simmer, covered, for 20 more minutes or until onions are tender. Serves six.

Note: This is a thin stew. If a thicker one is wanted, at the end of cooking time blend 1 to 2 tablespoons flour with 2 to 3 tablespoons water. Cook the stew uncovered, stirring frequently, for 5 more minutes or until stew has thickened.

Thursday

Chicken Breasts in Cream Sauce

Saffron Rice with Mushrooms
Chicken Breasts in Cream Sauce
Peas Cooked with Lettuce and Shredded Prosciutto
Strawberries Romanoff

2 cups well-flavored, strong chicken bouillon
2 cups heavy cream
6 medium chicken breasts, halved, skinned, and boned
½ cup butter
juice of 2 lemons
2 tablespoons dry sherry
salt
freshly ground pepper
¼ cup minced parsley

In a very large saucepan combine chicken bouillon and heavy cream. Over medium heat bring to boil. Reduce heat to low. Simmer, uncovered, for 30 minutes or until liquid is reduced by about half. Cool and reserve. Trim any ragged ends off chicken breasts. Heat butter in one very large or in two frying pans; the pans must have tight lids and be large enough for chicken pieces side by side. Sprinkle with juice of 1 lemon. Over medium heat cook breasts for 2 minutes or until whitish and opaque. Turn and cook for 2 minutes longer or until the other side is the same. Cover the pans with tightly fitting lids or tie aluminum foil over the top. Cook the chicken breasts in a slow, preheated 325° oven for about 15 minutes. Test doneness by pressing a few of the breasts with a finger; the meat should feel springy. Transfer the breasts to a heated platter and keep warm in oven. To the pan juices (if you are using 2 frying pans, combine the pan juices in one) add the reserved cream mixture. Over high heat bring to boil. Cook for 3-4 minutes, stirring constantly, until sauce is thickened. Reduce heat to low and stir in the juice of remaining lemon, and sherry. Check the seasoning, add salt and pepper if necessary. Pour sauce over the chicken breasts and sprinkle with parsley. Serves six.

Friday

Bow Noodles with Three Cheeses

Bow Noodles with Three Cheeses
Chicken Marengo
Fresh or Frozen Buttered Lima Beans
Chocolate Mousse

fine dry bread crumbs
12 ounces egg noodle bows (about 6 cups)
2 tablespoons butter
1 cup freshly grated Parmesan cheese
1 cup diced Swiss cheese
1 cup diced Mozzarella cheese
3 cups Thin White Sauce

Coat a buttered 3-quart baking dish generously with bread crumbs. Cook the egg noodle bows in plenty of rapidly boiling salt water until barely tender. Drain well. Put bows in a bowl and toss well with the butter and Parmesan cheese. Add Swiss cheese and Mozzarella and toss again. Turn half of the bows into the baking dish and top with half of the Thin White Sauce. Top with remaining bows and top these with remaining Thin White Sauce. Sprinkle 2-3 tablespoons grated bread crumbs over top. Bake in a preheated 350° oven for 25 minutes or until golden brown. Serves six.

Thin White Sauce

3 tablespoons butter
3 tablespoons flour
½ teaspoon salt
⅛ teaspoon freshly ground pepper
1 cup milk or Half and Half

Heat butter in a heavy saucepan. Stir in flour, salt and pepper. Cook over medium heat, stirring constantly, until smooth. Stir in milk or Half and Half. Cook, stirring all the time, until sauce is thickened and smooth. Reduce to lowest possible and put an asbestos plate over the heat. Cook sauce for 10 more minutes, to remove any taste of raw flour. Stir frequently. Three cups.

Saturday

All-American Barn Dance and Birthday Party for Twenty

Country Ham* **Turkey**
Tossed Green Salad **Potato Salad**
Jellied Cucumber Salad
Watermelon Pickles
Corn Bread
Barbecued Limas* **Deviled Eggs**
Birthday Cake

**Recipe in book*

Drinks:

Cider, Almadén Grenache Rosé, Concannon Zinfandel Rosé (California) or any other good French or American Rosé Wine, Beer, Soft Drinks

A birthday barn dance party for all ages can be expanded in numbers with very little trouble since the food is flexible. Set up one long table, covered with a colorful paper tablecloth, for the foods and place them on hot trays. You will need a 12-pound country ham and a 15-pound turkey to serve twenty. Put the plates, flatware and napkins on another, similarly covered table. Have the wines, soft drinks and glasses (plastic glasses are permissible) in another location, away from the food. In order to keep the drinks cold, store them in plastic buckets filled with ice.

Place small (bridge) tables around the edge of the barn leaving the center free for dancing. Make simple tablecloths out of inexpensive red, white and blue materials (the edges can be pinked, and don't have to be sewn) and cover the tables with these cloths. Wrap the flatware in napkins made from the same materials as the tablecloths and tie them with contrasting ribbons. Decorate the barn with ballons and bunting. Make sure heaters are available; the night could be cool. Pre-slice the meats to save time. Stuff the eggs with different fillings. Have everything except the birthday cake ready and set out before calling people to come to eat. Make a ceremony out of bringing in the birthday cake lit up by candles — and make sure there are plates and forks ready for serving.

Country Ham

If the ham has a heavy coating of mold on it, which many country cured hams do, soak in cold water to cover for 24 hours. Then scrub thoroughly with a stiff brush. Rinse well and place the ham in a large kettle of simmering water to cover, skin side down. Simmer covered for 18 minutes per pound, or 16 minutes if you like a harder ham. For the last hour of cooking, add 1 quart cider and ½ cup brown sugar. When the ham is cooked, the small bone at the shank end will wiggle easily. Remove the ham from the water immediately and cool it at room temperature. Preheat the oven to 325°. Cut the rind and heavy skin off the ham, leaving most of the fat. Score the fat in a diamond pattern. If you wish, place one whole clove in each diamond pattern. Make a paste consisting of equal parts of dry yellow mustard moistened with water to a stiff paste and brown sugar. Spread this paste evenly over the fat. Bake the ham for 1 hour. Cool and serve at room temperature, sliced very thinly. Twenty servings.

Barbecued Limas

4 pounds dried lima beans
1 pound salt pork, diced small
½ cup butter
4 tablespoons salad oil
4 onions, thinly sliced
5 tablespoons Dijon mustard
5 tablespoons bottled steak sauce
1 tablespoon salt
2 tablespoons chili powder
4 cups tomato sauce
2 tablespoons paprika

Because you are using such a large amount of dried beans, it would be easier to boil and bake them in two batches. For the baking you will need two 5-quart casseroles. Soak the beans overnight in cold water to cover. Drain. Put half the beans into a large kettle and cover with water. Add half of the salt pork. Cover and bring to boil. Reduce heat to low and simmer covered for about 30–40 minutes until tender but not mushy. Drain, saving 2 cups bean broth. Put the remaining beans and pork with water to cover into the kettle and cook like the first batch. Drain, again saving 2 cups of bean broth. Combine butter and oil in a deep frying pan and cook the onions until golden brown. Stir into the onions the mustard, steak sauce, salt, chili powder and tomato sauce. Simmer uncovered for 5 minutes, stirring frequently. Put the beans and the pork into two 5-quart casseroles. Divide the sauce into equal parts. Mix one part of the sauce with the pork and beans in one casserole. Bake uncovered in a preheated 400° oven for 1 hour, basting and moistening with the reserved bean broth during the cooking. Use about 1½ to 2 cups broth for each casserole. Fifteen minutes before the beans are done, sprinkle with paprika.

JULY

The most immediate and exquisite of all pleasures on a day or night when the heat rises straight into the air from the ground is the sudden touch of frost on tongue and palate. This is true for summer drinks and for the icy desserts of the season. But it is not true for unsweet foods, with the possible exception of soups, though even these are spoiled by overchilling, for extreme cold deadens flavors. When making a dish that needs to be chilled, rather than cool, you must exaggerate the seasonings or you won't taste them. Just melt ice cream to room temperature and you'll see what I mean — it is cloyingly sweet.

The old adage of something hot on the hottest day holds as true as ever, be it only a cup of hot consommé. And beware of too much ice in your drinks if you want to be well enough to enjoy summer.

JULY

	FAMILY FARE	
	LUNCHES	**DINNERS**
Sunday	Peaches and Cream Salmon Casserole and Creamed Mushrooms* Popovers	Poached Salmon Steaks Sauce Mousseline Steamed New Potatoes Green Beans Vinaigrette Clafoutis*
Monday	Danish Bacon and Egg Omelet* Corn Bread Watermelon	Marinated Pork for a Cold Supper* Mustard Pickled Beets Mixed Vegetables in Mayonnaise Potato Salad Fresh Raspberry Sherbet
Tuesday	Egg Noodles and Cottage Cheese Casserole* Sliced Tomatoes Fruit and Cookies	Curried Calf's Liver* Yellow Rice (with saffron or turmeric) Guacamole Salad Fresh Peaches Stewed in Vanilla Syrup
Wednesday	Tomatoes Filled with Tuna Fish Salad Rice Salad Blueberry Orange Bread* with Butter and Blueberry Jam	Cold Roast Chicken American Ratatouille* Potato Salad with French Dressing Assorted Cheeses and Crackers Melon
Thursday	Country Risotto* Cheese French Bread	Brown Chicken Fricassee with Madeira* Broiled Tomatoes Sautéed Mushrooms Browned Potatoes Peach Ice Cream
Friday	Baked Eggs, Mushrooms and Shrimp in Cheese Sauce* Sliced Tomatoes Watermelon	Fillets of Sole Coq d'Or* Tiny Boiled New Potatoes Cucumber Salad Fresh Apricot Pie
Saturday	French Fried Potatoes Cucumber Salad Blueberry Betty*	Zucchini Soup Cold Meat Loaf with Chutney Glaze* Rice Salad Vanilla Ice Cream with Fresh Sliced Peaches

QUICK & EASY Dinners For Two	BUDGET DINNERS	ENTERTAINING
Lamb Curry Rice Uncooked Mango Chutney* Green Beans Vinaigrette Fresh Lemon Ice	Baked Short Ribs* German Potato Salad Tomatoes and Cucumber Vinaigrette Watermelon	Melon and Prosciutto Mango Chicken* Yellow Rice Chutney Red Radish Salad Deep-Dish Blackberry Pie with Cream
Summer Vegetable Stew* Stuffed Eggs on Watercress Open Peach Tart	Salmon Salad Tomatoes a la Crème* Marinated Potatoes and Cucumbers Fruit Salad	Ham Baked with Sherry* Spoon Bread Poached Apples Pennsylvania Dutch Coffee Cake* Cider Coffee Tea Milk
Grilled Chicken Mushroom Sauce* Grilled Eggplant Slices Sautéed Cherry Tomatoes Fresh Peaches and Raspberries in Kirsch	Eggs in Tomato Shells* Sautéed Peppers, Onions and Celery Blueberry Muffins Ice Cream	Schinkenfleckerln* (Austrian Ham and Noodles) Tossed Green Salad Cheese Platter: Brie, Bel Paese, Port Salut, Sharp Cheddar French Goat Cheese, Boursin Triple Cream Assorted White and Brown Breads and Crackers Fruit
Veal Cutlet Parmigiana Corn on the Cob Tomato Salad with Fresh Basil and Mustard Dressing Uncooked Blueberry Compote*	Sautéed Fish Fillets Creamed Potatoes Mixed Garden Vegetable Casserole* Angel Pie	Persian Pancake Omelet with Vegetables* Cold Roast Beef Remoulade Sauce Salad of White Beans and Tomatoes Fresh Peach Ice Cream Cookies
Thick Cold Cucumber Soup* Broiled Lamb Chops Stewed Tomatoes and Okra Coffee Ice Cream	Cold Chicken Zucchini and Potato Mousaka* Green Salad Strawberries and Cream	Jellied Madrilène with Diced Avocado Chicken Curry Rice Chutney Cold Marinated Zucchini* Coffee Granita with Whipped Cream
Garlic Broiled Shrimp Venetian Rice and Peas* Cucumbers and Tomatoes Melon with Vanilla Ice Cream	Pasta with Striped Bass Sauce* Mixed Green Salad with Herbs Fruit and Cheese	Oeufs en Gelée (French Eggs in Aspic) Broiled Shrimp Homemade Lemon Mayonnaise Small Boiled New Potatoes in Their Skins Tomato Salad with Herbs Riz a l'Impératrice*
Hot Tomato Soup Made with Fresh Tomatoes Tuna, Potato and Onion Dinner Salad* Tossed Green Salad Crackers and Cheese Tray	Chicken, Spinach and Noodles* Green Beans and Radish Salad Peaches	Shrimp in Beer* Lemon Butter Sauce Wilted Cucumber Sauce Marinated Green Beans and Tomatoes French Bread Fresh Fruit Salad Almond Cake*

FAMILY FARE LUNCHES

July

Sunday **Salmon Casserole and Creamed Mushrooms**

Peaches and Cream
Salmon Casserole and Creamed Mushrooms
Popovers

1 can (1 pound) salmon
2 cups fresh white bread crumbs
½ cup pitted black or pimiento-stuffed olives, sliced
1 cup grated Swiss or Cheddar cheese
½ cup minced parsley
1 cup light cream or milk
3 eggs
salt
freshly ground pepper
1 medium onion, grated
juice of 1 lemon
Creamed Mushrooms

Drain, bone and flake the salmon into a bowl. Add bread crumbs, olives, cheese and parsley. Mix well. Beat together the cream, eggs, salt, pepper and onion. Stir into salmon mixture. Stir in lemon juice. Turn into a buttered 1½-quart baking dish. Place into a baking pan containing 1 inch of hot water. Bake uncovered in a preheated 350° oven for 45 minutes or until set. Serve with Creamed Mushrooms on the side. Serves six.

Creamed Mushrooms

4 tablespoons butter
1 pound mushrooms, thinly sliced
1 tablespoon fresh lemon juice
salt
freshly ground pepper
1 cup heavy cream

Heat butter in a heavy saucepan and add mushrooms. Cook over high heat, stirring constantly, for about 5 minutes. Stir in lemon juice and season with salt and pepper. Turn heat to low and add cream. Cook, without a cover, stirring frequently, for another 5 minutes. Serves six.

Monday

Danish Bacon and Egg Omelet

Danish Bacon and Egg Omelet
Corn Bread
Watermelon

½ pound lean sliced bacon (preferably Danish bacon, canned)
6 eggs
1 tablespoon flour
salt
freshly ground pepper
¼ cup chopped chives or 2 tablespoons grated onion

As with all omelets, it is better and easier to make two rather than doubling the recipe for one large omelet. Cook the bacon in a frying pan until golden brown and just beginning to crisp heavily. Drain and crumble. Pour off all but 4 tablespoons of fat from frying pan. Beat together the eggs, flour, salt, pepper and chives. Heat the bacon fat. Pour the egg mixture into the hot fat. When the omelet is beginning to set, sprinkle crumbled bacon over it. Lift the cooked omelet edges with a fork so that the uncooked portion runs underneath. Cook over low heat until golden brown and set. Fold and serve hot on a heated platter or, for a harder omelet, turn on a plate and slide again into the frying pan uncooked side down. Brown lightly on the uncooked side and serve.

Tuesday

Egg Noodles and Cottage Cheese Casserole

Egg Noodles and Cottage Cheese Casserole
Sliced Tomatoes
Fruit and Cookies

6 lean bacon slices
3 cups cooked and drained medium egg noodles
salt
freshly ground pepper
2 cups creamed or dry cottage cheese
2 eggs
½ cup heavy cream
4 tablespoons butter
½ cup fine dry bread crumbs

Cook the bacon in a heavy large skillet until crisp and brown. Crumble coarsely and pour the bacon and its own fat into a bowl. Add noodles and toss with 2 forks. Season with salt and pepper. In another bowl, beat together the cottage cheese, eggs and heavy cream. Turn one third of the noodle mixture into a generously buttered 2-quart baking dish. Top with half of the cheese mixture. Top this with another third of the noodles. Top the noodles with the remaining half of the cheese mixture and end up with a layer of noodles. Heat butter in the frying pan in which the bacon was cooked. Stir the bread crumbs into the butter and cook, stirring constantly, for 2 minutes or until they are well coated with butter. Sprinkle over the noodles. Bake in a preheated oven 350° for about 30 minutes or until set, with golden brown crumbs. Six servings.

Wednesday

Blueberry Orange Bread

Tomatoes Filled with Tuna Fish Salad
Rice Salad
Blueberry Orange Bread with Butter and Blueberry Jam

¼ cup boiling water
2 tablespoons butter
½ cup + 2 tablespoons fresh orange juice
3 tablespoons grated orange rind
1 egg
1 cup sugar
2 cups flour
1 teaspoon baking powder
¼ teaspoon baking soda
½ teaspoon salt
1 cup blueberries, picked over
2 tablespoons honey

Combine in a bowl, boiling water and butter. Stir until butter is melted. Add ½ cup of orange juice and 2½ tablespoons of orange rind. In another bowl, beat together the egg and sugar until light. Sift together the flour, baking powder, baking soda and salt. Add the flour mixture gradually and alternately with the orange liquid, to the egg and sugar. Beat until smooth. Fold in the blueberries. Turn the batter into a well buttered and floured 9 × 5 × 3-inch pan or a 1½-quart cake mold. Bake in a preheated 325° oven for about 1 hour 10 minutes. Line a cake rack with waxed paper and turn the loaf onto it. Blend together honey with remaining 2 tablespoons or orange juice and remaining ½ tablespoon of orange rind. Spoon over the hot loaf. Cool completely before slicing. One nine-inch loaf.

Thursday

Country Risotto

Country Risotto
Cheese
French Bread

1 cup dry white navy beans
3½ cups chicken or beef bouillon
2 medium potatoes, cut into ½-inch slices
2 large carrots, sliced
2 large zucchini, thinly sliced
2 leeks, white and green parts, sliced, or 1 bunch green onions, white and green parts, sliced
1 turnip, cut into ½-inch cubes
1 cup raw long-grain rice
2 pounds fresh peas, shelled or 1 10-ounce package frozen peas
salt
freshly ground pepper
¼ teaspoon ground sage
¼ cup melted butter
freshly grated Parmesan cheese

Pour boiling water over beans, cover and let stand for 1 hour. Drain. Put beans into a large kettle, add cold water to cover and simmer covered for 45 minutes. Add 3 cups of bouillon and bring to boil. Add the potatoes, carrots, zucchini, leeks and turnip. Cook uncovered over high heat for about 4 minutes. Add rice and the remaining ½ cup of bouillon. Cook covered over medium heat, stirring frequently, until rice is almost tender. Add the peas, salt and pepper to taste. Cook covered until the rice and peas are tender, about 15 minutes. If the risotto is too liquid, cook uncovered to reduce the liquid. If too thick, add a little more bouillon. Stir sage into the melted butter and stir into the risotto Serve with grated Parmesan cheese. Six servings.

Friday

Baked Eggs, Mushrooms and Shrimp in Cheese Sauce

Baked Eggs, Mushrooms and Shrimp in Cheese Sauce
Sliced Tomatoes
Watermelon

8 hard-cooked eggs, shelled
3 tablespoons mayonnaise
2 tablespoons minced sweet pickle
1½ teaspoons vinegar
½ teaspoon dry mustard
salt
freshly ground pepper
3 tablespoons butter
½ pound mushrooms, thinly sliced
1 pound cooked shelled and deveined shrimp
Cheese Sauce

Cut eggs into halves lengthwise. Remove yolks and mash them to a smooth paste with the mayonnaise, sweet pickle, vinegar, mustard, salt and pepper. Refill the whites with this mixture. Heat butter in a frying pan and cook the mushrooms over high heat for 3–4 minutes or until barely golden but still firm. Spread mushrooms over the bottom of a large baking dish. Lay the egg halves side by side, in one single layer, over the mushrooms. Top with shrimp. Spoon the Cheese Sauce over shrimp. Bake in a preheated 400° oven for 15 minutes or until thoroughly heated through and golden. Six servings.

Cheese Sauce

4 tablespoons butter
3 tablespoons flour
2 cups hot milk
salt
freshly ground pepper
dash Tabasco
1 cup grated mild Cheddar or Swiss cheese

Heat butter in a saucepan. Stir in flour. Cook, stirring constantly, for about 1 minute. Stir in the hot milk all at once. Cook, stirring all the time, until sauce is smooth and thickened. Season with salt, pepper and Tabasco. Cook over lowest heat, preferably over an asbestos plate, for 5–10 more minutes, stirring frequently. This is to remove the raw flour taste all too frequent in white sauces. Stir in cheese and cook only until the cheese is melted. Cool before using. About two cups.

Saturday

Blueberry Betty

French Fried Potatoes
Cucumber Salad
Blueberry Betty

4 cups washed fresh blueberries or thawed frozen blueberries, drained
juice of 1 large lemon
½ cup firmly packed brown sugar
4 cups ½-inch fresh white bread cubes, without crusts
¼ cup sugar
1 teaspoon ground cinnamon
2 tablespoons butter, cut into small pieces
1 cup heavy cream

Mix together the blueberries, lemon juice and brown sugar. Spread half of the mixture in a shallow baking dish. Mix together the bread cubes, sugar and cinnamon. Put half of this mixture over the berries. Top it with the remaining berries, and top these with the remaining bread cubes. Dot with butter. Bake in a preheated 350° oven for 25 – 30 minutes. Serve warm, with cream on the side. Makes four to six servings.

FAMILY FARE DINNERS

July

Sunday

Poached Salmon Steaks
Sauce Mousseline
Steamed New Potatoes
Green Beans Vinaigrette
Clafoutis

Clafoutis

3 pounds pitted sweet black cherries
2 tablespoons fresh lemon juice
3 tablespoons Kirsch (optional)
½ cup butter
½ cup + 1 tablespoon sugar
1 tablespoon grated lemon rind
¼ teaspoon ground nutmeg
3 eggs
1 cup flour

A French fruit dessert. To pit the cherries, use either a new hairpin or a special cherry pitter, a small, inexpensive tool available at hardware stores. Combine the cherries, lemon juice and Kirsch in a bowl and let stand at room temperature for 30 minutes. Cream the butter with ½ cup sugar, lemon rind, and nutmeg until very soft and light. Beat in the eggs, one at a time, beating well after each addition. Beat in flour. Turn batter into a well buttered and floured 9-inch spring form pan. With a slotted spoon, lift out the cherries from their juice and spread them over the batter. Blend the remaining 1 tablespoon of sugar with the cherry juice and dribble over cherries and batter. Bake in a preheated 375° oven for 40 minutes or until set. Serve warm, lukewarm or cooled, but not chilled. Six servings.

Monday

Marinated Pork for a Cold Supper

Marinated Pork for a Cold Supper
Mustard
Pickled Beets
Mixed Vegetables in Mayonnaise
Potato Salad
Fresh Raspberry Sherbet

3 pounds boned loin of pork (weigh after boning)
1 large onion stuck with 4 cloves
2 bay leaves
1 tablespoon salt
Marinade:
2 cups white or cider vinegar
1 large onion, sliced
2 bay leaves
5 peppercorns
5 parsley sprigs

Place meat in a large saucepan and add enough water to just cover the meat, onion, bay leaves and salt. Bring to boil, lower the heat to low and skim. Simmer covered about 1½ to 1¾ hours or about 35 minutes to the pound. Cool the meat in its cooking liquid. Drain, trim off excess fat and slice thinly. Place the meat in a deep bowl or serving dish, (do not use aluminum), cover with marinade and refrigerate for 4 hours or overnight. At serving time, drain and scrape off the vegetables. Dribble a little drained marinade over the meat to keep moist. Serves six.

To make the marinade: Combine all the ingredients and cook for 5–8 minutes. Cool before using on the sliced meat.

Tuesday

Curried Calf's Liver

Curried Calf's Liver
Yellow Rice (with saffron or turmeric)
Guacamole Salad
Fresh Peaches Stewed in Vanilla Syrup

½ cup plain yogurt
juice of 1 large lemon
1 tablespoon salad oil
1 tablespoon Madras curry powder
2 teaspoons salt
1 teaspoon freshly ground pepper
1½ pounds calf's liver, ¼-inch thick and cut into 4-inch pieces
4 tablespoons butter
1 large onion, thinly sliced
1 tablespoon flour
1 cup heavy cream

Combine the yogurt, lemon juice, salad oil, curry powder, salt, and pepper in a deep bowl, do not use aluminum. Mix well. Drop in the liver pieces, turning them with two spoons in marinade to make sure they are coated on all sides. Refrigerate for about 30 minutes. Heat butter in a heavy deep frying pan and and cook the onion slices until soft and golden. Remove the onion slices with a slotted spoon to a plate, cover and keep warm. Drain the liver pieces. Heat the butter in the frying pan to foaming. Over moderate heat, cook the liver pieces, a few at a time, for about 3 minutes, turning over once. As they turn golden brown, transfer them with a slotted spoon to a heated serving dish, cover and keep warm. Return the onions to the frying pan and stir in flour. Cook for 1 minute. Stir in cream. Cook, stirring constantly, until sauce is thickened and very hot. Pour the sauce over liver and serve immediately. Serves six.

Wednesday

American Ratatouille

Cold Roast Chicken
American Ratatouille
Potato Salad with French Dressing
Assorted Cheeses and Crackers
Melon

1 medium eggplant, peeled and cut into 2-inch cubes
2 tablespoons salt
½ cup olive oil (it *must* be olive oil)
2 large onions, thinly sliced
2 garlic cloves
2 large green or red sweet peppers, cut into rings and seeded
4 large tomatoes, peeled and choppe
4 small zucchini or yellow squash, sliced, or mixed squash
1 cup fresh okra, sliced
2 cups fresh kernel corn, scraped off the cob
freshly ground pepper
3 tablespoons minced fresh basil leave or 1 tablespoon dried basil
⅓ cup minced parsley

Sprinkle eggplant with about 2 tablespoons of salt and place in a colander. Weigh down with a plate topped by a large full bowl of water or a can of beans or other canned food. Place in the sink and let stand for about 30 minutes to drain off excess moisture. Heat olive oil over very low heat in a heavy casserole. The oil must be warm, but it should not smoke. *Cook* — but do *not* fry — over low heat the onions, garlic cloves, and peppers in the warm oil for 30 minutes or until very soft. Add the drained eggplant, tomatoes, zucchini, okra, and corn. Season with salt, but taste first as the eggplant may be salty, and pepper. Add basil and parsley. Simmer, covered, over low heat for 15 minutes. Uncover and simmer for 15-25 minutes longer to let excess moisture evaporate. Ratatouille should be neither soupy nor dry. Serves six.

Note: Other vegetables, such as mushrooms, may be added to this vegetable stew. Use your own taste as a guide. The thing to remember is that the vegetables are *stewed*, not fried, in the oil.

Thursday

Brown Chicken Fricassee with Madeira

Brown Chicken Fricassee with Madeira
Broiled Tomatoes
Sautéed Mushrooms
Browned Potatoes
Peach Ice Cream

1 4-5 pound chicken, cut into pieces
½ cup flour
1 teaspoon salt
¼ teaspoon freshly ground pepper
4 tablespoons butter
1 medium onion, thinly sliced
2-3 cups hot chicken bouillon
1 cup Madeira or dry sherry
2 bay leaves
1¾ cups heavy cream, lightly whipped

Cut any fat off the chicken pieces. If wanted, remove the skins. Coat chicken on all sides with flour mixed with salt and pepper. Heat butter in a heavy frying pan. Over high heat, brown the chicken pieces. Transfer the chicken pieces to a casserole. Add onion to the pan juices and brown. Add the onion to the chicken, together with 2 cups of bouillon, Madeira and bay leaves. Bring to boil. Simmer, covered, over low heat for 45 minutes to 1 hour, or until the chicken is tender. (Skinned chicken pieces will take a shorter cooking time). Check for moisture; if necessary, add a little more chicken bouillon. Remove the chicken to a deep heated serving dish and keep hot. If necessary, boil down to 2 cups the liquid in which the chicken was cooked. Stir in cream. Heat through but do not boil. Pour the sauce over the chicken pieces. Four to six servings.

Friday

Fillets of Sole Coq d'Or

Fillets of Sole Coq d'Or
Tiny Boiled New Potatoes
Cucumber Salad
Fresh Apricot Pie

¾ cup butter
2 tablespoons salad oil
2 tablespoons lemon juice
2 tablespoons minced parsley
salt
freshly ground pepper
6 large fillets of sole
2 teaspoons curry powder
1 teaspoon tomato paste
1 tablespoon minced chutney
6 slices pineapple, preferably fresh
2 tablespoons flour
1 cup fish stock or chicken bouillon
1 cup heavy cream
paprika

Heat ¼ cup of butter and the salad oil in a large frying pan. Stir in lemon juice, parsley, about ½ teaspoon salt and ¼ teaspoon pepper. Cook for 1 minute. Add fish, 2 or 3 pieces at a time, depending on size of frying pan. Cook until delicately browned on both sides, turning over once. This should take 3-5 minutes on each side, depending on thickness. The fish is ready when it flakes; do not overcook. Place fillets in overlapping pieces on a large, heated serving platter. Cover loosely with foil and keep hot in a low 200° oven. Heat remaining ½ cup of butter in another frying pan and stir in curry powder, tomato paste and chutney. Cook, stirring constantly, for about 2 minutes. Add pineapple slices, a few at a time if frying pan is not large enough to hold them all without touching. Cook over medium heat for 6 minutes or until golden brown, turning over once. Place pineapple slices around fish, cover again with the foil and keep hot. Stir flour into frying pan in which the pineapple was cooked. Cook for about 2 minutes. Do not let it brown. Stir in fish stock or bouillon. Cook over high heat, stirring constantly, until liquid has cooked down to about ½ to ¾ cup. Reduce heat and stir in heavy cream. Cook over low heat, stirring constantly, until sauce is smooth. Add salt and pepper to taste. Spoon sauce over fish, but not the pineapple, and serve hot, sprinkled with paprika. Serves six.

Saturday

Cold Meat Loaf with Chutney Glaze

Zucchini Soup
Cold Meat Loaf with Chutney Glaze
Rice Salad
Vanilla Ice Cream with Fresh Sliced Peaches

¼ cup orange juice
2 slices white bread, crusts removed
1½ pounds lean ground beef
1 egg
3 tablespoons minced onion
2 tablespoons minced parsley
salt
freshly ground pepper
2 tablespoons orange juice concentrate
2 tablespoons soy sauce
½ cup any favorite chutney
1 garlic clove

Heat the orange juice in a small saucepan and soak bread in it. Put the bread, ground beef, egg, onion and parsley into a bowl. Mix well and season with salt and pepper. Mix thoroughly, preferably using hands. Shape into a loaf and place into a baking pan. Put the orange juice concentrate, soy sauce, chutney and garlic clove into a blender. Puree to a smooth mixture. Spoon half of it over the meat loaf and reserve the other half. Bake in a preheated 350° oven for 30 minutes. Spoon the remaining glaze over the meat loaf and bake for 30 minutes longer. Remove to a serving platter, cool and slice. Serves four to six.

QUICK & EASY DINNERS FOR TWO

July

Sunday

Uncooked Mango Chutney

Lamb Curry
Rice
Uncooked Mango Chutney
Green Beans Vinaigrette
Fresh Lemon Ice

1 ripe mango, weighing about 1½ pounds
2 tablespoons fresh lemon juice or more
1 tablespoon grated or finely diced fresh ginger
1 garlic clove, mashed
½ teaspoon salt
½ cup grated fresh coconut
Tabasco to taste

Uncooked chutneys are part of Indian curry dinners. They are easy, but must be made only a short time before serving, and they will only keep a day in the refrigerator. Peel the mango. Cut the flesh into ¼-inch cubes, put them in a bowl and toss with lemon juice. Add the ginger, garlic, salt, coconut and mix well. Stir in Tabasco, beginning with about 3 drops and increasing to taste. Cover and refrigerate.

Note: If fresh coconut is not available, use dry *unsweetened* coconut, to be found in health stores. Soak the coconut in lukewarm water to cover for 15 minutes, or until plumped, and drain.

Monday

Summer Vegetable Stew

Summer Vegetable Stew
Stuffed Eggs on Watercress
Open Peach Tart

1 large carrot, diced
1 large potato, peeled and diced
2 celery stalks, sliced
2 small zucchini, sliced
¼ head small cabbage, chopped
½ cup peas, fresh or frozen
½ cup lima beans, fresh or frozen
1 tomato, peeled and chopped
1 sweet green or red pepper, sliced
1 white turnip, diced
1-2 cups water
salt
freshly ground pepper
½ teaspoon any dried herb or
 2 tablespoons minced basil, thyme, tarragon, chives or any combination of herbs
¼ cup olive oil (it
 must be olive oil)

This is a method rather than a recipe, because the amount of the ingredients used does not really matter, besides giving a definite flavor to the dish. The main thing is to have fresh vegetables and to cook them quickly. Any vegetables may be used. Those listed here are just a guide line, to be varied according to taste. Serve with sour cream or freshly grated Parmesan cheese. Combine all the vegetables and 1 cup of water (use 2 or more cups if a thinner stew is desired) in a heavy saucepan. Season with salt and pepper and add the herbs. Bring quickly to boil. Stir in olive oil. Lower the heat. Simmer covered for 10 minutes or until the vegetables are just tender.

Tuesday

Mushroom Sauce

Grilled Chicken
Mushroom Sauce
Grilled Eggplant Slices
Sautéed Cherry Tomatoes
Fresh Peaches and Raspberries in Kirsch

1 tablespoon minced onion
2 tablespoons minced parsley
¼ cup minced bacon or prosciutto
1 tablespoon olive oil
1 tablespoon butter
¼ pound mushrooms, thinly sliced
1 teaspoon flour
1 small tomato, peeled, seeded and chopped
½ cup dry white wine
¼ cup beef bouillon or water
salt
freshly ground pepper
¼ teaspoon dried thyme

Combine the onion, parsley and bacon on a chopping board. Mince together to a paste — this affects the taste of the dish. Heat the olive oil and butter and cook the onion mixture for 2-3 minutes. Add the mushrooms and cook, stirring constantly, 3 minutes longer. Sprinkle with flour and stir in tomato, wine and bouillon. Season with salt, pepper, and thyme. Cook over medium heat for 3-4 more minutes.

Wednesday

Uncooked Blueberry Compote

Veal Cutlet Parmigiana
Corn on the Cob
Tomato Salad with Fresh Basil and Mustard Dressing
Uncooked Blueberry Compote

1 pint blueberries
sugar to taste
dry red wine

Pick over, wash and drain the blueberries. Put them in a bowl and add sugar to taste. Add enough wine to barely cover the berries. Chill in the freezer compartment of the refrigerator.

Thursday

Thick Cold Cucumber Soup

Thick Cold Cucumber Soup
Broiled Lamb Chops
Stewed Tomatoes and Okra
Coffee Ice Cream

2 cups plain yogurt
⅓ cup chopped walnuts
2 cups peeled diced cucumber
1 garlic clove, mashed
salt
freshly ground pepper

Beat the yogurt with a wire whisk or an egg beater until somewhat liquified. Add all the other ingredients and blend. Chill in freezing compartment of the refrigerator. At serving time, add an ice cube to each serving.

Friday

Venetian Rice and Peas

Garlic Broiled Shrimp
Venetian Rice and Peas
Cucumbers and Tomatoes
Melon with Vanilla Ice Cream

2 tablespoons butter
1 very small onion, minced
1 slice prosciutto or ham, minced
1 cup fresh shelled peas or
½ package frozen peas
¾ cup long grained rice
1¾ cups hot chicken bouillon
(you can use a cube)
salt
freshly ground pepper
¼ cup freshly grated Parmesan cheese

Heat butter in a heavy saucepan and cook the onion until soft and just golden. Add prosciutto and peas. Cook 5 minutes longer. Stir in the rice. Cook, stirring constantly, until rice is opaque, about 2-3 minutes. Add hot chicken bouillon. Season with salt and pepper, but go easy on the salt as the bouillon may be salty. Cover the saucepan. Cook over low heat, stirring frequently, for 15 minutes or until rice is tender but not mushy. If it looks like it is sticking, add a tablespoon or two more bouillon. Sprinkle with Parmesan cheese and serve very hot.

Saturday

Tuna, Potato and Onion Dinner Salad

Hot Tomato Soup Made with Fresh Tomatoes
Tuna, Potato and Onion Dinner Salad
Tossed Green Salad
Crackers and Cheese Tray

4 tablespoons olive oil
2 tablespoons vinegar or more
to taste
salt
freshly ground pepper
1 medium red onion, thinly
sliced
2 freshly cooked large potatoes,
peeled and sliced
¼ cup minced parsley
1 tablespoon capers
1 7-ounce can tuna fish,
drained and coarsely flaked

Combine and mix well the olive oil, vinegar, salt and pepper. In a glass or china bowl, make alternate layers of onion and potato slices. Sprinkle with parsley and capers. Add the dressing and toss gently with a fork. Let stand at room temperature for 15 minutes. Add the tuna and gently toss again. Cover with foil or plastic wrap and keep at room temperature for 30 minutes. Do not chill.

BUDGET DINNERS

July

Sunday

Baked Short Ribs

Baked Short Ribs
German Potato Salad
Tomatoes and Cucumber Vinaigrette
Watermelon

6 pounds short ribs, cut into 3-inch pieces
1 cup canned or fresh chopped tomatoes
1 cup beef bouillon
1 cup dry red wine
½ cup minced onion
3 tablespoons prepared horseradish or 1 tablespoon grated fresh horseradish
1 teaspoon salt
freshly ground pepper
3 parsley sprigs
2 bay leaves

Trim any excess fat off the short ribs and lay them in one layer in a baking pan. Brown under the broiler, turning once. Transfer the meat to a large, deep casserole. Mash the tomatoes and combine them with all the other ingredients. Pour over the short ribs. Cook covered in a preheated 350° oven for 2½ hours. Remove the ribs to a heated platter. Strain the sauce over the ribs. Makes four to six servings.

Monday

Tomatoes a la Crème

Salmon Salad
Tomatoes a la Crème
Marinated Potatoes and Cucumbers
Fruit Salad

6 large firm ripe tomatoes
3 tablespoons butter
salt
½ cup heavy cream
freshly ground pepper

Do not peel the tomatoes. Cut off a thin slice at the stem and blossom ends. Then cut the tomatoes into halves crosswise. Heat the butter in a large frying pan, preferably one that can go to the table. When it is bubbling, put in the tomatoes, cut side down. Puncture the rounded side with the point of a knife in 2 or 3 places. Cook over medium heat for 5 minutes. Turn over. Sprinkle with salt. Cook for 5 more minutes. Turn, to let the juices run out. Turn again to bring cut side up. Pour in the cream and mix with the pan juices. Check the salt and season with pepper. When the sauce is bubbling and very hot, serve immediately. Four servings.

Tuesday

Eggs in Tomato Shells

Eggs in Tomato Shells
Sautéed Peppers, Onions and Celery
Blueberry Muffins
Ice Cream

6 large firm ripe tomatoes
salt
freshly ground pepper
4 slices bacon, fried and crumbled
1 tablespoon minced fresh basil
6 teaspoons butter
6 eggs
¼ cup freshly grated Parmesan cheese
6 buttered toast rounds

Cut a small slice off the blossom and stem end of each tomato. With a grapefruit spoon or serrated knife, slice around the inner rim of the tomatoes and scoop out most of the pulp. Turn the tomatoes upside down on a plate to drain for 10 minutes. Turn right side up and place in a buttered shallow baking dish. Season with salt and pepper. Sprinkle equal amounts of bacon and basil into each tomato, as well as 1 teaspoon of butter. Break an egg into each tomato. Bake without a cover in a preheated 350° oven for 20-25 minutes until the egg whites and yolk are firm, but the yolk still runny. Sprinkle with Parmesan cheese and run quickly under broiler to melt cheese. Place each tomato on a round of buttered toast and serve hot. Serves four to six.

Wednesday

Mixed Garden Vegetable Casserole

Sautéed Fish Fillets
Creamed Potatoes
Mixed Garden Vegetable Casserole
Angel Pie

4 carrots, quartered
4 white turnips, quartered
10 white onions, whole if small, halved if large
salt
freshly ground pepper
1 tablespoon minced chervil
1 tablespoon minced chives
¼ cup melted butter
2 cups shelled fresh lima beans
2 cups green beans, cut into 1-inch pieces
½ head Romaine lettuce, shredded

Butter a large, deep baking dish. In it place the carrots, turnips, onions, salt, pepper, chervil, chives and butter. Cover and place in a cold oven. Turn on the heat to 375°. Cook for 15 minutes. Add the limas, the beans and the Romaine lettuce. Toss everything. Cover and cook for another 15 minutes. Makes four to six servings.

Thursday

Zucchini and Potato Mousaka

Cold Chicken
Zucchini and Potato Mousaka
Green Salad
Strawberries and Cream

3 pounds zucchini
3 pounds potatoes
¼ cup olive oil
2 medium onions, minced
2 garlic cloves, minced
1 cup tomato sauce
½ cup minced parsley
1 tablespoon minced fresh basil
salt
freshly ground pepper

Wash zucchini, cut off ends but do not peel. Cut zucchini into ¼-inch thick lengthwise strips. Peel and wash potatoes. Cut them also into ¼-inch thick lengthwise strips. Heat 2 tablespoons of oil in a large deep frying pan and cook the onions and garlic, stirring frequently, until onions are soft. Add the tomato sauce, parsley, basil, salt and pepper. Simmer for 3 minutes. Grease a deep 4-quart baking dish. Layer the potatoes and zucchini in it, beginning and ending with a layer of potatoes. Before topping zucchini with the last layer of potatoes, pour tomato sauce over the vegetables and top with potatoes. Drizzle the remaining oil over the potatoes. Bake in a preheated 350° oven for 1¼ hours, basting the potatoes occasionally. When done, the potatoes should be crisp and the moisture almost absorbed. Serves four to six.

Friday

Pasta with Striped Bass Sauce

Pasta with Striped Bass Sauce
Mixed Green Salad with Herbs
Fruit and Cheese

2 tablespoons salad or olive oil
1 garlic clove, minced
1 tablespoon minced fresh basil
1 tablespoon minced fresh dill weed
2 tablespoons minced parsley
4 ripe tomatoes, peeled and chopped
½ cup dry white wine
1½ pounds fresh fish fillets such as striped bass
1 pound freshly cooked pasta

This sounds to be an unlikely pasta sauce, but is a surprisingly very good and popular one. Heat the oil in a large frying pan. Cook the garlic, basil, dill and parsley for no more than 2–3 minutes. Add the tomatoes and wine. Reduce the heat and simmer, uncovered, for 15 minutes or until thickened. Cut the fish into 1-inch pieces and add to the sauce. Simmer for 5 minutes. Serve over freshly cooked, drained pasta. Makes four to six servings.

Saturday

Chicken, Spinach and Noodles

Chicken, Spinach and Noodles
Green Beans and Radish Salad
Peaches

2 2½-3 pound fryers, cut into pieces
1 quart chicken bouillon
½ pound wide noodles
4 tablespoons butter
4 tablespoons flour
1 cup heavy cream
salt
freshly ground pepper
1 teaspoon ground nutmeg
1½ cups tomato sauce
3 tablespoons minced chives or green onion tops
2 pounds spinach or 3 10-ounce packages frozen spinach, cooked and thoroughly drained dry
¾ cup freshly grated Parmesan cheese

Put chicken pieces into a large kettle and add chicken bouillon. Cover and bring to boil. Reduce heat and skin. Simmer, covered, for 20-30 minutes or until chicken is completely cooked. Strain and reserve broth. Cool and chill broth sufficiently to be able to take off any fat that has risen to the surface. Cool the chicken pieces, then skin and cut off the meat in large pieces. Reduce chicken broth over high heat to about 2 cups. Cook noodles in plenty of boiling salted water until not quite tender. Drain and reserve. Heat butter in a saucepan, stir in flour and cook for 2 minutes. Add the reduced chicken broth and cook, stirring constantly, until thick and smooth. Stir in cream. Over lowest possible heat, preferably over an asbestos plate or in the top of a double boiler over hot water, cook the sauce covered for 20 minutes. Season with salt, pepper and nutmeg. Mix ¾ cup of sauce with spinach. Spread over bottom of a buttered shallow 9 × 12-inch baking dish. Spread noodles over spinach. Pour tomato sauce over noodles and sprinkle with chives. Arrange the chicken pieces on top. Cover with remaining cream sauce and sprinkle with Parmesan. Bake in preheated 350° oven for 30 minutes or until browned and bubbly.

ENTERTAINING

July

Sunday

Mango Chicken

Melon and Prosciutto
Mango Chicken
Yellow Rice
Chutney
Red Radish Salad
Deep-Dish Blackberry Pie with Cream

2 3½-pound chickens, cut into serving pieces (no backs or wing tips)
2 tablespoons butter
2 tablespoons salad oil
2 large onions, thinly sliced
2 mangoes, peeled and chopped (2 to 3 cups pulp)
or
2 cups stoned fresh apricots, chopped or 1 cup dried apricots, plumped in lukewarm water for 1 hour
or
2 to 3 cups peeled, seeded, and chopped papaya
¼ cup mango chutney, chopped
½ cup chicken bouillon or water
salt
freshly ground pepper
¼ teaspoon nutmeg
grated rind of 1 lime, green part only
juice of 1 lime

A mildly exotic dish that won't frighten those who fear exotic food. Apricots or papayas may be substituted for the mangoes, but mangoes are best. Remove skin and every trace of fat from chicken. (This will eliminate a lot of fat found in the skin). Wash the chicken pieces and pat dry. Heat butter and oil in a large, deep frying pan and cook chicken pieces over medium heat until golden brown on all sides. Transfer them to a heavy casserole. Add onions to the frying pan. Cook, stirring constantly, over low heat, until they are very soft but still white. Add mangoes or other fruit and mango chutney. Raise heat to medium and cook mixture for 3 more minutes, stirring constantly. Stir in chicken bouillon. Season with salt, pepper, and nutmeg. Stir in lime rind. Pour sauce over the chicken. Cover and cook in a preheated 350° oven for 30-45 minutes or until chicken is cooked; cooking time depends on the size of the pieces. Check occasionally for moisture; if the sauce looks too thick, add a little more chicken bouillon. Remove from oven and stir in the lime juice. Serve as is or, much better, clear chicken pieces of fruit and onions and transfer chicken to a hot serving dish. Keep warm in oven. Pour sauce into a blender and blend until smooth. Pour sauce back into the casserole and heat through before ladling over chicken. Do not let the sauce boil again. Serves four to six.

Monday

Ham Baked with Sherry

Ham Baked with Sherry
Spoon Bread
Poached Apples
Pennsylvania Dutch Coffee Cake
Cider
Coffee Tea Milk

6 large slices of cooked ham
1 tablespoon butter
1 tablespoon flour
2 teaspoons tomato paste
¾ cup dry sherry (or port, madeira, or marsala if preferred)
½ cup heavy cream
salt
freshly ground pepper

Have ham at room temperature. Heat the butter in a small saucepan. Stir in the flour and tomato paste. Cook, stirring constantly, about 1 minute. Stir in the wine and cook 2 minutes longer, stirring constantly. Reduce heat to lowest possible and stir in the cream. Season with very little salt and pepper since the ham will be salty. Arrange the ham in overlapping slices in a flat buttered baking dish. Spoon the sauce over the meat. Cook in a preheated moderate 350° oven about 5 minutes, or until the ham is heated through. Serves four to six.

Tuesday

Schinkenfleckerln (Austrian Ham and Noodles)

Schinkenfleckerln
Tossed Green Salad
Cheese Platter: Brie, Bel Paese, Port Salut, Sharp Cheddar, French Goat Cheese, Boursin, Triple Cream
Assorted White and Brown Breads and Crackers
Fruit

1 pound wide noodles, broken into 1-or 1½-inch pieces
1 pound lean cooked ham
¾ cup butter
6 eggs, separated
1½ cups sour cream
salt
freshly ground pepper

Traditionally, the dish is made with little square noodles available in Hungarian and Czech groceries. Wide noodles will also serve, but before cooking they should be broken into 1-or 1½-inch pieces. Cook noodles in plenty of boiling salted water until three-quarters done, almost tender. Drain and reserve. Cut ham into ½-inch dice. Put noodles and ham into a big bowl and mix with fork. Beat butter until soft and creamy. Beat in egg yolks, beating well after each addition. Beat in sour cream. The longer these ingredients are beaten, the lighter the dish; an electric handbeater is recommended. Add egg mixture to noodles and ham, and mix thoroughly. Season to taste with salt and pepper. Beat egg whites until stiff. Fold them into ham mixture. Spoon into a well-buttered 10-to-12-cup baking dish that can go to the table. Bake in a preheated 350° oven for 35-40 minutes or until top is crisp and golden. Serve immediately. Serves six.

Wednesday

Persian Pancake Omelet with Vegetables

Persian Pancake Omelet with Vegetables
Cold Roast Beef
Remoulade Sauce
Salad of White Beans and Tomatoes
Fresh Peach Ice Cream
Cookies

8 eggs
1 medium onion, grated
2 tablespoons flour
4 cups very finely shredded Romaine lettuce
¾ cup minced spring onions
½ cup minced parsley
1 teaspoon dried basil
1 teaspoon salt
freshly ground pepper
½ to 1 teaspoon ground saffron
½ cup olive or salad oil

Beat the eggs until light. Beat in the onion, flour, lettuce, spring onions, parsley, dried basil, salt, pepper, and saffron. Beat to mix thoroughly. Heat oil in a 10-inch frying pan until it just begins to get hazy. Pour in the egg mixture. Remove from heat, cover the frying pan, and place in a preheated 350° oven for about 25 minutes. After 15 minutes' baking time, lift the underside of the pancake with a spatula or a knife. If it is browned, cut the pancake into 4 or 6 pieces and turn each piece to cook on the other side. Cook, uncovered, for 10 more minutes or until the bottom is golden brown. Transfer to a flat serving dish and serve either warm or lukewarm, but not chilled. Four to six servings.

Thursday

Cold Marinated Zucchini

Jellied Madrilène with Diced Avocado
Chicken Curry
Rice
Chutney
Cold Marinated Zucchini
Coffee Granita with Whipped Cream

8 medium zucchini, about 5 inches long
olive oil for frying
1 cup mild vinegar
½ cup olive oil
1 garlic clove, mashed
2 tablespoons minced fresh basil or 1 teaspoon dried basil
salt
freshly ground pepper
salad greens
4 tablespoons minced parsley

Trim zucchini and scrape lightly with a knife to remove any waxy coating. Wash and dry. Cut zucchini into ¾-inch slices. Heat about ¼ inch olive oil in a heavy frying pan until oil is hazy. Carefully fry a few zucchini slices at a time for about 2 minutes on each side, turning once. The zucchini should be golden but still crisp. Drain on paper towels and cool. In a small saucepan combine the vinegar, olive oil, garlic, basil, salt and pepper. Simmer over medium heat for 5 minutes. Cool to lukewarm. In the meantime line a salad bowl with salad greens. Pile the fried zucchini in orderly rows on the greens. Pour the marinade over zucchini and sprinkle with parsley. Serve immediately. Serves six.

Note: If zucchini is to be refrigerated, do not pile them on salad greens, as the greens will wilt under the marinade. Put the fried zucchini carefully into a bowl, pour the marinade over them, and refrigerate. At serving time pour off any excess marinade, pile on salad greens and sprinkle with parsley.

Friday

Riz a l'Impératrice

Oeufs en Gelée (French Eggs in Aspic)
Broiled Shrimp
Homemade Lemon Mayonnaise
Small Boiled New Potatoes in Their Skins
Tomato Salad with Herbs
Riz a l'Impératrice

⅓ cup finely diced glacé lemon peel
⅓ cup finely diced citron peel
⅓ cup finely diced glacé orange peel
⅓ cup finely diced glacé cherries
⅔ cup Kirsch or very light rum

Combined the fruit and Kirsch in a bowl. Mix well. Cover and let stand at room temperature serveral hours or overnight. *Note:* If a glacé fruit mix is used, the pieces of fruit must be cut again, since they are coarsely cut in these mixes.

½ cup water
½ cup sugar
¾ cup untreated long or short grain rice (do not use processed rice)
2 cups milk
1 2-inch piece vanilla bean or 1 tablespoon vanilla flavoring
2 tablespoons (2 envelopes) unflavored gelatin
⅓ cup cold water
1 cup vanilla custard or thin vanilla pudding (optional)
2 cups heavy cream
red currant jelly
Raspberry Sauce (see below)

Combine water and sugar in a large, heavy saucepan and bring to boil. Wash rice in a strainer under running cold water to remove excess starch. Drain and add to boiling syrup, stirring as you add rice to avoid lumps. Cook over low heat, stirring constantly, for 5 minutes. Drain rice and reserve the cooking syrup. In the top of a double boiler scald milk with vanilla bean. (If vanilla flavoring is used, add it to the cooked rice). Add rice and stir well to mix. Cover. Cook over boiling water for 1 hour, or until almost all milk has been absorbed by the rice. Stir frequently. The rice should be creamy but not liquid. Sprinkle the gelatin over the water and mix. (If vanilla custard is used, use an additional tablespoon of gelatin.) Heat gelatin to liquify and stir into hot rice. (This works better than stirring cold solid gelatin into the rice.) Blend thoroughly and cool. If a vanilla custard is used, stir into cool rice mixture. In a large bowl whip the cream until it is thick but still soft. Stir glacé fruit and their liquid into the whipped cream. Add the rice pudding and mix well. Rinse a 2-quart mold with cold water. Line mold with a thin layer of red currant jelly. Pack rice mixture into mold and refrigerate overnight. Unmold on a deep platter; the red currant jelly will drip prettily over the rice. Serve with Raspberry Sauce.

Raspberry Sauce: Simmer together 2 boxes frozen raspberries with ½ cup sugar until raspberries are very soft. Strain through a sieve or puree in a blender. Add ½ cup Kirsch or light rum and chill before serving.

Saturday

Fourth of July Picnic for Eight

Shrimp in Beer*
Lemon Butter Sauce
Wilted Cucumber Sauce
Marinated Green Beans and Tomatoes
French Bread
Fresh Fruit Salad
Almond Cake*
Drinks:

Cold Beer, any inexpensive imported German Moselle or Rhine Wine, California Rieslings or White or Red Mountain Jug Wines, Soft drinks

**Recipe in book*

This seafood picnic can be prepared any place you can build a fire. All of the food, except the shrimp, is prepared at home, packed in plastic containers and taken to the picnic site. An alternative to the Lemon Butter Sauce for the shrimp might be a Vinaigrette made with lemon juice.

Take inexpensive china plates and glassware with you, or very good quality plastics. Don't forget a pile of large paper napkins and a paper tablecloth. You will also need:

- a large kettle that can go over a charcoal fire
- a medium saucepan to reheat the butter sauce
- cutting board
- serrated knife
- long handled strainer or scoop for scooping shrimp from kettle to plate
- corkscrew, can opener
- salt, pepper
- charcoal, some kindling material
- matches
- little paper or plastic or other cups for individual sauce servings

On hot days, put the shrimp, salads and fruit into thermos boxes and bags. Carry salad dressings in separate containers and pour over salads about half an hour before serving. Keep drinks chilled in thermal bags or let them rest in a nearby stream or water, tied to the shore with long strings. Clean up after yourself, including shrimp peels. Carry some large paper bags for this.

Shrimp in Beer

4 cans beer or ale
2 large garlic cloves, peeled
1 lemon, sliced
1 tablespoon salt
2 tablespoons chopped parsley
dash of Tabasco
3 bay leaves
4 stalks fresh dill weed
2 celery stalks, with leaves
4 pounds shrimp

Combine all the ingredients except the shrimp in a large kettle. Bring to boil. Simmer without a cover for 10 minutes. Add the shrimp. Return to boil. Cook for 3–5 minutes or until the shrimp turn pink. Remove from heat. Scoop from kettle onto plates. Peel and eat with fingers, dipping into Lemon Butter Sauce or Vinaigrette. Makes eight servings.

Almond Cake

3 eggs, separated
¾ cup sugar
⅓ cup orange liqueur
¼ teaspoon almond extract
¾ cup flour
¾ cup finely ground blanched almonds
½ cup (1 stick) butter, melted
⅛ teaspoon salt
confectioners' sugar

Beat the egg yolks until thick and light. Gradually, about 2–3 tablespoons at a time, beat in ½ cup plus 2 tablespoons of sugar. Beat in orange liqueur and almond extract. Beat in flour and ground almonds, beating well after each addition. Stir in melted butter. Beat the egg whites with the salt until frothy. Beat in remaining sugar, a tablespoon at a time, and beat until stiff but not dry. Fold the egg whites into batter. Grease and flour a 1½-quart cake pan or mold or 3 small loaf pans. Turn the batter into the pan and bang once or twice on the table to remove air holes. Bake in a preheated 350° oven for about 30 minutes. Cool the cake in the pan for about 10 minutes. Turn out onto rack. When completely cooled, dust with confectioners' sugar.

AUGUST

If you were really convinced that the best summer lunch is good bread, good cheese, good wine or beer and some good fresh fruit, your life would be much easier and people would thank you for it. I think summer is the time to savor food, and savoring means small, exquisite quantities rather than portions meant to appease hunger. Investigate portable foods for impromptu city lunches out of doors when you cannot picnic in the country. There are parks in our cities, and outdoor benches; there are sandwiches and sliced meats, cheeses and fruits and perhaps a superdelicious cookie or two that can make lunch in a city summer truly a refreshing pause in the day's occupation.

AUGUST

FAMILY FARE

	LUNCHES	DINNERS
Sunday	Melon Crème Lorraine* Brioches Cream Cheese and Bar-le-Duc	Cold Circassian Chicken with Walnuts* Mixed Vegetable Salad and Lemon French Dressing Chick Pea Salad Hot Chocolate Soufflé
Monday	Cold Curried Chicken Soup* Cucumber and Radish Sandwiches Plum Pie	Ham and Corn Chili* Mexican Rice Green Salad Pears and Cheeses
Tuesday	Cheese and Potato Salad* Tomatoes and Cucumbers Peach Shortcake	A Cup of Hot Consommé, with Sherry Cold Veal Loaf* Assorted Pickles Watermelon Rind Relish Chick Pea Salad Coffee Ice Cream
Wednesday	Western Egg Sandwiches* Potato Chips Ice Cream and Chocolate Cookies	Sweet and Sour Shrimp* Boiled Rice Sautéed Zucchini Custard Peach Pie
Thursday	The Sultan's Delight* Chick Pea Salad Blueberries and Cream	Lamb Kidneys with Sherry* Dry White Rice Pureed Broccoli Chocolate Mousse
Friday	Cold Vichyssoise* Salad Niçoise Brown Bread and Butter Blueberry Flummery	Sole Bonne Femme* Steamed New Potatoes Broiled Tomatoes Watercress with Lemon French Dressing Baked Peaches with Ice Cream
Saturday	Broiled Canadian Bacon Corn Timbales on Fried Tomatoes* French Bread Fresh Fruit Salad	Roast Roman Lamb Roman Stuffed Tomatoes* Green Salad Zuppa Inglese

QUICK & EASY Dinners For Two	BUDGET DINNERS	ENTERTAINING
Roast Chicken Roast Potatoes Italian Zucchini* Blueberry Cobbler	Baked Ham Deviled Corn* Macaroni Salad Date Cupcakes and Peaches	Cold Zucchini Soup Cold Virginia Ham Lentil Salad* Sliced Tomatoes and Basil Lemon Sherbet
Vichyssoise Main Dish Cheese Salad* Sliced Tomatoes Peaches with White Wine	Halibut with Spicy Sauce* Panfried Potatoes and Onions Cucumbers in Sour Cream and Dill Fresh Fruit	Chicken Salad with Fresh Lemon Mayonnaise Rice Salad with Freshly Cooked Peas Beans, Diced Carrots, and Lemon French Dressing Green Salad Sacher Torte*
Chicken Livers with Sage* Rice and Peas Cold Cooked Carrots with Lemon French Dressing Watermelon	Ham Mousse* Corn on the Cob Tomatoes Filled with Chive Cream Cheese Lemon Sherbet	Piperade (Basque Scrambled Eggs with Vegetables)* Croutons Pâté de Foie Gras Watercress Salad with Lemon French Dressing Peach Melba Made with Fresh Peaches and Raspberries
Veal with Lemon* Thin Buttered Noodles Mixed Green Salad with Mushrooms and Avocado Peach Cobbler	Stuffed Eggplant* Baked Tomato Halves Syrian Bread Sweet Cherries	Melon and Prosciutto Lamb Stew with Parsley and Lemon* Small New Boiled Potatoes Blueberry Tart
Barbecued Chicken Caucasian Plum Sauce* Chick Pea Salad Cucumbers and Tomatoes Vanilla Ice Cream with Blueberry Sauce	Zucchini Soup Salade Niçoise* French Bread Fresh Peach Pie	West Indian Callaloo* Hot Corn Sticks Assorted Cold Cuts and Cheeses Breads and Crackers Peach Pie
Piquant Shrimp* Fresh Corn Pudding Watercress Baked Peaches Filled with Ground Almonds	Haddock Casserole* Potato Chips Green Beans Peaches and Cream	Iced Watercress Soup Veal Scallopine Fried Zucchini Stuffed Tomatoes with Rice Peaches in Champagne* Almond Cookies
Green Noodles with Basil* Salade Niçoise Chilled Cantaloupe	Egg Noodles with Three Cheeses* Green Salad Fresh Fruit Salad	Cold Curried Chicken Breasts* Cold Rice Salad with Vegetables French Bread Butter in a Crock Brie Cheese and Apples Grapes Walnut Cookies

FAMILY FARE LUNCHES

August

Sunday

Crème Lorraine

Melon
Crème Lorraine
Brioches
Cream Cheese and Bar-le-Duc

6 slices bacon
1½ cups (6 ounces) grated Swiss cheese
1½ cups (6 ounces) freshly grated Parmesan cheese
2 cups heavy cream
2 eggs, well beaten
salt
freshly ground pepper

This is lighter and more delicate than a regular cheese soufflé. Cook the bacon until crisp. Break into small pieces rather than crumbling. Beat together the cheeses, heavy cream, eggs, and bacon pieces. Salt and pepper to taste. Turn into a 1½-quart baking dish. Bake in a preheated 350° oven for 35 minutes or until set. Makes four servings.

Monday

Cold Curried Chicken Soup

Cold Curried Chicken Soup
Cucumber and Radish Sandwiches
Plum Pie

1 tablespoon butter
1 medium onion, minced
2 tart apples, peeled, cored and thinly sliced
2 teaspoons curry powder or to taste
1 tablespoon flour
2 cups chicken bouillon
salt
freshly ground pepper
½ cup dry sherry or dry white wine
½ cup minced cooked chicken, preferably white meat
1 cup light cream, well chilled

Heat butter in a saucepan and cook the onion and apples until very soft but still white. Stir in curry powder and cook 2 minutes longer. Stir in flour and chicken bouillon. Taste and then season with salt and pepper; the bouillon may be salty. Stir in sherry. Bring to boil, reduce heat to very low and simmer for 10 minutes. Cool and blend in a blender or strain through a fine sieve. Chill. At serving time, add chicken and cream, mix well. Makes three servings.

Tuesday

Cheese and Potato Salad

Cheese and Potato Salad
Tomatoes and Cucumbers
Peach Shortcake

6 large potatoes, freshly boiled
½ pound Swiss or sharp Cheddar cheese, in one piece
1 cup diced celery
½ cup chopped walnuts
1 cup mayonnaise
½ teaspoon dry mustard
1 teaspoon Worcestershire sauce
salt
freshly ground pepper
salad greens
6 hard-cooked eggs, stuffed or plain, cut into halves

Peel the potatoes. Cut the potatoes into 1-inch cubes and the cheese into ½-inch cubes. Combine the potatoes, cheese, celery, walnuts, mayonnaise, mustard and Worcestershire sauce in a bowl and mix well. Check the seasonings; if necessary, add a little salt and pepper. Refrigerate for 1 hour. Line a salad bowl with salad greens. Pile the cheese salad on the greens and garnish with eggs. Makes four to six servings.

Wednesday

Western Egg Sandwiches

Western Egg Sandwiches
Potato Chips
Ice Cream and Chocolate Cookies

6 tablespoons butter
1 medium onion, minced
1 garlic clove, minced
2 cups chopped cooked ham
10 eggs, slightly beaten
¾ cup milk
salt
freshly ground pepper
½ teaspoon ground marjoram
12 slices buttered toast

Heat butter in a frying pan. Add the onion, garlic and ham. Cook over low heat, stirring frequently, for 5 minutes or until onion is soft. Combine the eggs and milk in a bowl. Beat well. Add the ham mixture. Mix well. Taste for seasoning; if necessary, add salt and pepper. Beat in marjoram. Spoon the mixture into a lightly buttered shallow 10-or 12-inch baking dish. Bake in a preheated 350° oven for 10-15 minutes or until firm. Cut into 6 pieces. Serve each piece between 2 slices of hot buttered toast. Makes six sandwiches.

Thursday

The Sultan's Delight

The Sultan's Delight
Chick Pea Salad
Blueberries and Cream

2 medium eggplants
2 tablespoons olive oil
1 pound ground lamb
2 medium onions, minced
½ cup dry red wine
2 cups chopped fresh tomatoes or 2 cups (1 1-pound can) canned tomatoes, undrained
salt
freshly ground pepper
2-3 tablespoons fresh minced basil leaves or 1 tablespoon dried basil
¼ cup beef bouillon
2 tablespoons melted butter
¼ cup grated Parmesan cheese

Prick the eggplants with a fork. Bake in a preheated 400° oven for 40 minutes or until tender. While the eggplants are baking, heat the olive oil in a heavy saucepan. Cook the lamb and onions, stirring constantly, until browned. Pour off any excess fat. Add wine and cook for 2-3 minutes or until wine has almost evaporated. Add the tomatoes, salt, pepper and basil. Simmer, covered, for about 20 minutes. Cut the baked eggplants into halves lengthwise. Scoop out the pulp with a teaspoon, without piercing shells. Put the pulp into a bowl and mash thoroughly, combine the lamb mixture and blend well. Place eggplant shells into a greased shallow baking dish. Divide lamb mixture into 4 parts and spoon into each of the four eggplant shells. Pour beef bouillon into baking dish. Sprinkle melted butter and Parmesan over shells. Bake in a preheated 350° oven for about 15-20 minutes. Serves four.

Friday

Cold Vichyssoise

Cold Vichyssoise
Salade Niçoise
Brown Bread and Butter
Blueberry Flummery

2 tablespoons butter
4 medium potatoes, thinly sliced
4 white medium onions, thinly sliced
4 leeks, white parts only, thinly sliced
OR
3 bunches green onions, white parts only, thinly sliced
1 large garlic clove, mashed
4 cups chicken bouillon
1 cup milk
1 cup heavy cream
salt
freshly ground pepper, preferably white
2 tablespoons minced chives or parsley

Heat butter in a large heavy saucepan. Add the potatoes, onions, leeks, garlic and 1 cup of chicken bouillon. Simmer, covered, over very low heat until the vegetables are very soft. Stir frequently. Add the remaining chicken broth. Simmer, covered, for 10 more minutes. Add the milk and cream. Bring to the boiling point but do not boil. Cool. Season with salt and pepper to taste. Puree the soup in a blender. If too thick, thin with a little cold milk. Chill very thoroughly. Check the seasoning before serving and sprinkle with chives. Six servings.

Saturday

Corn Timbales on Fried Tomatoes

Broiled Canadian Bacon
Corn Timbales on Fried Tomatoes
French Bread
Fresh Fruit Salad

1 cup fresh corn cut from the cob
6 tablespoons heavy cream
½ teaspoon salt
1 teaspoon sugar
1 teaspoon dry mustard
1 teaspoon paprika
2 eggs
4 thick tomato slices, fried

Combine the corn, heavy cream, salt, sugar, mustard and paprika in a blender top. Blend for 30 seconds. Add the eggs and blend 30 seconds longer. Pour the mixture into 4 generously buttered individual custard cups. Set the cups in a baking pan filled with 1½ inches of hot water. Cover with foil. Bake in a preheated 350° oven for 20 minutes. Remove the foil and bake for 10 minutes longer or until firm. Invert each cup onto a slice of fried tomato. To do this, run a knife around the edges of the custard cups first. Makes four servings.

FAMILY FARE DINNERS

August

Sunday

Cold Circassian Chicken with Walnuts

Cold Circassian Chicken with Walnuts
Mixed Vegetable Salad and Lemon French Dressing
Chick Pea Salad
Hot Chocolate Soufflé

3 quarts water
1 medium onion
1 large carrot, cut into pieces
1 celery stalk, cut into pieces
½ cup parsley sprigs
1 teaspoon salt
1 teaspoon cayenne pepper
1 4-5 pound chicken
3 slices white bread, without crusts, cubed
2½ cups walnut meats
grated rind from 1 lemon
juice of 1 lemon
1 tablespoon paprika

In a large kettle, combine the water, onion, carrot, celery, parsley, salt and cayenne pepper. Bring to boil. Lower heat and simmer, covered, for 10 minutes. Remove all excess fat from chicken and add the bird to broth. Bring to boil, skim and reduce heat to low. Simmer, covered, for 1 to 1½ hours or until the chicken is tender. Cool chicken in bouillon. Remove 1½ cups chicken bouillon and put in refrigerator or freezer. After the fat has risen to the top of the reserved bouillon, remove it. Combine the bread and 1 cup of reserved chicken bouillon in a blender top. Cover and blend at high speed. Turning off the motor each time, gradually add walnuts. Blend to a paste. If too thick, add a little of remaining ½ cup of reserved chicken consommé, 2 tablespoons at a time. Blend in lemon rind and lemon juice.

Remove the chicken from its cooking liquid and reserve bouillon for soup. Skin the chicken. Slice it neatly and arrange slices on a platter. Spread the chicken with the walnut sauce and sprinkle with paprika. Serves four to six.

*Save about ½ cup white chicken meat for a Curried Chicken Soup.

Monday

Ham and Corn Chili

Ham and Corn Chili
Mexican Rice
Green Salad
Pears and Cheeses

2 tablespoons butter
¼ cup minced onion
1 garlic clove, mashed
1 small green pepper, cut into thin strips
2 teaspoons chili powder, or more to taste
2 tablespoons flour
1 to 1½ cups beef bouillon
1 cup chopped canned tomatoes, with their juice
3 cups leftover or cooked ham cut into 1-inch cubes
salt
freshly ground pepper
1 cup cooked corn kernels

Heat butter in a heavy saucepan. Add the onion, garlic and pepper. Cook over low heat, stirring constantly, until the onion and pepper strips are soft. Stir in chili powder and cook stirring all the time, 2 minutes longer. Stir in flour, 1 cup of bouillon and tomatoes. Bring to boil, lower heat and cook, stirring frequently for about 10 minutes. If the sauce looks too thick, stir in remaining ½ cup of bouillon. Add the ham, mix well and simmer covered for 5 more minutes. Taste for seasoning; if necessary, add a little more salt and pepper. Add the corn and cook for 3-5 minutes longer, or until the corn is thoroughly heated through. Serves four to six.

Tuesday

Cold Veal Loaf

A Cup of Hot Consommé, with Sherry
Cold Veal Loaf
Assorted Pickles
Watermelon Rind Relish
Chick Pea Salad
Coffee Ice Cream

2 tablespoons butter
1 medium onion, minced
2 pounds ground veal
½ pound bacon, ground
salt
freshly ground pepper
2 tablespoons minced parsley
1 tablespoon grated lemon rind
1 tablespoon fresh lemon juice
½ cup fine dry bread crumbs
2 tablespoons tomato sauce
¼ cup milk or light cream
1 egg
2 tablespoons melted butter or bacon fat
tomato sauce

Heat butter in a saucepan and cook the onion until soft but not brown. Combine the onion and all the other ingredients except the bacon fat in a large bowl and mix well. Shape into a loaf and turn into a 9-inch loaf pan. Brush the top with bacon fat. Cook in a preheated 350° oven for about 1 hour. Serve warm, with tomato sauce, or cold, thinly sliced. Makes four to six servings.

Wednesday

Sweet and Sour Shrimp

Sweet and Sour Shrimp
Boiled Rice
Sautéed Zucchini
Custard Peach Pie

2 pounds cooked shelled deveined shrimps (if large, cut into pieces)
2 cups pineapple chunks, drained
2 tablespoons grated fresh ginger root
1 green pepper, seeded and cut into thin strips
1 big cucumber, peeled, seeded and cut into ½-inch cubes
½ cup butter
1 cup unsweetened pineapple juice
1 tablespoon sugar
⅓ cup cider vinegar
2 tablespoons soy sauce
1 tablespoon cornstarch
2 tablespoons water

Fresh ginger root is found in Oriental groceries and many vegetable markets. Combine the shrimp, pineapple chunks, ginger roots, green pepper and cucumber in a bowl and mix well. Heat butter in a large, heavy saucepan. Add the shrimp mixture and cook over medium heat, stirring constantly, for about 2 minutes. Stir in the pineapple juice, sugar, vinegar and soy sauce. Blend the cornstarch with water to a smooth paste and stir into the shrimp mixture. Cook over medium heat, stirring constantly, until the sauce is clear and thickened and the dish thoroughly heated through. Six servings.

Thursday

Lamb Kidneys with Sherry

Lamb Kidneys with Sherry
Dry White Rice
Pureed Broccoli
Chocolate Mousse

12 lamb kidneys
2 tablespoons butter
2 tablespoons olive oil
¼ cup minced shallots or onion
⅓ cup dry sherry or Madeira
1½ cups chicken bouillon
3 tablespoons flour
1 tablespoon Worcestershire sauce
1 tablespoon fresh lemon juice
salt
freshly ground pepper

Trim kidneys by removing all outer membrane and fat. Cut kidneys into halves lengthwise. Remove the white membrane in the center. Cut kidneys crosswise into ½-inch slices. Wash quickly under running water. Dry thoroughly between paper towels. Heat butter and olive oil in a saucepan. Add the kidneys and cook over medium heat, stirring constantly, for 2-3 minutes or until the kidneys are just beginning to brown. Pour off any excess fat. Add the shallots and cook for 1 minute longer. Add sherry and cook for 2 more minutes. Combine the chicken bouillon and flour to a smooth mixture. Stir into the kidneys and mix well. Bring the mixture slowly to boil. Cook over low heat, stirring constantly, for about 5 minutes. Stir in Worcestershire sauce and lemon juice. Check the seasoning; if necessary, season with a little salt and pepper. Heat through but do not boil and serve very hot. Serves four.

Friday

Sole Bonne Femme

Sole Bonne Femme
Steamed New Potatoes
Broiled Tomatoes
Watercress with Lemon French Dressing
Baked Peaches with Ice Cream

6 fillets of sole, washed and dried thoroughly
½ cup dry white wine or dry vermouth
½ cup fish stock or chicken bouillon
juice of 1 lemon
salt
freshly ground pepper
6 tablespoons butter
1 tablespoon flour
2 egg yolks, beaten
1 cup thinly sliced mushrooms

Lay fillets of sole side by side in a well buttered shallow baking dish. Top with wine, fish stock and half of the lemon juice. Sprinkle with salt and pepper. Cover with aluminum foil. Cook in a preheated 350° oven for 10-15 minutes or until fish flakes. Lower oven temperature to 200°. Drain juices from baking dish into a saucepan. Cover fish again with foil and keep warm in low oven. Stir 2 tablespoons of butter into fish juices. Cook, stirring constantly until butter is melted. Stir in flour. Cook, stirring all the time, until sauce is slightly thickened. Remove from heat. Sir 2 tablespoons of sauce into beaten egg yolks. Return egg yolk mixture to sauce and blend thoroughly. Keep sauce warm over hot water or over low heat and an asbestos plate. Quickly cook mushrooms in remaining butter until still very firm and white. Add mushrooms to sauce and mix well. Stir in remaining lemon juice. Place fillets of sole in a warmed oven proof dish or platter. Pour sauce over fish. Run under broiler for 2-3 minutes or until sauce is golden and bubbly. Serves four to six.

Saturday

Roman Stuffed Tomatoes

Roast Roman Lamb
Roman Stuffed Tomatoes
Green Salad
Zuppa Inglese

8 large ripe but firm tomatoes
½ cup olive oil
⅓ cup minced parsley
2 garlic cloves, minced
1 cup long grain rice
2 cups hot chicken bouillon
salt
freshly ground pepper
½ teaspoon ground thyme *or* 2 tablespoons minced fresh basil leaves

Cut a slice from the stem end of each tomato. Scoop out the centers into a bowl, using a spoon. Do not break the shells. Strain tomato pulp and reserve the juice. Place tomatoes into a lightly oiled shallow baking dish. Sprinkle each tomato with a little olive oil, using 2 to 3 tablespoons of oil. Heat remaining oil in a heavy saucepan and cook parsley and garlic for 1 minute. Add rice. Cook over medium heat, stirring constantly, for 3 minutes or until the rice is opaque. Add hot chicken bouillon. Cover and cook over low heat for 10 minutes, or until the rice is three-quarters done. Remove from heat and season with salt and pepper. Stir in thyme or basil leaves. Fill tomatoes with the rice mixture. Pour the reserved tomato pulp into the baking dish with the tomatoes to the depth of ¼ to ½ inch. Bake in a preheated 350° oven for 30 minutes or until rice is tender and the liquid in the pan absorbed. Baste occasionally with the pan liquids. May be eaten warm or cold, but not chilled. Serves six.

QUICK & EASY DINNERS FOR TWO

August

Sunday

Roast Chicken
Roast Potatoes
Italian Zucchini
Blueberry Cobbler

Italian Zucchini

2 tablespoons olive oil
2 zucchini, trimmed and sliced
2 garlic cloves, peeled but left whole
about ⅓ cup beef or chicken bouillon or water
salt
freshly ground pepper
¼ teaspoon ground marjoram or any favored herb

Heat olive oil in a heavy saucepan. Add zucchini, garlic and bouillon. Season with salt and pepper and stir in marjoram. Cook, covered, over medium heat, stirring frequently, until the zucchini are tender and reasonably, but not totally dry.
Note: The liquid needed in this dish depends on the size of the zucchini and that of the saucepan. Add a little more bouillon or water if needed, or respectively, cook without a cover to reduce the pan liquid.

Monday

Main Dish Cheese Salad

Vichyssoise
Main Dish Cheese Salad
Sliced Tomatoes
Peaches with White Wine

4 medium potatoes, freshly cooked and peeled
½ lb. Swiss cheese, in one piece
1 cup diced celery
¼ cup chopped walnuts (optional)
¾ cup mayonnaise, thinned with 1 tablespoon light or heavy cream
½ to 1 teaspoon dry mustard, or to taste
½ teaspoon Worcestershire sauce
lettuce
cucumber slices

Cut the potatoes and cheese into ½-inch cubes. Add celery and walnuts. Stir in the mayonnaise, mustard and Worcestershire sauce. Blend well by tossing with 2 forks. Refrigerate for 1 hour. Serve on lettuce and garnish with cucumber slices.

Tuesday

Chicken Livers with Sage

Chicken Livers with Sage
Rice and Peas
Cold Cooked Carrots with Lemon French Dressing
Watermelon

½ pound chicken livers
salt
freshly ground pepper
10 fresh sage leaves, finely chopped or 1 tablespoon dried sage, crumbled or 1½ teaspoons ground sage
2 tablespoons butter
1 slice bacon, minced
¼ cup dry white wine

Trim the chicken livers, and if very large, cut into halves. Season with salt and pepper. Roll in sage until coated on all sides. When no fresh sage is available, use dry sage, preferably the dry leaf sage or, if there isn't any, ground sage. Heat together the butter and bacon. Add chicken livers. Cook over medium heat 3 minutes, stirring occasionally. Add wine. Cover and cook 1-2 minutes longer. Do not overcook, but some people like chicken livers well done whereas others do not.

Wednesday

Veal with Lemon

Veal with Lemon
Thin Buttered Noodles
Mixed Green Salad with Mushrooms and Avocado
Peach Cobbler

1 pound boneless veal
flour
2 tablespoons butter
juice of 1 large lemon
salt
freshly ground pepper
⅓ cup dry white wine

Trim all fat, gristle and membrane from the veal. Cut into 1½-inch pieces. Coat with flour and shake off excess. Heat butter in a heavy frying pan. Over high heat, stirring constantly, cook the veal for 2-3 minutes or until golden brown. Stir in lemon juice and season with salt and pepper. Reduce heat to lowest possible. Simmer, shaking the pan frequently, for 3-5 minutes. Add wine. Simmer for 5-10 minutes longer or until the meat is tender. Stir frequently. If necessary to avoid scorching, add a little more wine, one tablespoon at a time. There should be only a little sauce in this dish.

Thursday

Caucasian Plum Sauce

Barbecued Chicken
Caucasian Plum Sauce
Chick Pea Salad
Cucumbers and Tomatoes
Vanilla Ice Cream with Blueberry Sauce

1 pound blue Italian plums, pitted
4 large garlic cloves, minced
salt
freshly ground pepper
1 teaspoon sugar

This is good for roast fowl, meats, barbecued and skewered dishes. Cook the plums in just enough water to cover. Drain and reserve the liquid. Rub the plums through a fine sieve or puree in a blender. Add the garlic, salt and pepper to taste and sugar. If necessary, stir in enough of the reserved plum liquid to make a puree the consistency of applesauce. Bring to boil. Reduce the heat and simmer for 5 minutes, stirring frequently. Serve hot in the house, or chilled on a picnic. About 1 cup.

Friday

Piquant Shrimp

Piquant Shrimp
Fresh Corn Pudding
Watercress
Baked Peaches Filled with Ground Almonds

½ to ¾ pound cooked shelled and deveined shrimp (if frozen, thaw)
½ cup water
2 tablespoons butter
salt
freshly ground pepper
2-3 tablespoons white or cider vinegar (do not use wine vinegar) or vinegar to taste

Put the shrimp into a heavy saucepan. Add water, butter, salt and pepper. Cook over low heat, stirring frequently with a fork, until the shrimp are thoroughly heated through. Stir in vinegar. Cook for 3-4 minutes or until the flavor of the vinegar has been absorbed by the shrimp. Taste and correct the seasonings and if wanted, add a little more vinegar. Serve with spoon bread or corn pudding.
Note: You can add Tabasco for a hotter dish and 1 or ½ teaspoon of powdered thyme or marjoram.

Saturday

Green Noodles with Basil

Green Noodles with Basil
Salade Niçoise
Chilled Cantaloupe

¾ pound green noodles
1 or 2 garlic cloves, crushed
½ to ¾ cup butter, at room temperature and cut into small pieces
2 teaspoons crushed dried basil leaves or 3 tablespoons fresh basil, minced
½ teaspoon salt
1 teaspoon freshly ground pepper
½ cup heavy cream, heated
¾ cup freshly grated Parmesan cheese

Cook noodles until al dente. Drain; return to cooking pot. Add all the other ingredients. Cover the cooking pot with lid and shake thoroughly to blend the ingredients or toss with a fork and serving spoon. Turn the noodles into a hot serving dish and serve immediately, with more Parmesan on the side.

BUDGET DINNERS

August

Sunday

Baked Ham
Deviled Corn
Macaroni Salad
Date Cupcakes and Peaches

Deviled Corn

4 slices bacon
1 medium onion, minced
1 tablespoon flour
1 teaspoon dry mustard
1 cup milk
1 teaspoon Worcestershire sauce
dash of Tabasco
1 tablespoon sugar
salt
3-4 cups fresh corn kernels

Cook bacon until crisp in a medium frying pan. Remove bacon and drain on paper towel. Pour off all but 2 tablespoons of bacon fat from the frying pan and cook onion until soft. Stir in flour and mustard, and cook, stirring constantly, for 2 minutes. Stir in milk and cook until thick and smooth. Stir in Worcestershire, Tabasco, sugar, salt and blend thoroughly. Stir in the corn kernels and cook over medium heat, stirring frequently, for 5 minutes or until the corn is tender. Crumble the bacon and sprinkle over the corn before serving. Four to six servings.

Monday

Halibut with Spicy Sauce

Halibut with Spicy Sauce
Panfried Potatoes and Onions
Cucumbers in Sour Cream and Dill
Fresh Fruit

1 halibut steak approximately 1 to 1½ inches thick and weighing about 2½ pounds
2 tablespoons butter
2 tablespoons Worcestershire sauce
¼ cup dry white wine
1 tablespoon Dijon mustard
salt
freshly ground pepper
dash of Tabasco
2 tablespoons minced parsley

Place the halibut steak skinside (if any) down into an oiled baking pan. In a small saucepan, combine all the other ingredients except the parsley. Bring to boil and pour over fish. Bake in a preheated 400° oven, basting occasionally, for 15-20 minutes. Test for doneness by inserting fork into the thickest part of the fish. If the tines pull out easily and leave small holes, the fish is cooked. Sprinkle with parsley before serving. Makes four to six servings.

Tuesday

Ham Mousse

Ham Mousse
Corn on the Cob
Tomatoes Filled with Chive Cream Cheese
Lemon Sherbet

1½ teaspoons unflavored gelatin
¼ cup cold water
1½ cups clear chicken bouillon
¼ cup dry sherry
2 eggs, separated
1 cup heavy cream, whipped
3 cups cooked ham, ground fine
½ cup seeded, finely chopped cucumber
½ cup minced parsley
salt
freshly ground pepper
salad greens
mustard mayonnaise

Sprinkle gelatin over the water and stir to dissolve. Heat chicken bouillon to boil. Stir in sherry and gelatin and stir until smooth. Beat the egg yolks. Stir egg yolks into chicken bouillon mixture. Cook over low heat, stirring constantly, until the mixture thickens. Remove from heat and cool. Beat the egg whites with a pinch of salt until stiff but not dry. Fold first the whipped cream and then the beaten egg whites into the first mixture. Gently fold the ham, cucumber and parsley into the mousse. Season with salt and pepper. Pour into an old 8-cup mold or bowl. Chill for several hours or until well set. Unmold onto a platter lined with salad greens. Serve with mustard mayonnaise. Serves six.

Wednesday

Stuffed Eggplant

Stuffed Eggplant
Baked Tomato Halves
Syrian Bread
Sweet Cherries

2 large eggplants
2 tablespoons butter
1 tablespoon salad or olive oil
1 medium onion, minced
1 garlic clove, minced
1 pound lean ground beef
¼ cup minced parsley
1 tablespoon minced fresh mint
1 teaspoon ground cinnamon
salt
freshly ground pepper
½ cup cooked rice
1 cup chopped fresh tomato
2 eggs
4 tablespoons freshly grated Parmesan cheese

Parboil the whole eggplants in boiling salted water to cover for 10 minutes. Cool slightly and split lengthwise. Remove the pulp with a spoon leaving a ½-inch rim around the edge. Chop the pulp coarsely. Heat butter and oil in a large frying pan. Cook the onion and garlic for 3 minutes or until soft. Add beef. Cook, stirring with a fork over medium heat, until the meat is browned. Stir in parsley, mint, cinnamon, salt, and pepper. Mix in rice, tomato and eggs, blending well. Fill the eggplant halves with the mixture and sprinkle with cheese. Bake in a preheated oven 350° for 30 minutes. Four servings.

Thursday

Salade Niçoise

Zucchini Soup
Salade Niçoise
French Bread
Fresh Peach Pie

12 small new potatoes, scrubbed, with skins left on
6 tablespoons olive oil
2 tablespoons wine vinegar
2 tablespoons minced shallots or onions
1 tablespoon minced fresh basil
2 tablespoons minced parsley
2 7-ounce cans tuna fish in olive oil
1 pound green beans, left whole and cooked but still firm
3 tomatoes, peeled and cut into sixths
6 hard-cooked eggs, quartered
salt
freshly ground pepper
12 anchovy fillets, drained

Cook the potatoes until tender, but not mushy. Drain well and place into a bowl. Pour half of the oil and vinegar over them and toss carefully, making sure that each potato is coated with dressing. Sprinkle in the shallots, basil and parsley. Drain the tuna fish and break into chunks. On a large round platter, place the tuna chunks in the middle. Arrange the other vegetables and the eggs around the tuna in a decorative manner. Sprinkle with salt and pepper. Lay the anchovies over the vegetables. Place the potatoes around the vegetables and sprinkle with the remaining oil and vinegar. Four to six servings.

Friday

Haddock Casserole

Haddock Casserole
Potato Chips
Green Beans
Peaches and Cream

2 pounds fresh haddock or cod in one piece
juice of 1 lemon
3 parsley sprigs
2 tablespoons fresh dill
2 tablespoons butter
2 tablespoons flour
½ cup heavy cream
salt
freshly ground pepper
dash of Tabasco
1 teaspoon Worcestershire sauce
2 cups cooked rice
1 sweet Spanish onion, very thinly sliced
½ cup fine dry bread crumbs
lemon wedges

Place the fish in a large, deep frying pan. Cover with water. Add lemon juice, parsley and dill. Bring to boil slowly. Reduce heat so that the water barely simmers, cover and simmer for 15 minutes or until the fish flakes easily. Remove fish from broth, and reserve. When cool, flake in large flakes. Strain the broth and measure 1¼ cups. Heat butter in a saucepan and stir in flour. Cook for 2 minutes. Add fish broth and, stirring constantly, add cream and cook until smooth and thickened. Season with salt, pepper, Tabasco and Worcestershire sauce. In a large, flat baking dish, holding about 2 quarts, spoon about half the rice over bottom. Top with half the onion rings and half of the fish. Repeat the layering, ending with fish. Pour sauce over everything and sprinkle with bread crumbs. Bake in preheated 350° oven for 30 minutes. Serve with lemon wedges. Serves four to six.

Saturday

Egg Noodles with Three Cheeses

Egg Noodles with Three Cheeses
Green Salad
Fresh Fruit Salad

2 cups creamed cottage cheese
1 package (8 ounces) cream cheese, at room temperature
1 package (7½ ounces) farmer's cheese, at room temperature
1 teaspoon salt
freshly ground pepper
1 tablespoon grated onion
¼ cup minced parsley
1 pound medium egg noodles

Combine all the ingredients, except the noodles, in one large bowl. Beat and stir to make a smooth mixture. Cook the noodles in plenty of boiling salt water until just tender, al dente. Drain well, place into a heated serving dish and toss with the cheeses. Serve immediately. Makes four servings.
Note: This recipe can easily be doubled.

ENTERTAINING

August

Sunday

Cold Zucchini Soup
Cold Virginia Ham
Lentil Salad
Sliced Tomatoes and Basil
Lemon Sherbet

Lentil Salad

3 cups dried lentils
1 large onion stuck with 3 cloves
1 carrot, cut up
1 bay leaf
the green tops of 2 celery stalks, or 2 celery stalks, cut up
2 garlic cloves
2 bunches scallions, white and green parts, thinly sliced
French dressing made with the juice of 2 lemons, ⅓ cup olive oil, 1 minced garlic clove, and ¼ teaspoon dried thyme
salt
freshly ground pepper
watercress
sliced radishes

Any lentil dish must be well seasoned. Put lentils into a large saucepan. Pour enough boiling water to cover them, with 2 inches of water to spare. Cover the saucepan and let lentils stand for 1 hour. Add the onion, carrot, bay leaf, celery, and garlic cloves. Bring to boil, skim, reduce heat to very low, and cover. Simmer for 20 minutes or until lentils are tender but not mushy; they must hold their shape. Do not overcook. Drain lentils in a strainer and remove vegetables. Put lentils into a salad bowl while they are still hot. Add the scallions, French dressing, and salt and pepper to taste. Let lentils cool at room temperature. Refrigerate for at least 2 hours to blend the flavors. At serving time, if necessary, pour off any excess dressing. Garnish with watercress and sliced radishes. Serves six.

Monday

Sacher Torte

Chicken Salad with Fresh Lemon Mayonnaise
Rice Salad with Freshly Cooked Peas, Beans, Diced Carrots, and Lemon French Dressing
Green Salad
Sacher Torte

½ cup sweet butter, at room temperature
1 cup superfine sugar or confectioners' sugar
6 eggs, separated
4 ounces (4 squares) semi-sweet cooking chocolate
2 tablespoons water
½ cup superfine sugar
1 cup sifted flour
1 cup apricot jam
2 tablespoons brandy
Chocolate Glaze (see below)

Cream butter until very soft and fluffy. Gradually beat in sugar, beating well after each addition. Beat in egg yolks, one at a time, beating well after each yolk. Beat until mixture is very thick and light. Melt semi-sweet chocolate in water over very low heat. Do not scorch. Cool completely. Beat melted chocolate into egg mixture. Beat egg whites until foamy. Gradually beat in ½ cup of superfine sugar. Beat until stiff. Fold flour into egg batter. Then fold in the beaten egg whites. Butter and flour an 8-inch spring pan. Turn the batter into it. Bang once or twice on counter to remove air holes. Bake in a preheated 350° oven for 1 hour or until it tests clean. Cool cake. Heat apricot jam with brandy. Stir to mix and strain through a fine sieve. Cool. Cut cake into halves. Spread half of the cake with half of the apricot mixture. Top with the other cake half. Spread remaining apricot mixture over top of cake. Let jam harden before glazing with Chocolate Glaze.

Chocolate Glaze

2 squares (2 ounces) semi-sweet chocolate
3 tablespoons water
2 tablespoons butter
¾ cup sifted confectioners' sugar

In a small saucepan over very low heat combine the chocolate, water, and butter. Cook, stirring constantly, until chocolate is melted. Remove from heat. Stir in sugar. Beat with a spoon until just smooth. Use immediately, since the glaze stiffens as it cools. If this happens, heat it up again, over very low heat, stirring constantly. The recipe makes one 8-inch Sacher Torte.

Tuesday

Piperade (Basque Scrambled Eggs with Vegetables)

Piperade (Basque Scrambled Eggs with Vegetables)
Croutons
Pâté de Foie Gras
Watercress Salad with Lemon French Dressing
Peach Melba Made with Fresh Peaches and Raspberries

¼ cup bacon fat or butter (bacon fat is better)
4 medium onions, thinly sliced
3 large green peppers, cut into strips
6 medium tomatoes, peeled, seeded, and coarsely chopped
salt
freshly ground pepper
1 garlic clove, minced
1 tablespoon fresh basil, minced, *or* herbs to taste
6 eggs
fried bread croutons

These scrambled eggs must be soft and creamy. Heat bacon fat in a heavy frying pan and cook onions stirring constantly, until soft and golden. They must not brown. Add the green peppers. Simmer, covered, over low heat for 10 minutes, stirring frequently to prevent sticking. Add the tomatoes, salt, and pepper, garlic clove, and basil. Simmer, covered, over very low heat for 10 - 15 minutes or until vegetables have become almost a puree, though the pepper strips should retain their shape somewhat. Stir frequently. Add eggs. Stir mixture with a fork until eggs are barely set. Remove from heat and stir again; the heat in the frying pan will finish cooking the eggs to a creamy consistency. Serve immediately with fried croutons, on very hot plates. Serves four to six.

Wednesday

Lamb Stew with Parsley and Lemon

Melon and Prosciutto
Lamb Stew with Parsley and Lemon
Small New Boiled Potatoes
Blueberry Tart

3 pounds boneless lean lamb
2 tablespoons salad oil
3 cups finely chopped parsley, no stems
2 lemons, cut into thick slices, without seeds
salt
freshly ground pepper
hot water
1 tablespoon butter kneaded with 1 tablespoon flour

Trim every bit of fat and gristle off the lamb. Cut lamb into 1-inch pieces. Heat salad oil in a deep casserole and over high heat, brown lamb on all sides. Reduce heat to low. Add the parsley, lemons, salt and pepper. Preferably use the flat-leaved so-called Italian parsley, which is more flavorful than the curly variety. Add just enough hot water to cover meat. Simmer, tightly covered, over low heat for 45 minutes or until meat is tender and the liquid reduced. Stir in the butter-flour mixture to thicken sauce. There should not be a great deal of sauce, just enough to cover the meat. Makes four to six servings.

Thursday

West Indian Callaloo

West Indian Callaloo
Hot Corn Sticks
Assorted Cold Cuts and Cheeses
Breads and Crackers
Peach Pie

¼ pound salt pork
2 pounds fresh spinach, washed, hard stems removed, and chopped
1 pound fresh okra, sliced
1 small onion, coarsely chopped
1 garlic clove, minced
1 small red hot pepper, seeded, or more to taste, minced, or Tabasco to taste
¼ teaspoon ground thyme
salt
freshly ground pepper
1 tablespoon butter
1 tablespoon olive oil
1½ pounds crab meat, flaked or 6 small fresh crabs

Pour boiling water over the salt pork, let stand 5 minutes to remove excess saltiness, drain and cut into small dice. Put the pork, spinach, okra, onion, garlic, and minced red hot pepper or Tabasco into a large kettle. Add the thyme and boiling water to cover. Season with salt and pepper. Simmer, covered, over low heat for 20 minutes or until vegetables are soft. Check for moisture; since the thickness of this soup depends on individual taste, more water may be necessary. Stir in butter and the olive oil. Add crab meat or crabs and simmer 20 minutes longer. If crabs are used (1 for each serving) remove and serve them on a separate plate, along with soup. Swiss chard or the tops of young beets may be used instead of spinach, and the soup may be as hot as your heart desires. Serves six.

Friday

Peaches in Champagne

Iced Watercress Soup
Veal Scallopine
Fried Zucchini
Stuffed Tomatoes with Rice
Peaches in Champagne
Almond Cookies

6 ripe, perfect peaches, chilled
1 bottle sweet champagne or Asti Spumante, well chilled
almond cookies

Just before beginning the meal, dip the peaches into boiling water and slip off the skins. Lay each peach in a wine glass. Refrigerate until serving time. Serve each guest a glass with a peach. Uncork the champagne and fill each glass. The champagne is to be sipped and the peach is to be eaten with a dessert fork and spoon. Serve with almond cookies. Serves six.

Saturday

Old Fashioned Box Supper for Two

Cold Curried Chicken Breasts*
Cold Rice Salad with Vegetables*
French Bread **Butter in a Crock**
Brie Cheese and Apples
Grapes **Walnut Cookies**
**Recipe in book*

The Box Supper for Two is an old American tradition, which, for charm and conviviality, is as good today as it was a hundred years ago. It is a good way to give a joint party and one at which each individual hostess can shine. Send out invitations asking each woman guest to provide a box or basket supper for two. Suggest on the invitation that imaginatively decorated boxes or baskets would be appreciated. On the day, assemble all the boxes and baskets in one spot. Have the host auction off each basket to the male guests in an informal fashion. Or else, number the boxes or baskets and give each man a number, or let him draw a number out of a box. When the number is called, the man steps forward to claim the basket and the lady who put it up.

As a hostess, you should provide the drinks, extra silver in case any is forgotten and places for people to sit. Tables and chairs for all are not necessary. A supply of blankets or mats to spread on the ground is a good idea.

If the party is to be held at night, hurricane lamps, and Japanese lanterns made by filling large brown paper bags full of sald and placing short, fat candles in them, provide light and enhance the atmosphere. Don't forget to have large trash bags or cans around, but totally out of sight.

The simplest way to fix a box supper is to take a shoe box, line it with clean white paper, and pack the food into it after wrapping in plastic or foil. However, this would be for a simple beach or similarly informal social, with food that can be eaten with the fingers, such as fried chicken etc.

Since this is a Party Box Supper, a box large and pretty enough should be produced, or made by papering one large enough with some decorative paper, inside out. Butter still, at least simpler, is to use a pretty basket. Remember that box or basket will be there for all to see and to bid on. Line box or basket with a pretty cloth and put the food, silver, napkins, salt and pepper on it, without crowding. Include French bread, a small crock of butter and a spreading knife. Carry the cookies in a little box and place the grapes in a small basket. You might also include some good cheese, such as a piece of Brie and an apple or pear.

As for the main dish, the Cold Curried Chicken Breasts on Rice Salad with Vegetables, serve it by placing the meat on a pretty dinner plate, with the Rice Salad alongside. Decorate the plate with a little watercress, a slice of tomato, a radish or any other touch of edible color. Cover each plate tightly with plastic wrap.

Drinks

Any good French, Swiss, Italian or American white wine, chilled but not frozen, such as a Pouilly Fuisse, a Fendant du Valais, a Verdicchio di Jesi or a Pinot Chardonny from California.

Cold Curried Chicken Breasts

2 whole chicken breasts, each weighing about 3/4 pound, skinned and boned, fat and gristle removed
good quality chicken broth, heated
3 egg yolks
1½ cups heavy cream
1 teaspoon curry powder
2 tablespoons butter, cut into small pieces
6 tablespoons dry sherry
salt
freshly ground pepper
grated rind of 1 lemon

Place chicken breasts in a deep frying pan. Cover with hot chicken broth. Simmer for 25-30 minutes or until meat is tender. Drain, reserving the broth for other uses. Cool completely. Split the chicken breasts into halves. Place two halves on a plate for 1 serving. In the top of a double boiler, beat together the egg yolks, cream and curry powder. Place *over,* not in hot water. Stir in butter, stirring until melted. Stir in sherry. Cook, stirring frequently, until the sauce is smooth and thickened. It should be the consistency of custard. Season with salt and pepper to taste. Pour sauce over the chicken breasts , cool and refrigerate. It will set when cold. Before serving, sprinkle with lemon rind. Two servings.

Cold Rice Salad with Vegetables

1 tablespoon salt
¾ cup long grain rice
3 tablespoons olive oil
1 tablespoon vinegar
salt
freshly ground pepper
¼ cup sliced radishes
¼ cup peeled, seeded and chopped cucumber
¼ cup minced green pepper
3 tablespoons minced chives
3 tablespoons minced parsley
2 tablespoons minced fresh basil leaves
1 teaspoon minced fresh tarragon leaves

Bring 2 quarts of water to boil and add 1 tablespoon salt. Pour in rice. Cook over high heat uncovered for 12 minutes. Pour into a strainer and rinse under running cold water. Drain thoroughly. Put rice into a non-metal bowl. Stir in the oil, vinegar, salt, pepper and mix well. Let stand at room temperature for 1 hour. Add the remaining ingredients and mix well. Refrigerate until ready to serve. Makes two servings.

SEPTEMBER

There are two schools of thought on the feeding of children. Should they be made to try a food at least once if this is done over their dead bodies, or should they be let stay in the rut of their eating patterns, provided that these eating patterns keep them healthy and happy? I honestly don't know which one is right. Surely, people, and children are people, should be exposed to all the lovely possibilities of the world of food, but on the other hand, is a diversified diet that important just because it is diversified? Does it really make a difference in life if you've never tasted Brussels sprouts? Mind you, this is the voice of experience speaking, ruling out junk foods firmly, but admitting that salami sandwiches and plenty of fresh fruit made a boy of mine, firm on saying no to vegetables, into the healthy father of two healthy children. Obviously, he also ate meat and potatoes, and salad and milk, but ignored beans and spinach and interesting foods like oysters and snails. All I can say is that as long as they are healthy and happy, leave them alone.

SEPTEMBER

FAMILY FARE

	LUNCHES	DINNERS
Sunday	Nantucket Scallops* Rice Cakes Melon Balls and Sponge Cake	German Sausages in Sour Cream Sauce* Mashed Potatoes Grated Sautéed Zucchini French Chocolate Cake
Monday	Pesto Sauce for Pasta* Spaghetti with Pesto Sliced Tomatoes Coconut Bars and Fruit	Givetch* Wheat or Barley Pilaf Raw Mushroom Salad Baked Custard with Stewed Peaches
Tuesday	Egg Salad Sandwiches Lettuce and Avocado Salad Baked Stuffed Pears*	Stuffed Zucchini* Potato Salad Fresh Fruit and Cheese
Wednesday	Broiled Frankfurters Zucchini and Tomato Casserole* Sliced Peaches and Cream	Swiss Steak Baked Potatoes Corn, Okra and Tomato Casserole Mocha Fromage*
Thursday	Spaghetti with Walnut Sauce* Green Salad Grapes	Swedish Seamen's Beef* Pickled Beets Cucumber Salad Bavarian Cream
Friday	Eby Heller's Chicken Corn Soup* Cooked Cauliflower and Watercress Salad Open Plum Tart	Shrimp and Pineapple* Boiled Rice Mango Relish Mixed Fruit Salad with Walnut Cookies
Saturday	Homemade Scrapple* Fried Apples Bacon Homemade Applesauce	Lemon Chicken* White Bean Salad Watercress and Radish Salad Butter Pecan Ice Cream with Caramel Sauce

QUICK & EASY Dinners For Two	BUDGET DINNERS	ENTERTAINING
Chicken in Port Wine* Zucchini and Tomatoes Thin Buttered Noodles Watercress Stewed Fresh Plums	Chicken Cacciatore* Spaghetti Broccoli Vinaigrette Pears, Apples and Cheese	Crumbed Meat Patties on Tomato Slices* Mushrooms Baked in Sour Cream Hot French Garlic Bread Cantaloupe Balls in a Sugar Syrup Flavored with Fresh Ginger
Antipasto of Salami, Tuna and Pimiento Fettucine with Ham Sauce* Sliced Tomatoes Grapes	Meat Loaf Baked Lima Beans with Cheese and Sour Cream* Baked Potatoes Vanilla Ice Cream with Fudge Sauce	Baked Eggplant, Mozzarella, Eggs, and Tomatoes* White Dried Bean Salad Cucumbers Vinaigrette Fresh Plum Tart
Steak Quick Bean Casserole* Tossed Green Salad Fresh Fruit	Deviled Lamb Riblets* Spanish Rice Lettuce and Avocado Salad Peach Cobbler	Chicken Liver Appetizers Poulet à la Crème Buttered Noodles Polonaise Peas Cooked with Lettuce Molded Cream Ring Filled with Fresh Fruit Salad*
Lamb Stew with Egg Sauce* Rice Buttered Green Beans Carrot Sticks Fresh Plum Pie	Pork and Cucumber Stew* Corn Bread Creamed and Buttered Cabbage Wedges Orange Chiffon Cake	Smoked Salmon on Toast Virginia Ham Corn Pudding* Homemade Cheesecake
Grilled Ham and Cheese Rolls* Barley Pilaff Green Peppers and Tomato Stew Deep Dish Apple Pie with Ice Cream	Baked Beef en Casserole* Mashed Potatoes Green Beans with Mustard Dried Apricot and Raisin Pie	Leeks Vinaigrette Lemon Beef* Barley Pilaf Buttered Lima Beans Fresh Peeled Peach in Glass of Champagne
Fried Fish Fillets Italian Pan-Fried Tomatoes* Corn on the Cob Brownies	Manhattan Clam Chowder* Corn Muffins Guava Jelly and Cream Cheese Crackers	Tomatoes Filled with Herbed Rice Deep-Fried Scallops Tartar Sauce Sautéed Zucchini Compote of Fresh Plums* Whipped Cream
Saltimbocca* Melting Potatoes Buttered Carrots and Onions Green Salad Nectarines	Frankfurter and Potato Stew Green Beans with Mustard Sauce* Orange and Onion Salad Apple Compote and Cookies	Ham Loaf* Spoon Bread Poached Apples Pennsylvania Dutch Coffee Cake* Served with Butter and Jam* Cider Coffee Tea Milk

FAMILY FARE LUNCHES

September

Sunday

Nantucket Scallops

Nantucket Scallops
Rice Cakes
Melon Balls and Sponge Cake

2 pounds scallops
½ cup dry white wine
1 tablespoon lemon juice
2 tablespoons minced parsley
1 tablespoon minced fresh dill weed
1 teaspoon salt
½ teaspoon freshly ground pepper
1 cup light cream
½ cup buttered bread crumbs

If the scallops are very large, cut them into halves or quarters. Place scallops into a generously buttered shallow baking dish. Combine the wine, lemon juice, parsley, dill weed, salt and pepper. Pour over the scallops. Mix gently. Pour cream over scallops. Sprinkle with buttered bread crumbs. Bake in a preheated 435° oven for about 15 minutes. If wanted, run quickly under the broiler to brown the top. Makes four to six servings.

Monday

Pesto Sauce for Pasta

Pesto Sauce for Pasta
Spaghetti with Pesto
Sliced Tomatoes
Coconut Bars and Fruit

1 cup olive oil
  (it must be olive oil)
3 large garlic cloves or
  garlic to taste
1 cup fresh basil leaves,
  firmly packed
1 cup freshly grated Parmesan
  or Romano cheese
⅔ cup pine nuts (pignoli)
  or walnuts
1 teaspoon salt

Combine all the ingredients in a blender. Cover and blend at moderate speed, scraping down the sides with a rubber spatula. If the mixture is too thick, add a little more olive oil, 2 tablespoons at a time. Makes about 1½ cups.

Note: This sauce freezes very well or pour it into a jelly jar. cover with a film of olive oil and plastic wrap and store in refrigerator. To use, spoon over cooked pasta and toss well. Three-quarters of a cup of sauce will dress 1 pound of cooked pasta. It is desirable to add 1 tablespoon of butter to the pasta together with the Pesto or use. 1 tablespoon for each serving, in vegetable soup or on cooked vegetables.

Tuesday

Baked Stuffed Pears

Egg Salad Sandwiches
Lettuce and Avocado Salad
Baked Stuffed Pears

6 large, ripe but firm pears
juice of 1 lemon
4 tablespoons honey
2 tablespoons butter
⅓ cup chopped walnuts
½ cup mixed glacé fruit,
  finely diced
2 cups orange juice
heavy cream

Wash the pears. Remove stem and cut fruit into halves lengthwise. Remove the core with a sharp knife and hollow out the cavity a little more for the stuffing. Place the pear halves side by side in a baking dish. Sprinkle with lemon juice to prevent discoloring. Heat together the honey and butter until both are melted. Mix the walnuts and glacé fruit. Stuff each pear cavity with a little of the mixture. Brush the honey butter over the pears and stuffing. Pour the orange juice around the pears into the baking dish. Bake uncovered in a preheated 350° oven for 30 minutes or until the pears are tender. Do not overbake. Serve warm, with cream on the side. Serves six.

Wednesday

Zucchini and Tomato Casserole

Broiled Frankfurters
Zucchini and Tomato Casserole
Sliced Peaches and Cream

¼ cup olive oil
1 small onion, minced
1 garlic clove, minced
4 large zucchini, cut into ¼-inch slices
2 tablespoons minced fresh basil leaves or 2 teaspoons dried basil
½ cup freshly grated Parmesan cheese
4 large tomatoes, peeled and sliced
salt
freshly ground pepper
½ cup fine dry bread crumbs
2 tablespoons melted butter

Heat olive oil in a frying pan and cook onion and garlic stirring constantly, for 3-4 minutes or until onion is soft. Add zucchini. Cook over medium heat, stirring constantly with a fork, for 3-5 minutes, or until turning golden but still firm. Place a layer of zucchini into a buttered 1½-quart baking dish. Sprinkle each layer with a little basil and Parmesan cheese. Top with a layer of tomatoes and sprinkle with a little salt and pepper. Repeat the process. Combine the bread crumbs and melted butter and sprinkle over the vegetables. Bake uncovered in a preheated 350° oven for 20 minutes or until golden brown. Serves six.

Thursday

Spaghetti with Walnut Sauce

Spaghetti with Walnut Sauce
Green Salad
Grapes

1 cup shelled walnuts
4 tablespoons olive oil
2 garlic cloves, minced
boiling water
½ cup minced parsley
2 tablespoons minced fresh basil leaves (optional)
salt
freshly ground pepper
1 pound spaghetti, cooked al dente, drained and very hot
freshly grated Parmesan cheese

Grind the walnuts in a nut grinder or ¼ cup at a time, in a blender. If ground in a blender, do not overblend or the walnuts will be pasty. Heat oil in a heavy saucepan and cook garlic for 2-3 minutes. Do not brown. Add the ground walnuts. Cook over low heat, stirring constantly, for 2 more minutes. Remove from heat. Stir in remaining oil and just enough boiling water to make a sauce the consistency of thick tomato sauce. Add parsley and mix well. Salt and pepper to taste. Pour the sauce over spaghetti and toss. Serve with grated Parmesan cheese on the side. Makes about one cup, or enough to dress 1 to 1½ pounds cooked spaghetti or pasta.

Friday

Eby Heller's Chicken Corn Soup

Eby Heller's Chicken Corn Soup
Cooked Cauliflower and Watercress Salad
Open Plum Tart

3 quarts water
1 4-pound stewing chicken, cut into pieces
2 teaspoons salt
¼ teaspoon freshly ground pepper
½ teaspoon saffron
2 cups narrow egg noodles
2 cups corn kernels, fresh or frozen
2 tablespoons minced parsley
2 hard cooked eggs, chopped

Eby Heller's a charming lady who wrote the best of all Pennsylvania Dutch cookbooks: The Art of Pennsylvania Dutch Cooking. Pour the water into a large kettle. Add the chicken, salt, pepper and saffron. Bring to boil. Lower heat. Simmer, covered, over low heat 1¼ hours or until chicken is tender; cooking time depends on the age of the chicken. Skim occasionally. Remove chicken from the stock and cool. Reserve the stock. Cut the breast and legs off the chicken and reserve for further use, such as in chicken pie or salad. Cut off all remaining meat from chicken, removing fat and gristle and cut into ½-inch cubes. Return the meat to chicken stock. Chill until all the fat has risen to top and can be easily removed. Reheat the stock to boil. Add noodles and corn. Reduce heat to moderate and cook uncovered for 10 minutes or until corn and noodles are tender. Check seasoning. Just before serving, stir in parsley and chopped eggs. Six to eight servings.

Saturday

Homemade Scrapple

Homemade Scrapple
Fried Apples
Bacon
Homemade Applesauce

3½ cups beef bouillon
1 teaspoon salt
¼ teaspoon freshly ground pepper
1 medium onion, minced
¼ cup minced parsley
3 bay leaves
3 pounds spareribs
2½ cups cornmeal
2 cups water
flour
shortening for frying

Combine the beef bouillon, salt, pepper, onion, parsley and bay leaves in a big kettle. Bring to boil and add spareribs. Reduce heat to low and simmer, covered, for 2½ hours. Remove meat from broth and strain the broth. Cut off all the meat from spareribs, and remove every bit of bone and gristle. Run meat through the fine blade of meat chopper. Return meat to broth and bring to boil. Stir cornmeal slowly into the water, beating hard to avoid lumps. Stir in about ⅓ of boiling broth. Cook over low heat, stirring frequently, for 10-15 minutes or until mixture is very thick. Pour scrapple into two 9 × 5 × 3-inch loaf pans. Chill. When ready to serve, cut the Scrapple into ½-inch slices. Coat the slices with flour. Fry in very little shortening until brown and crisp. Two nine-inch loaves.

FAMILY FARE DINNERS

September

Sunday

German Sausages in Sour Cream Sauce

German Sausages in Sour Cream Sauce
Mashed Potatoes
Grated Sautéed Zucchini
French Chocolate Cake

8 German Bratwurst sausages
2 tablespoons butter
¼ to ½ cup chicken or beef bouillon
1 tablespoon flour
½ teaspoon salt
1 cup sour cream

Drop sausages into boiling water to cover. Let stand 5 minutes. Drain sausages and dry thoroughly with paper towels. Heat butter in a large frying pan. Cook the sausages, turning over frequently, over moderate heat for 5-7 minutes or until golden on all sides. Add ¼ cup of bouillon to the frying pan. Reduce heat to very low. Cook uncovered for about 15 minutes, turing over once. If the frying pan looks dry, add a little more chicken bouillon. Transfer sausages to a heated deep serving platter, cover with foil and keep warm in a low oven. Beat the flour and salt into sour cream. Add this mixture, a few tablespoons at a time and stirring constantly, to the juices in frying pan. Cook over low heat for about 5 minutes or until sauce is thickened. Do not let boil. Pour sauce over the sausages and serve very hot. Serves four to six.

Monday

Givetch

Givetch
Wheat or Barley Pilaf
Raw Mushroom Salad
Baked Custard with Stewed Peaches

¼ cup butter
2 pounds lean boneless lamb, cut into 1½-inch pieces
2 medium onions, chopped
1½ cups water
½ pound green beans, sliced
½ cauliflower, broken into flowerets
2 medium zucchini, thickly sliced
2 large green peppers, cut into strips
3 large tomatoes, chopped
¼ pound fresh okra, trimmed and sliced
salt
freshly ground pepper
½ teaspoon ground marjoram
juice of 1 lemon
plain yogurt or sour cream

Heat butter in a large, heavy casserole which can go to the table. Over high heat, brown meat on all sides. Add onions and 1 cup of water. Simmer, covered, over low heat for about 30 minutes or until meat is half cooked. Stir occasionally. Add all the other ingredients except the lemon juice. Bring to boil. Reduce heat to very low and simmer, covered, for 20-30 minutes or until vegetables are tender but still firm. Stir and check frequently for moisture; if necessary, add remaining water. Remove from heat and stir in the lemon juice. Serve from the casserole, with yogurt or sour cream on the side. Six servings.

Tuesday

Stuffed Zucchini

Stuffed Zucchini
Potato Salad
Fresh Fruit and Cheese

1 pound ground beef or lamb
1 large onion, grated
¼ cup long grain raw rice
½ cup tomato juice
¼ cup minced dill weed
salt
freshly ground pepper
8 to 9 large zucchini (about 6 inches long)
3 tablespoons butter
1½ cups chicken bouillon
lemon wedges

Combine the meat, onion, rice, tomato juice, dill weed, salt and pepper to taste in a bowl. Mix well. Scrape and wash zucchini. Cut off the stem end, scoop it out a little and reserve. With an apple corer or a sharp knife, scoop out zucchini leaving a ⅓-inch shell. Throw away scooped out pulp. Fill each zucchini with a little of the meat mixture, pushing it down with the handle of a spoon. When full, cover with the stem end. Place a rack on the bottom of a heavy saucepan. Arrange zucchini side by side on rack. If any filling is left, shape it into small balls and place on top of zucchini or between them. Dot with butter and pour bouillon around vegetables. Cover with waxed paper or aluminum foil. Place a plate on top of the zucchini to weigh it down during cooking. Cover and cook over medium heat for 1 hour or until zucchini are tender. Check occasionally for moisture; if necessary, add a little more bouillon. Transfer to a serving dish and pour pan juices over vegetables. Serve with lemon wedges. Serves six.

Wednesday

Mocha Fromage

Swiss Steak
Baked Potatoes
Corn, Okra and Tomato Sassorole
Mocha Fromage

1 package unflavored gelatin
¾ cup cold strong coffee
3 eggs
¾ cup sugar
¼ cup cocoa (preferably Dutch-processed cocoa)
1 cup heavy cream
⅓ cup grated semisweet chocolate

Sprinkle gelatin into coffee and stir. Set the bowl with the gelatin in a pan of hot water and heat until the gelatin is liquid. Beat the eggs, sugar and cocoa until light and doubled in volume. Beat in the gelatin mixture. Whip the cream until stiff. Add the egg mixture to the whipped cream and blend thoroughly. Pour into 6 individual little soufflé dishes or parfait glasses. Cover and chill until firm. Sprinkle top with grated chocolate before serving. Makes four to six servings.

Thursday

Swedish Seamen's Beef

Swedish Seamen's Beef
Pickled Beets
Cucumber Salad
Bavarian Cream

2 pounds chuck or round or other boneless lean beef
salt
freshly ground pepper
6 bay leaves, crumbled
1 12-ounce can beer or ale
⅓ cup flour
⅔ to 1 cup butter
2 pounds raw potatoes, peeled and sliced
3 large carrots, sliced
3 large onions, sliced

Cut the meat into 1-inch squares which are about ¼-inch thick. Sprinkle with salt and pepper. Place in a deep bowl (do not use aluminum) and sprinkle with crumbled bay leaves. Pour beer over meat. Refrigerate for 4 hours or overnight. Drain meat and dry it. Reserve marinade. Coat meat with flour. Heat ⅓ of the butter in a frying pan and cook meat over high heat for 2 minutes, or until golden on both sides. Reserve meat. Cook potatoes in the same frying pan for 3 minutes or until golden and reserve. Add a little more butter and cook carrots for 3 minutes. If necessary, add again a little more butter and cook onions until soft and golden. In a buttered 2½-quart casserole, arrange alternate layers of potatoes, meat, carrots and onions. The first and last layers should be potatoes. Pour reserved marinade over the mixture. Cover with a lid or tie on aluminum foil. Bake in a preheated 350° oven for 1 hour or until meat and vegetables are tender. Check occasionally for moisture; if too dry, add a little more beer or water, about ¼ cup at a time. Serves six.

Friday

Shrimp and Pineapple

Shrimp and Pineapple
Boiled Rice
Mango Relish
Mixed Fruit Salad with Walnut Cookies

2 tablespoons salad oil
3 green or red sweet peppers, sliced
1 tablespoon grated fresh ginger *or* 1 teaspoon ground ginger
1 garlic clove, minced
2 pounds raw shrimp, shelled and deveined
1 tablespoon soy sauce
1 tablespoon dry sherry
1 cup chopped fresh pineapple or pineapple bits, drained

Heat salad oil in a casserole which can go to the table. Add the peppers, ginger and garlic. Cook over medium heat, stirring constantly, for 3-4 minutes or until peppers are almost soft. Add the shrimp and cook, stirring all the time, for 2 minutes longer. Add the soy sauce, sherry and pineapple. Simmer, covered, for 3-5 more minutes or until the shrimp are cooked and the dish heated through; cooking time depends on the size of the shrimp. Makes four to six servings.

Saturday

Lemon Chicken

Lemon Chicken
White Bean Salad
Watercress and Radish Salad
Butter Pecan Ice Cream with Caramel Sauce

1 4-5 pound roasting chicken
salt
freshly ground pepper
3 lemons
1 large parsley bunch
3 tablespoons olive oil
1 large onion, minced
1 tablespoon ground turmeric
2 cups hot chicken bouillon
2 garlic cloves
Green Sauce

Trim all excess fat off chicken. Wash and dry chicken inside out. Sprinkle the cavity with salt and pepper. Cut 1 of the lemons into quarters. Rub the chicken inside out with lemon. Put two of the lemon quarters into cavity. Wash parsley thoroughly and cut off stems. Stuff parsley into cavity of chicken. Truss chicken. Heat olive oil in a saucepan large enough to hold chicken and cook onion until soft. Stir in half of the turmeric. Cook, stirring constantly, for 2 minutes. Rub the chicken with remaining turmeric. Put chicken into saucepan. Cook over medium heat, turning once or twice, until chicken is a deep yellow on all sides. Add hot chicken bouillon, garlic, a little salt and pepper. Grate the rind of 1 of the remaining lemons and add to chicken. Squeeze the juice of the two remaining lemons and add to chicken. Bring to boil. Reduce heat to very low. Cover saucepan tightly. Simmer for 1 hour or until chicken is tender, but not overcooked. Cool the chicken but do not chill. Slice the meat off the bones and arrange on a platter. Garnish with parsley and serve with Green Sauce. Serves six.

QUICK & EASY DINNERS FOR TWO

September

Sunday

Chicken in Port Wine

Chicken in Port Wine
Zucchini and Tomatoes
Thin Buttered Noodles
Watercress
Stewed Fresh Plums

1 large chicken breast, split
2 tablespoons butter
1 tablespoon salad oil
1 small onion, minced
1 garlic clove, mashed
1 cup port wine
salt
freshly ground pepper
½ teaspoon ground thyme
1 bunch watercress

Skin chicken breast halves and trim off any fat. Heat butter and oil in a deep frying pan and cook onion and garlic for 2-3 minutes. Add chicken breast pieces and brown on both sides. Add port wine, salt, pepper and thyme. Bring to boil. Lower heat and simmer, covered, for 15 minutes or until tender. If necessary to prevent scorching, add a little hot water, but not much at a time since there should be just a little sauce. Put into a heated serving dish and garnish with watercress, which takes the place of salad.

Monday

Fettucine with Ham Sauce

Antipasto of Salami, Tuna and Pimiento
Fettucine with Ham Sauce
Sliced Tomatoes
Grapes

½ pound prosciutto or smoked ham
4 tablespoons butter
½ pound freshly cooked hot fettucine or fine noodles
⅓ cup freshly grated Parmesan cheese

Cut the fat from ham and dice small. Cut ham into ¼-inch cubes. Put the ham fat into a casserole that can go to the table and which is big enough to hold the fettucine. Add butter to the ham fat. Heat both until just hot; they must not brown. Add diced ham and toss. Heat through but do not brown. Add cooked hot fettucine and sprinkle with Parmesan cheese. Toss to mix well and serve immediately.

Tuesday

Quick Bean Casserole

Steak
Quick Bean Casserole
Tossed Green Salad
Fresh Fruit

½ medium onion, minced or 2 large minced shallots
2 slices bacon, minced
1 tablespoon olive oil
1 large fresh tomato, peeled and chopped or 1 cup Italian style drained tomatoes
½ teaspoon ground thyme, marjoram or dried basil, or herbs to taste
1 1-pound can kidney, pinto, or any other beans or chick peas, drained
3-4 green onions, thinly sliced, green and white part (optional)
salt
freshly ground pepper.

In a casserole, combine the onion, bacon and olive oil. Cook over medium heat, stirring constantly, until onion is soft and golden. Add the tomato and the herb. Cook over high heat, stirring constantly, for 3-4 minutes or until tomato is soft. Add beans and green onions. Cook over low heat until thoroughly heated through. Do not overcook or the beans will be too soft. Season with salt and pepper.

Wednesday

Lamb Stew with Egg Sauce

Lamb Stew with Egg Sauce
Rice
Buttered Green Beans
Carrot Sticks
Fresh Plum Pie

1 pound lean boneless lamb
2 slices minced bacon
1 tablespoon minced onion
1 tablespoon butter
salt
freshly ground pepper
1 tablespoon flour
⅓ cup dry white wine
½ teaspoon ground marjoram
2 egg yolks or 1 large egg yolk
1 tablespoon fresh lemon juice
2 tablespoons minced parsley

Trim any fat and cut lamb into 1½-inch cubes. In a deep frying pan, combine the lamb, bacon, onion and butter. Cook over medium heat, stirring constantly, until lamb is golden, but not browned. Season with salt and pepper and sprinkle with flour. Stir well. Add the wine and marjoram. Cook, stirring constantly, for 3-4 minutes or until wine has evaporated. Add enough hot water to almost, but not quite, cover meat. Simmer, covered, over low heat, stirring frequently, for 20 minutes or until meat is tender. If the dish looks like it is scorching, add a little more hot water, but do not make it soupy. Beat together the egg yolks and lemon juice. Remove lamb from heat and stir in sauce. Keep in a warm place on the stove, but not over direct heat, for 3-4 minutes or until the sauce has set without curdling. Sprinkle with parsley and serve very hot.

Thursday

Grilled Ham and Cheese Rolls

Grilled Ham and Cheese Rolls
Barley Pilaff
Green Peppers and Tomato Stew
Deep Dish Apple Pie with Ice Cream

Dijon or other prepared mustard
8 thin slices boiled ham
8 ½-inch sticks Swiss or Cheddar cheese

Spread mustard on one side of the ham slices. Place 1 stick of cheese on each slice. Roll and secure with toothpicks. Place on greased broiler rack on the lower shelf of the broiler. Broil under medium heat until browned on all sides, turning once.

Friday

Italian Pan-Fried Tomatoes

Fried Fish Fillets
Italian Pan-Fried Tomatoes
Corn on the Cob
Brownies

6 large firm Italian-type
plum tomatoes
salt
freshly ground pepper
1 teaspoon dried oregano
or basil *or* marjoram
⅓ cup olive oil
¼ cup water

Use plum tomatoes because they are firmer and tastier. Wash the tomatoes and cut into halves lengthwise. Put each half, cut side up, into a shallow frying pan. Sprinkle the tomatoes with salt, pepper and oregano or other herb. Combine the oil and water and sprinkle over the tomatoes. Over medium heat, cook the tomatoes for about 7 minutes, shaking the pan occasionally so they will not stick. If too dry, sprinkle with a little more oil and water, one tablespoon at a time; the dish should not be soupy. Turn the tomatoes carefully with a pancake turner and cook for 2-3 minutes longer, shaking the pan frequently. To serve, turn them cut side up on a heated serving dish.

Saturday

Saltimbocca

Saltimbocca
Melting Potatoes
Buttered Carrots and Onions
Green Salad
Nectarines

4 slices veal scallopini,
about ¼-inch thick
freshly ground pepper
about ¾ teaspoon ground sage
4 thin slices prosciutto or smoked
ham, larger than the meat
wooden toothpicks
2 tablespoons butter
1 teaspoon olive oil
⅓ cup dry white wine

Place the scallopini between two sheets of waxed paper. Pound them with a rolling pin or a filled bottle until they are as thin as possible without tearing the meat — about ⅛-inch thick. Sprinkle with pepper and ground sage. Place ham slices on the scallopini; the ham should cover them. "Stitch" each scallopini with a wooden toothpick to keep meat and ham together. Heat butter and olive oil in a large frying pan which will accomodate the scallopini in one layer, or use two pans, each one with heated butter and oil. Arrange the scallopini in frying pans, meatside down. Cook over medium heat for about 3-5 minutes, depending on their thinness. Turn and cook 2 minutes longer on the ham side. Transfer to a heated serving platter and keep hot. Add wine to the frying pan, scraping up the brown bits at the bottom, bring to boil and spoon over the meat.

BUDGET DINNERS

September

Sunday

Chicken Cacciatore

Chicken Cacciatore
Spaghetti
Broccoli Vinaigrette
Pears, Apples and Cheese

¼ cup salad oil
3 pounds chicken parts, fat trimmed off
1 cup minced onion
½ cup minced celery
1 medium carrot, minced
1 garlic clove, minced
½ or 1 green pepper, minced
2 8-ounce cans tomato sauce
½ cup water or dry red or white wine
salt
freshly ground pepper
½ teaspoon dried thyme or marjoram or to taste

Heat salad oil in a large, deep frying pan. Over high heat, brown the chicken parts on all sides. Transfer them to a casserole. Add the onion, celery, carrot, garlic and green pepper to frying pan. If necessary to prevent scorching, add a little more oil. Cook over medium heat, stirring constantly, for 5 minutes or until the vegetables are soft. Add tomato sauce, wine, salt, pepper and thyme. Bring quickly to boil. Pour the sauce over the chicken. Simmer, covered for about 20 minutes. Uncover and simmer 10 minutes longer. Makes four to six servings.

Monday

Baked Lima Beans with Cheese and Sour Cream

Meat Loaf
Baked Lima Beans with Cheese and Sour Cream
Baked Potatoes
Vanilla Ice Cream with Fudge Sauce

2 10-ounce packages frozen lima beans
2 cups sour cream
2 tablespoons flour
2 tablespoons grated onion
½ teaspoon dried thyme or marjoram or curry powder
1 cup grated Swiss or Cheddar cheese
salt
freshly ground pepper
1 cup fresh white bread crumbs or stuffing mix
¼ cup melted butter

Drop the lima beans into boiling salted water and cook for 2 minutes. Drain. Put sour cream into a bowl. Stir in flour, grated onion, thyme and cheese. Mix well. Check the seasoning; if necessary, add some salt and pepper. Fold in the lima beans. Turn into a buttered 2-quart baking dish. Top with bread crumbs and sprinkle with melted butter. Bake in a preheated 350° oven 35 minutes or until golden brown and bubbly. Makes six servings.

Tuesday

Deviled Lamb Riblets

Deviled Lamb Riblets
Spanish Rice
Lettuce and Avocado Salad
Peach Cobbler

3-4 pounds lamb riblets
3 tablespoons Dijon mustard
1 cup flour
salt
freshly ground pepper
½ cup salad oil
½ cup minced onion
1 tablespoon paprika
¾ cup chili sauce
¼ cup lemon juice
2 cups beef bouillon

Trim all excess fat off the lamb. Spread the meat with Dijon mustard. Sprinkle with flour, salt and pepper. Heat oil in a large heavy frying pan. Over high heat, cook the meat until browned on all sides. Transfer the meat to a casserole. Add the onion to frying pan and stir in paprika. Cook, stirring constantly, for 3 minutes or until onion is soft. Stir in chili sauce and lemon juice. Mix well. Stir in beef bouillon. Bring to boil and pour over the lamb riblets, scraping up all the brown bits at the bottom of the frying pan. Simmer, covered, over low heat for about 1 hour. Check the seasoning; if necessary, add a little more salt and pepper. Six servings.

Wednesday

Pork and Cucumber Stew

Pork and Cucumber Stew
Corn Bread
Creamed and Buttered Cabbage Wedges
Orange Chiffon Cake

2 pounds lean boneless pork, cut into 1½-inch cubes
salt
freshly ground pepper
2 tablespoons salad oil
2 medium onions, thinly sliced
2 garlic cloves, minced
1 cup thinly sliced celery
1 green pepper, cut into strips
1 cup hot water
2 teaspoons dried rosemary, crumbled
2 large cucumbers
½ cup tomato sauce or 1 large tomato, peeled and chopped

Sprinkle the meat with salt and pepper. Heat oil in a large saucepan. Add the pork, in 2 or 3 batches, and over high heat, brown well on all sides. Transfer the pork to a heated dish and keep warm. Add onion, garlic, celery and green pepper to the pan juices. Cook over medium heat, stirring constantly, for about 5 minutes, or until tender. Return the meat to saucepan. Add water and rosemary. Simmer, covered, over low heat for 1½ hours, or until the meat is tender but not overcooked. While the pork is cooking, peel the cucumbers and cut into quarters lengthwise. With a spoon, scoop out the seeds. Cut the cucumber quarters into 1-inch pieces. Add cucumber pieces and tomato sauce to the pork. Check the seasoning and add, if necessary, salt and pepper. Cook for 5 minutes longer or until heated through. Serves four to six.

Thursday

Baked Beef en Casserole

Baked Beef en Casserole
Mashed Potatoes
Green Beans with Mustard
Dried Apricot and Raisin Pie

2 tablespoons butter
2 tablespoons salad oil
2½ pounds stewing beef, fat trimmed off and cut into 1½-inch pieces
2 cups chopped onions
2 garlic cloves, minced
3 tablespoons flour
½ cup chopped celery
1 8-ounce can tomato sauce
1½ cups sour cream
2 tablespoons Worcestershire sauce
2 tablespoons minced parsley

Heat butter and oil in a large frying pan. Over high heat, in small amounts, brown the meat on all sides. Transfer to a deep 3-quart casserole. Add onion and garlic to the frying pan. Cook, stirring constantly, until soft. Stir in flour and cook for 1 minute longer. Add celery, tomato sauce, sour cream and Worcestershire sauce. Mix well. Simmer gently over low heat for 5 minutes. Pour over the meat in the casserole. Cook uncovered in a preheated 325° oven for 1½ hours, or until the meat is tender. Sprinkle with parsley before serving. Makes six servings.

Friday

Manhattan Clam Chowder

Manhattan Clam Chowder
Corn Muffins
Guava Jelly and Cream Cheese
Crackers

¼ lb. salt pork, cut
into very small dice
1 large onion, thinly sliced
½ green pepper, chopped
½ cup diced celery
¼ cup diced carrot
½ cup diced turnip
3 cups diced potatoes
3 cups water
salt
freshly ground pepper
1 pint clams and their liquid
½ teaspoon dried thyme
2 cups tomato juice
2 tablespoons tomato paste
4 tablespoons minced parsley

Cook the salt pork in large, heavy saucepan until crisp. Pour off all but 1 tablespoon of the fat and cook the onion, green pepper, celery, carrots and turnip until soft and golden. Add the potatoes, water and 1 teaspoon salt and pepper to taste. Chop the clams and add them to the soup with their liquid. Add thyme, tomato juice and stir in tomato paste. Bring to boil. Lower the heat and simmer, covered, for 15 minutes or until the potatoes are soft. Sprinkle with parsley before serving. Four to six servings.

Saturday

Green Beans with Mustard Sauce

Frankfurter and Potato Stew
Green Beans with Mustard Sauce
Orange and Onion Salad
Apple Compote and Cookies

1 pound green beans,
cut into 2-inch lengths
2 tablespoons water
2 tablespoons salad or
olive oil
2 egg yolks, at room temperature
1 teaspoon dry mustard
½ cup hot beef bouillon
2 teaspoons vinegar or to taste
salt
freshly ground pepper

Put the beans into a saucepan with a tight-fitting lid; this is essential. Add water and oil. Cover tightly. Cook over very low heat, tossing frequently, for about 10 minutes. Do not uncover the saucepan. The beans should be crisp but tender. In a saucepan, beat together the eggs and mustard. Stir in hot beef bouillon. Cook over very low heat, stirring constantly, until thickened. Stir in vinegar, salt and pepper. Add the beans and toss. Cook over very low heat, stirring all the time, for 3-4 minutes longer, or until the beans are well coated with the sauce. Serve hot. Four servings.

ENTERTAINING

September

Sunday

Crumbed Meat Patties on Tomato Slices

Crumbed Meat Patties on Tomato Slices
Mushrooms Baked in Sour Cream
Hot French Garlic Bread
Cantaloupe Balls in a Sugar Syrup Flavored with Fresh Ginger

2 pounds ground steak
3 tablespoons grated onion
4 tablespoons freshly grated Parmesan cheese
1 large egg, beaten
grated rind of 1 lemon
juice of ½ lemon
¼ cup minced parsley
salt
freshly ground pepper
fine dry bread crumbs
4 tablespoons butter
6 slices large, firm, ripe tomatoes
Boston lettuce

In a bowl combine the meat, onion, Parmesan Cheese, egg, lemon rind and juice, parsley, salt and pepper to taste. Mix thoroughly and shape into flat patties — about 12. Dip the patties on both sides in bread crumbs. Heat butter in a frying pan and cook the patties over moderate heat — 2 to 3 minutes on each side or until crisp. Place 2 patties on top of each other on each tomato slice. Line a serving dish with lettuce leaves and arrange the tomatoes and meat patties on lettuce. Serves six.

Note: This dish is also good lukewarm. Take on picnics, but do not chill.

Monday

Baked Eggplant, Mozzarella, Eggs, and Tomatoes

Baked Eggplant, Mozzarella, Eggs, and Tomatoes
White Dried Bean Salad
Cucumbers Vinaigrette
Fresh Plum Tart

4 small eggplants
salt
2 large ripe but firm tomatoes, peeled and cut into ¼-inch slices
4 anchovies, drained and minced, or to taste
3 hard-cooked eggs, sliced
1 8-to 10-ounce Mozzarella cheese, cut into ¼-inch slices
freshly ground pepper
1 cup parsley sprigs, preferably Italian parsley
¼ cup fresh basil leaves or 2 to 3 tablespoons dried basil
2 garlic cloves
⅓ cup olive oil

Trim stems off and cut eggplants into ¼-inch slices. Sprinkle a little salt on each slice and lay them in a colander. Stand the colander in sink or over a bowl. Let eggplant slices stand at room temperature for about 30 minutes to drain off excess liquid. Blot them dry with paper towels. Spread each tomato slice with a little minced anchovy. In a shallow ovenproof dish that can go to the table, make well-overlapping rows of eggplant, egg slices, tomato and mozzarella slices, in this order. Sprinkle with very little salt (eggplant and anchovies are salty) and pepper. Mince together to a paste the parsley, basil, and garlic cloves. Sprinkle this mixture over the vegetables and cheese and sprinkle with olive oil. Cover the dish with foil tied on with string. Bake in a preheated 350° oven for 30 minutes. Remove the foil and bake for about 10 minutes longer, allowing excessive moisture to evaporate. Serve either hot or cold, but not chilled. Serves three to four.
Note: If you need more servings, it is better to make two separate dishes rather than double the recipe.

Tuesday

Molded Cream Ring Filled with Fresh Fruit Salad

Chicken Liver Appetizers
Poulet a la Creme
Buttered Noodles Polonaise
Peas Cooked with Lettuce
Molded Cream Ring Filled with Fresh Fruit Salad

3 eggs, separated
½ cup superfine sugar
1 teaspoon vanilla flavoring
2 tablespoons (2 envelopes) unflavored gelatin
¼ cup milk
2 cups heavy cream, whipped
sugar
fresh fruit salad

Beat the egg yolks, sugar and vanilla with an electric beater until thick and lemon-colored. Sprinkle the gelatin over milk and dissolve over hot water. Stir into the egg mixture. Whip the egg whites until stiff and glossy. Fold into the egg mixture. Then fold in whipped cream. Rinse a 1½-or 2-quart ring mold with cold water. Sprinkle inside with sugar. Spoon in the cream. Chill until the cream is thoroughly set and cold. Unmold on a platter. Fill the inside of the ring with a colorful fresh fruit salad and arrange some decorative pieces of fruit around the ring. Serves four to six.

Wednesday

Corn Pudding

Smoked Salmon on Toast
Virginia Ham
Corn Pudding
Homemade Cheesecake

2 tablespoons butter
2 tablespoons flour
1 cup light cream or
  Half and Half
2½ cups drained kernel corn
⅓ cup finely diced green pepper
⅓ cup finely diced pimiento
3 eggs, separated
salt
freshly ground pepper
2 slices crispy fried bacon,
  crumbled

Heat butter in a heavy saucepan. Stir in flour. Cook, stirring constantly, for 2 minutes, but do not brown. Stir in cream. Cook, stirring all the time, until the mixture is smooth and thickened. Add the corn, green pepper, and pimiento. Stir to mix well. Remove from heat and beat in the egg yolks, one at a time, beating well after each addition. Season with salt and pepper to taste. Stir in bacon. Beat the egg whites until stiff. Fold into the corn mixture. Turn into a buttered 2-quart baking dish. Cook in a preheated 350° oven for 30 minutes or until golden and puffy. Serve immediately. Serves six.

Thursday

Lemon Beef

Leeks Vinaigrette
Lemon Beef
Barley Pilaf
Buttered Lima Beans
Fresh Peeled Peach in
  Glass of Champagne

4 juicy lemons
4 pounds top round, in one piece
½ cup olive oil
salt
freshly ground pepper
2 cups cold beef bouillon

Cut one of the lemons into thin rounds and squeeze another lemon. Trim fat off meat. Rub meat on all sides with lemon slices and reserve lemon slices. Put meat into a bowl, but do not use aluminum. Combine olive oil and lemon juice. If not tart enough, add more lemon juice. Sprinkle over meat, making sure it is well coated. Arrange half of reserved lemon slices under meat and half on top. Cover bowl and refrigerate for 3 days, turning meat twice a day. Before cooking, drain and dry meat between paper towels; throw away lemon slices but reserve marinade. Put meat into a baking pan and sprinkle lightly with salt and pepper. Roast in a preheated 400° oven for 1½ hours or until tender. Baste every 10 minutes with a little of the marinade and cold beef broth. When meat is ready, slice and keep warm on a heated serving platter. Squeeze remaining 2 lemons. Bring liquid in roasting pan to boil, scraping up the brown bits at the bottom. If too thin, boil it down; if the right consistency for gravy, leave as is. Remove from heat, stir in lemon juice, and check seasoning. There should be only a little gravy since this is not a gravy dish. Sprinkle gravy over meat slices to keep them moist. Serves six to eight.

Note: If you want a less lemony dish, use two or three lemons instead of four, remembering that lemons vary in size and acidity.

Friday

Compote of Fresh Plums

Tomatoes Filled with Herbed Rice
Deep-Fried Scallops
Tartar Sauce
Sautéed Zucchini
Compote of Fresh Plums
Whipped Cream

3 pounds very ripe blue Italian plums, washed and stoned
1 cup sugar, or to taste
1 2-inch stick cinnamon (optional)

Combine the plums, sugar, and cinnamon in a heavy casserole. Cover tightly. Cook in 300° oven for 2 hours or until the plums are cooked and juicy. Chill before serving. Serves six.
Note: This slow cooking in the oven, without water, brings out all the deliciousness of the fruit. Cherries can be cooked in the same way.

Saturday

Cider Breakfast for Eight

Ham Loaf*
Spoon Bread
Poached Apples
Pennsylvania Dutch Coffee Cake*
Served with Butter and Jam
Cider
Coffee Tea Milk

**Recipe in book*

Some of one's friends can be entertained at breakfast very nicely. Children are invited too, of course. Make sure to ask people who are early risers and who have something to say at that hour of the morning.

This is a seated meal, and if you have an attractive kitchen, have it there. Unless you are using one long table, seat the children at their own table. They will finish sooner and make more of a mess. Let them get up to play when they have finished eating.

Set the table or tables for Fall with chrysanthemums or a bowl of polished apples in the center and use bright placemats and napkins. Colorful tablecloths, mats and napkins can be made easily and inexpensively by cutting them out of one large sheet, machine hemming along the edges.

Put a pitcher of cider and a crock of butter on each table. Use hot trays on a side table or counter to keep the foods warm throughout the meal. Make more coffee than you think necessary and make sure that your coffee is strong and very hot. Have both hot milk and cream to go with the coffee.

Saturday

Ham Loaf

1 pound smoked ham, ground
1 pound lean pork, ground
1¼ cups fresh white bread crumbs
¾ cup milk
2 bay leaves, crumbled
1 tablespoon Dijon mustard
¼ teaspoon ground cloves
3 tablespoons dry sherry or Madeira
salt
1 large or 2 small eggs, beaten
1 tablespoon dark brown sugar

Grind the ham and pork *together*. This makes a bettter loaf, but if you obtain it, mix them together thoroughly. Soak 1 cup of bread crumbs in milk. Mix together the meat, bay leaves, mustard, cloves and sherry. Taste for salt; you may need a little, depending on the ham. Stir in the bread crumbs and eggs. Mix thoroughly. Pack the mixture into a 9-or 10-inch loaf pan. Sprinkle the remaining crumbs and the sugar over the mixture. Set the pan into a larger pan with 1 inch of water. Bake for 1¼ to 1½ hours in a preheated 350° oven, or until thoroughly set. Remove from oven and pour off any liquid. Loosen loaf and turn it out on a platter, crumb side up. Let stand for 5 minutes for better slicing or serve cold. Eight servings.

Pennsylvania Dutch Coffee Cake

1 egg
1 cup sugar
1½ teaspoons baking powder
½ teaspoon salt
½ cup sifted brown sugar
sour cream
1½ cups flour
¼ cup butter
1 tablespoon cinnamon

Break the egg into a measuring cup and fill the cup with sour cream to make 1 cup of egg and cream mixture. Sift the flour, sugar, baking powder and salt into a bowl. Add the egg and cream mixture and stir quickly to mix. Do not overstir. Place the dough into a greased and floured 8-or 9-inch pie plate. Dot with butter and sprinkle with brown sugar and cinnamon. Bake in a preheated 350° oven for 25–30 minutes. Serve warm, with butter and jam.

OCTOBER

"Guests, however inconvenient, must be honored," was my parents' motto. But honoring guests now is different than in my parents' time. For one thing, people eat much less and they prefer simple menus and non-restaurant food, because restaurants can't make good home food. Sophisticated restaurant diners love to come to a house where they are served delicious old fashioned boiled dinners, chicken fricassees, corn puddings and blueberry cobbler. A sure-fire way of pleasing guests is to specialize in a few such dishes because then the hostess needs not look further — her guests would be disappointed not to be served her specialties. Guests are also honored by jolly hostesses who have prepared everything beforehand, so that they don't have to come back to their guests with the patient air of a tired saint, because of last-minute fussing in the kitchen.

OCTOBER

FAMILY FARE

	LUNCHES	DINNERS
Sunday	Cheese Soufflé Canadian Bacon Cranberry Cobbler*	Roast Lamb White Beans and Jerusalem Artichokes* Orange and Onion Salad Pumpkin Pie
Monday	Cold Lamb Sandwiches with Chutney Belgian Tomato Salad* Baked Apples	Garlic Chicken with Toast* Carrots Vichy Braised Onions Fresh Fruit Salad and Cookies
Tuesday	Cold Cuts Avocado Coleslaw* Applesauce	Old Fashioned Chicken Fricassee* Dumplings Buttered Lima Beans Prune and Apricot Pie
Wednesday	Scotch Broth* Carrot Sticks Ice Cream	Flank Steak Strips Piquant* Chutney Pilaf Cooked with Bouillon Tossed Green Salad Custard Pie
Thursday	Minestrone Easy Graham Bread* with Jam and Jellies Pears and Grapes	Chicken with Chestnuts and Port* Baked Yams Buttered Broccoli Apple Crisp with Ice Cream
Friday	Tuna, Bean and Onion Salad* Watercress Chocolate Cupcakes	Baked Salmon with Capers* Parsley Potatoes Cucumber Salad Apple Kuchen with Whipped Cream
Saturday	Frittata with Frankfurters* Waldorf Salad Apple Pie	Broiled Marinated Lamb Chops Broiled Fruit Compote* Belgian Endives and Shredded Red Beets Salad Pears, Grapes, Cheese and Crackers

QUICK & EASY Dinners For Two	BUDGET DINNERS	ENTERTAINING
Chicken Breasts with Cream* Polenta Green Beans with Water Chestnuts Pears and Cheese	Roast Chicken Cheese and Potato Pie* Mixed Green Salad Chocolate Mousse	Hot Consommé with Sherry Shrimp Salad Spinach, Mushroom, and Bacon Salad with Tomato Slices Rice Torte*
Cabbage Soup* Hamburgers Sliced Tomatoes Ice Cream with Brandied Fruit Cookies	Beef Stew with Peas* Yellow Rice with Mushrooms Waldorf Salad Jam Cake	Baked Zucchini and Eggs* Cold Roast Chicken and Salad Cheese Tray Apples, Pears, and Grapes
Sausages Wine Mustard* Hot Potato Salad Sautéed Zucchini Plum Pie	Portuguese Green Potato Soup* Marinated Tomatoes French Bread Cheese Tray and Apples and Pears	Hot Cream of Watercress Soup Lemon Grilled Chicken Baked Potatoes Mushrooms Pickled in Wine* Pumpkin Soufflé
Veal with Mushrooms and Peppers* Parsleyed Potatoes Broiled Tomatoes Pound Cake, Ice Cream and Fudge Sauce	Meat Loaf Acorn Squash Filled with Pears* Avocado, Lettuce and Radish Salad Apple Pie	Matrosenfleisch* Buttered Noodles Sprinkled with Toasted Poppy Seeds Brussels Sprouts with Lemon Sauce Watercress and Red Radish Salad Vanilla Ice Cream with Brandied Fruit
Eggs in Anchovy Sauce* Yellow Rice Sautéed Eggplant Green Salad Apple Compote and Cookies	Crumbed Eggs with Tomato Sauce* Green Beans and Scallions French Fried Potatoes Apple Custard Pie	Belgian Endive and Avocado Salad Beef Bourguignon Boiled Potatoes Broccoli Puree Dried Apricot and Fresh Pear Compote* Heavy Cream
Fish Fillets Baked with Herbs* Boiled Potatoes Zucchini Salad Melonballs in Liqueur	Savory Baked Fish a la Grecque* Potato Salad Cucumber Salad Apple Custard and Cookies	Melon with Lime Beef en Daube* Saffron Rice Red and Green Pepper Salad Zucchini Salad with Green Sauce Chocolate Mousse
Spaghetti with Clam and Wine Sauce* Cold Roast Beef Tossed Green Salad Sliced Tomatoes with Mustard Dressing Ice Cream and Cookies	Chicken with Lemon Sauce* Rice Buttered Whole Leaf Spinach Vanilla Ice Cream with Hot Fudge Sauce	Chili Party for Twelve

FAMILY FARE LUNCHES

October

Sunday

Cheese Soufflé
Canadian Bacon
Cranberry Cobbler

Cranberry Cobbler

1½ cups fresh cranberries
1⅓ cups water
1½ cups sugar
1 tablespoon cornstarch
2 tablespoons butter
1 cup flour
2 teaspoons baking powder
½ teaspoon salt
½ teaspoon ground ginger
1 cup milk
grated rind of 1 orange
¼ cup chopped walnuts

Pick over the cranberries, throwing away any that are soft or bruised. Combine the cranberries and water in a saucepan. Cook over high heat for 5 minutes, or until the berries are beginning to burst. Mix 1 cup of sugar with cornstarch and stir into the cranberries. Turn down heat to low. Simmer slowly, stirring frequently, until the berries are thick and syrupy. Turn the cranberries into a 1½-quart deep baking dish. Cream butter with the remaining ½ cup of sugar. Sift together flour, baking powder, salt and ginger. Add to the egg mixture alternately with milk, beginning and ending with flour. Stir in orange rind. Pour the batter over the cranberries. Sprinkle with nuts. Bake in a preheated 350° oven for 30 minutes or until the batter is firm and lightly browned. Serve hot with vanilla ice cream. Serves six.

Monday

Belgian Tomato Salad

Cold Lamb Sandwiches with Chutney
Belgian Tomato Salad
Baked Apples

6 large, firm, ripe tomatoes
salt
freshly ground pepper
6 tablespoons olive oil
2 tablespoons mild vinegar or to taste
2 teaspoons Dijon mustard
2 tablespoons grated onion or shallot
¼ cup minced parsley
¼ teaspoon dried thyme

The tomatoes are vastly improved by this dressing which is also very good on cooked vegetables like green beans, carrots, broccoli. Peel the tomatoes. Plunge them into boiling water for 1 minute. Carefully slip off the peel and cut off the blossom end. Chill the tomatoes before cutting into thin slices. Arrange the slices in a shallow serving dish in overlapping rows. Combine all the remaining ingredients and blend thoroughly. Sprinkle over the tomatoes and refrigerate from 1 to 3 hours. Six servings.

Note: Onion lovers may place a thin slice of onion on each tomato before sprinkling them with the dressing.

Tuesday

Avocado Coleslaw

Cold Cuts
Avocado Coleslaw
Applesauce

1 large ripe avocado
¼ cup lemon juice
3 cups shredded cabbage
¼ cup chopped green pepper
1 tablespoon minced onion
10 radishes
⅓ cup mayonnaise
2 teaspoons ketchup
1 teaspoon salt
dash of Tabasco
salad greens

To ripen an avocado rapidly, place it in the flour canister — after washing and drying or wiping it clean. The darkness and warmth of the canister hastens the ripening process. Peel and cut the avocado into ½-inch cubes. Put into a bowl and sprinkle and toss with lemon juice. Let stand for 15 minutes. Drain. Combine the avocado, cabbage, green pepper and onion in a bowl. Slice 5 radishes and add to the vegetables. Blend together the mayonnaise, ketchup, salt and Tabasco. Pour over the vegetables and toss lightly. Serve in a salad bowl lined with salad greens and garnish with the remaining 5 radishes, cut into halves. Four to six servings.

Wednesday

Scotch Broth

Scotch Broth
Carrot Sticks
Ice Cream

2 pounds neck of lamb
or ribs
8 cups water
½ cup medium barley
1 teaspoon salt
2 large carrots, cut into
½-inch dice
1 medium turnip, cut into
½-inch dice
1 celery stalk, thinly sliced
4 medium onions, cut into quarters
freshly ground pepper

Put the lamb into a deep kettle and add water. Bring to boil. Lower heat, cover and simmer for 1½ hours. Skim whenever needed. Strain the soup and reserve the meat. Chill broth until the fat has risen to the top and solidified. Remove fat and return broth to the kettle. Add barley and salt. Simmer, covered, for 20 minutes or until the barley is half done. While the barley is cooking, cut the meat from the bones and discard them. Cut the meat into ½-inch pieces. Return the meat to the barley broth and add carrots, turnip, celery and onions. Taste the seasoning and add more salt and pepper. Simmer, covered, for 30 minutes to 1 hour until the vegetables are tender. Six servings.

Thursday

Easy Graham Bread

Minestrone
Easy Graham Bread
with Jam and Jellies
Pears and Grapes

1½ cups graham flour, unsifted
2 cups unbleached white flour
2 teaspoons baking soda
1 teaspoon salt
½ cup light brown sugar
½ cup molasses or honey
2 cups buttermilk

This bread has a chewy texture and an excellent homemade flavor. Measure the graham flour by spooning it into a cup; do not sift it. Sift together the white flour, baking soda, salt and brown sugar. Add the graham flour and stir to blend. Add the molasses or honey and buttermilk. Stir thoroughly to blend. The batter will be heavy. Grease 1 9 × 5-inch or 2 7 × 3-inch loaf pans. Spoon in the batter. Bake in a preheated 350° oven for 1 hour 10 minutes. Turn out onto racks to cool. Makes one 9 × 5-inch loaf.

Friday

Tuna, Bean and Onion Salad

Tuna, Bean and Onion Salad
Watercress
Chocolate Cupcakes

3 cups canned cannelini or other white beans
½ medium red onion, thinly sliced
6 tablespoons olive oil
2 tablespoons vinegar
1 teaspoon salt
freshly ground pepper
½ teaspoon ground marjoram
2 7-ounce cans tuna, drained
½ cup minced parsley

Drain the beans and put them into a strainer. Run cold water through them until the water runs clear. Drain on paper towels. Combine the beans and onion in a salad bowl. Pour oil and vinegar over the beans and season with salt, pepper and marjoram. Toss gently with a fork. Marinate at room temperature for 2 hours. Drain the tuna and break into bite-size chunks. Place on top of the beans and sprinkle with parsley. Makes four to six servings.

Saturday

Frittata with Frankfurters

Frittata with Frankfurters
Waldorf Salad
Apple Pie

6 tablespoons butter
1 medium onion, thinly sliced
½ green pepper, minced
4 frankfurters, cut into very thin rounds
6 eggs, beaten
½ cup grated Parmesan cheese
salt
freshly ground pepper
2 tablespoons minced parsley or dill weed

Heat butter in a large, heavy frying pan and cook the onion and pepper for 3 minutes or until soft. Add the frankfurters. Cook over low heat, stirring frequently, for 5 minutes or until the frankfurters are golden brown. Add the eggs, Parmesan, salt and pepper to taste and parsley. Mix well. Cook until the eggs are set. Cut into wedges and serve immediately. Makes four servings.

FAMILY FARE DINNERS

October

Sunday

Roast Lamb
White Beans and Jerusalem Artichokes
Orange and Onion Salad
Pumpkin Pie

White Beans and Jerusalem Artichokes

2 pounds Jerusalem artichokes
salted water
2 tablespoons olive oil
1 garlic clove, minced
¼ cup minced parsley
2 teaspoons dried basil
1 cup chopped fresh tomatoes or canned tomatoes, drained
salt
freshly ground pepper
1 1-pound 4-ounce can cannelini beans drained or 1 pound Great Northern white beans, cooked and drained

Jerusalem artichokes are not related to the usual globe artichokes. They are knotty tubers which grow underground and are dug up in the fall, winter and spring. Their flavor is distinctive and excellent with beans. Scrub the Jerusalem artichokes with a brush to remove any dirt. Pare the skin as you would peel a potato. Place the artichokes into a saucepan with salted water to cover. Bring to boil. Lower heat. Simmer, covered, for 5 minutes or until easily pierced with a knife. Drain and cool. Cut into ½-inch slices. Heat oil in a large, deep frying pan and cook garlic, parsley and basil for 2 minutes. Add tomatoes and season with salt and pepper. Cook over medium heat, stirring frequently, for about 5-10 minutes. Add beans and Jerusalem artichokes. Mix together gently with a fork and simmer until thoroughly heated through. Six servings.

Monday

Garlic Chicken with Toast

Garlic Chicken with Toast
Carrots Vichy
Braised Onions
Fresh Fruit Salad and Cookies

¼ cup salad oil
1 large onion, diced
2 large carrots, sliced
4 celery stalks, sliced
2 2½-to 3-pound chickens, cut into pieces (no backs)
salt
freshly ground pepper
juice of 2 lemons
20 to 30 garlic cloves, peeled and left whole
6 slices buttered or fried toast

Heat oil in a frying pan and cook, stirring constantly, the onion, carrots and celery until soft. With a slotted spoon, transfer the vegetables to a casserole with a tight-fitting lid or to a clay pot. Remove any fat from chicken pieces and if desired, skin them. Lay the chicken pieces on top of vegetables. Sprinkle with salt, pepper and lemon juice. Put the garlic around and on the chicken pieces. Cover tightly; *this is essential,* because the chickens must cook in their own juices. Cook in a preheated 350° oven for 1 hour. Do not uncover during cooking or until ready to serve. Serve each dinner with some of the garlic and a slice of buttered toast. The garlic is to be mashed with a fork and spread on the buttered toast. Serves six.

Note: In spite of the large number of garlic cloves, this dish is fragrant rather than offensive.

Tuesday

Old Fashioned Chicken Fricassee

Old Fashioned Chicken Fricassee
Dumplings
Buttered Lima Beans
Prune and Apricot Pie

1 4-5 pound roasting or stewing chicken, cut into pieces
well flavored chicken broth
6-8 celery stalks with green tops, cut into pieces
½ medium onion
2 teaspoons salt
4 tablespoons butter
3 tablespoons flour
1 cup light or heavy cream
¼ cup minced parsley

Remove all excess fat from chicken pieces and put into a large, heavy saucepan. Add enough chicken bouillon to cover. Add celery and onion. Bring to boil and skim. Lower heat. Simmer, covered, over very low heat for about 1 hour. Add salt. Continue to simmer until chicken is tender but not overcooked. A roasting chicken will take about 1½ hours, a stewing chicken may take as long as 3 hours. Test for doneness with a skewer. When chicken is cooked, transfer to a heated serving dish and keep hot in a low oven. Skim the fat off the broth and strain it into another saucepan. Cook it down to 1½ cups, skimming off fat as the broth cooks. Heat butter and stir in flour. Cook stirring constantly, for 2 minutes. Combine the chicken stock and cream and stir into butter mixture. Cook, stirring all the time, until sauce is thick and smooth. Set in a pan of hot water over medium heat, and cook for 10 minutes longer, stirring frequently. This is to remove any raw flour taste. Pour the sauce over chicken pieces and sprinkle with parsley. Serves six.

Wednesday

Flank Steak Piquant

Flank Steak Piquant
Chutney
Pilaf Cooked with Bouillon
Tossed Green Salad
Custard Pie

1 large flank steak weighing 2-3 pounds pounded thin
flour
3 tablespoons olive oil
1 large onion, thinly sliced
1 garlic clove, minced
1 teaspoon ground thyme
½ teaspoon ground ginger
½ teaspoon curry powder or more to taste
hot beef bouillon
salt
dash of Tabasco

Cut the steak against the grain into 2-inch wide strips and coat with flour, shaking off excess. Heat oil in a large deep frying pan or in a casserole; it must have a tight fitting lid. Add the onion, garlic, thyme, ginger and curry powder. Cook, stirring constantly, for 3-4 minutes or until the onion is soft. Add just enough hot bouillon to cover the meat; the amount depends on the size of the cooking pan used. Season with salt and Tabasco, cover tightly and transfer to a preheated 325° oven. Cook for 1 hour or until the meat is tender. Check for moisture; if necessary, add a little more hot bouillon, 2 tablespoons at a time, but do not raise the liquid level.

Thursday

Chicken with Chestnuts and Port

Chicken with Chestnuts and Port
Baked Yams
Buttered Broccoli
Apple Crisp with Ice Cream

2 pounds chestnuts in shells
2 tablespoons butter
2 tablespoons oil
2 2½-to 3-pound frying chickens, cut into pieces (no backs)
salt
freshly ground pepper
juice of 1 lemon
½ cup boiling water
3 cups chicken bouillon
1 tablespoon cornstarch
1 cup port wine

To peel the chestnuts: Put into a deep saucepan, add enough cold water to reach 1 inch above the chestnuts, cover and bring to boil. Turn off heat. Remove nuts 3 or 4 at a time and peel with a sharp knife. Keep the saucepan with remaining nuts covered. Remove the outer shell and the inner skin. As long as the chestnuts stay warm and wet they will peel easily. Reserve the chestnuts. Heat butter and oil in a large deep frying pan and cook chicken pieces until golden brown on all sides. Sprinkle the meat with salt, pepper and lemon juice. Add the water and cover pan tightly. Simmer, over very low heat, for 40-50 minutes or until tender. As the chickens are cooking, combine chestnuts and chicken bouillon in a saucepan. Cover and simmer over medium heat for 15-20 minutes or until chestnuts are tender but keeping their shape. Do not overcook. Drain into another saucepan, reserving chestnuts. Over high heat, cook chicken bouillon down to 2 cups. Stir cornstarch into port wine to make a smooth mixture and stir into chicken bouillon. Cook over slow heat, stirring constantly, until sauce is glossy and thickened. Place chicken on a deep serving platter and garnish with chestnuts. Pour sauce over chicken, but not over the chestnuts. Serves four to six.

Friday

Baked Salmon with Capers

Baked Salmon with Capers
Parsley Potatoes
Cucumber Salad
Apple Kuchen with Whipped Cream

6 salmon steaks, about 1½ inches thick
½ cup fresh lemon juice
⅔ cup melted butter
salt
freshly ground pepper
¼ cup dry vermouth or dry white wine or dry sherry
⅓ cup chopped capers
¼ cup minced parsley

Rub the salmon steaks with some of the lemon juice and coat them on both sides with some of the butter, using a pastry brush. Season with salt and pepper. Place fish side by side in a baking dish. Combine remaining lemon juice and melted butter. Cook fish in a preheated 425° oven for about 20 minutes, basting it every 5 minutes with lemon butter. Do not turn. Place cooked fish on a heated serving platter. Stir vermouth, wine or sherry into the pan juices. Stir in capers and parsley. Bring quickly to boil and pour over the salmon steaks. Serves six.

Note: This dish can be made with any thick fish steaks. Adjust the baking time according to the fish, though 20 minutes is a good average.

Saturday

Broiled Fruit Compote

Broiled Marinated Lamb Chops
Broiled Fruit Compote
Belgian Endives and Shredded Red Beets Salad
Pears, Grapes, Cheese and Crackers

1 1-pound package mixed dried fruit
2 large grapefruits, in sections
2 large oranges, in sections
2 large bananas, cut into ¼-inch slices
1 8-ounce can pineapple chunks in juice
½ cup light brown sugar, firmly packed
1 teaspoon ground nutmeg

Simmer the dried fruit in water to cover until soft. Drain. In a buttered shallow baking dish, and in one layer, arrange the fruits as follows: put the grapefruit and orange sections in 1 or 2 overlapping rows around the edges of the baking dish. Follow with a layer of the banana slices. Place the cooked dried fruit in the center of the dish. Sprinkle the pineapple chunks and their juice over the other fruit. Then sprinkle brown sugar and nutmeg over all the fruit. Broil about 4 inches away from the heat until the fruit is bubbly and glazed. Make sure the sugar does not burn. Serve hot. Makes four to six servings.

QUICK & EASY DINNERS FOR TWO

October

Sunday

Chicken Breasts with Cream

Chicken Breasts with Cream
Polenta
Green Beans with Water Chestnuts
Pears and Cheese

1 large chicken breast, halved
1 tablespoon butter
1 tablespoon salad oil
2 tablespoons minced shallots or onions
2 tablespoons water or dry white wine
2 tablespoons brandy (optional)
¼ cup heavy cream
1 egg yolk
salt
freshly ground pepper
juice of ½ lemon
2 tablespoons minced parsley

Remove the skin and excess fat from the chicken breast halves. Wash and dry. Heat butter and oil in a heavy frying pan. Over moderate heat, cook the chicken breasts for 5 minutes, turning once, or until golden. Push the meat to one side and add shallots. Cook, stirring constantly, until shallots are soft. Mix them with the chicken breasts. Add water or wine. Cover and cook over low heat 5 more minutes, or until just tender; cooking time depends on the size of the breasts. Transfer to a hot serving dish and keep hot. Add brandy to the pan juices and scrape up the brown bits at the bottom. Bring to a quick boil. Beat together the cream and egg. Add to the pan juices. Over low heat, simmer for 2-3 minutes or until heated through. Season with salt and pepper. Stir in lemon juice. Pour sauce over the chicken breasts and sprinkle with parsley.

Monday

Cabbage Soup

Cabbage Soup
Hamburgers
Sliced Tomatoes
Ice Cream with Brandied Fruit
Cookies

½ head (about ½ pound) cabbage, shredded
1 celery stalk, diced
1 carrot, diced
1 leek, sliced
1 turnip, diced
5 slices bacon *or* a small ham bone
salt
freshly ground pepper
¼ teaspoon ground thyme
freshly grated Parmesan cheese

Wash and drain all the vegetables into a heavy saucepan. Add enough cold water to cover and reach 2 inches above the vegetables. Add bacon and season with salt, pepper and thyme. Bring to boil. Lower heat, cover and simmer over very low heat for 30 minutes. Check the moisture; for a thinner soup add a little more hot water, 2 tablespoons at a time. For a stew-like soup, cook uncovered. Remove bacon or ham bone before serving with grated Parmesan.

Note: Leftover soup may be pureed in the blender. Add about 3 cups milk or enough milk for desired consistency and heat through but do not boil. Check the seasonings.

Tuesday

Wine Mustard

Sausages
Wine Mustard
Hot Potato Salad
Sautéed Zucchini
Plum Pie

Use as a cocktail spread or for meat sandwiches, corned beef and sausages. Blend together dry mustard and enough dry white wine to make a creamy mixture. Cover and let stand for at least 30 minutes to let the flavors mellow.

Wednesday

Veal with Mushrooms and Peppers

Veal with Mushrooms and Peppers
Parsleyed Potatoes
Broiled Tomatoes
Pound Cake, Ice Cream and Fudge Sauce

4 tablespoons olive oil
½ pound boneless veal, trimmed and cut into 2-inch strips
2 sweet green or red peppers, trimmed and cut into strips
½ pound mushrooms, sliced
salt
freshly ground pepper
1 to 1½ cups chopped fresh tomatoes or canned Italian tomatoes
½ teaspoon oregano

Heat olive oil in a casserole. Add veal. Cook over medium heat, stirring constantly, for about 2 minutes. Add the peppers and mushrooms. Cook, stirring constantly, for 2 more minutes. Season with salt and pepper. Stir in tomatoes and oregano. Simmer, covered, for about 15 minutes, stirring occasionally.

Thursday

Eggs in Anchovy Sauce

Eggs in Anchovy Sauce
Yellow Rice
Sautéed Eggplant
Green Salad
Apple Compote and Cookies

2 tablespoons butter
1 tablespoon flour
1 cup milk or ½ cup milk and ½ cup light cream or Half and Half
1 tablespoon anchovy paste
cayenne or Tabasco to taste
4 hard-cooked eggs, coarsely chopped
salt

Heat butter and stir in the flour. Cook, stirring constantly, for 1 minute. Stir in milk or cream mixture. Cook, stirring all the time, until the sauce is smooth and thickened. Stir in the anchovy paste and cayenne. Cook for 1 minute longer. Add eggs and if necessary, season with salt. Simmer over very low heat for about 3 minutes. Serve on hot buttered toast or rice.

Friday

Fish Fillets Baked with Herbs

Fish Fillets Baked with Herbs
Boiled Potatoes
Zucchini Salad
Melonballs in Liqueur

1 pound fish fillets, fresh or thawed and dried
salt
freshly ground pepper
⅓ cup minced parsley
2 tablespoons minced basil *or* 1 tablespoon minced fresh thyme *or* rosemary
juice of ½ lemon
¼ cup fine dry bread crumbs
¼ cup olive oil
lemon wedges

Oil a shallow baking pan and spread the fish in it in a single layer. Season lightly with salt and pepper. Sprinkle parsley and the herb over the fish. Sprinkle lemon juice over the herb. Top with bread crumbs. Drizzle olive oil over the bread crumbs. Bake uncovered in a preheated 350° oven for 10-15 minutes or until the fish flakes and the top is crisp. Serve with lemon wedges.

Saturday

Spaghetti with Clam and Wine Sauce

Spaghetti with Clam and Wine Sauce
Cold Roast Beef
Tossed Green Salad
Sliced Tomatoes with Mustard Dressing
Ice Cream and Cookies

2 tablespoons olive oil
1 tablespoon butter
2 tablespoons minced onion
1 small garlic clove, mashed
½ cup minced parsley
1 8-ounce can minced clams
½ cup dry white or red wine
salt
freshly ground pepper
½ lb. thin spaghetti, freshly cooked al dente and well drained
freshly grated Parmesan cheese

Heat olive oil and butter together. Add the onion, garlic clove and parsley. Cook, stirring constantly, for 2-3 minutes. Add the clams and wine. Cook over medium heat for 3-4 minutes or until the sauce is hot and a little reduced. Check the salt and season with pepper. Put the spaghetti into a deep hot serving dish. Add the sauce and toss. Sprinkle with some grated Parmesan cheese and serve some more on the side.

BUDGET DINNERS

October

Sunday

Cheese and Potato Pie

Roast Chicken
Cheese and Potato Pie
Mixed Green Salad
Chocolate Mousse

4 tablespoons butter, at room temperature
4 medium potatoes (a little over a pound)
salt
freshly ground pepper
1 cup shredded Swiss cheese
3 tablespoons grated onion
2 eggs
1 cup milk
dash of Tabasco
¾ teaspoon dry mustard
2 tablespoons minced parsley

Grease the bottom and sides of a 9-inch deep pie pan with 2 tablespoons of butter. Peel the potatoes. Shred them on the coarse side of a grater. Drain them well and squeeze them dry on a paper towel. Spread the potatoes in the pie pan. Sprinkle with 1 tablespoon of salt and a little pepper. Press the potatoes onto the bottom and sides of the pie pan to form a shell. Spread the cheese over the potatoes. Dot with remaining butter and drizzle with grated onion. Beat eggs with milk, about ¼ teaspoon salt, Tabasco, mustard and parsley. Pour over the cheese in the potato shell. Bake in a preheated 375° oven for 40–50 minutes or until the pie is set, golden brown at the edges and tests clean. Let stand for 5 minutes before cutting. Six servings.

Monday

Beef Stew with Peas

Beef Stew with Peas
Yellow Rice with Mushrooms
Waldorf Salad
Jam Cake

3 tablespoons butter
1 large onion, minced
½ cup minced parsley
2 pounds boneless chuck, all fat trimmed off, cut into 1½-inch pieces
2 tablespoon flour
salt
freshly ground pepper
1 teaspoon ground cumin
½ teaspoon curry powder
1¾ cups hot water
grated rind of 1 lemon
2 10-ounce packages frozen peas, thawed and drained
juice of 1 lemon (optional)

This is an adaptation of a recipe from Morocco. Heat butter in a large, heavy saucepan or casserole and cook the onion and parsley until the onion is soft and golden. Add the beef. Over high heat, stirring constantly, brown the beef on all sides. Reduce heat to medium. Stir in flour, a little salt and pepper, cumin and curry powder. Cook, stirring all the time, 3 minutes longer. Reduce heat to very low. Add water and lemon rind. Mix well. Simmer, covered, for 1 hour and 30 minutes or until the beef is tender. Add the peas and cook for 5 minutes longer. Remove from heat and stir in lemon juice. Serves six.

Tuesday

Portuguese Green Potato Soup

Portuguese Green Potato Soup
Marinated Tomatoes
French Bread
Cheese Tray and Apples and Pears

8 cups boiling water *or* 8 cups boiling chicken or beef bouillon
4 large potatoes, peeled and cut into 1-inch cubes
salt
freshly ground pepper
1 pound fresh greens, shredded (spinach, kale, lettuce, dandelions, etc.)
½ pound mild or hot Polish or Italian sausage

Put water or bouillon into a large saucepan and cook potatoes until tender. Season with salt and pepper; but go easy on the salt since the bouillon and sausage may be salty. Drain the potatoes and reserve broth. Coarsely mash the potatoes with a fork or a potato masher and return to the broth. Do not use a blender because blenders plasticize potatoes. Bring to boil and add the greens. Lower heat to medium and cook for about 3-5 minutes, until the greens are barely tender. Check the seasoning. While the potatoes are cooking, cook the sausage by either simmering in water or frying in a pan over low heat. Make sure the sausage is cooked through. Slice the sausage and add to the soup. Serve hot. Serves four to six.

Wednesday

Acorn Squash Filled with Pears

Meat Loaf
Acorn Squash Filled with Pears
Avocado, Lettuce and Radish Salad
Apple Pie

3 large acorn squash
¼ cup butter
2 medium onions, minced
salt
freshly ground pepper
½ teaspoon ground ginger
½ teaspoon ground mace
3 tablespoons light or dark brown sugar
3 tablespoons Bourbon whiskey or water
2 large pears, peeled, cored and cut into ¼-inch dice

Cut the squash into halves lengthwise and remove the seeds. Place the squash halves side by side in a baking dish, open side up. Pour 1 inch of water into the baking dish. Cover with foil. Bake in a preheated 400° oven for 25-30 minutes or until the squash is three quarters done. While it is baking, heat butter in a frying pan and cook the onion until soft and golden. Season with a little salt and pepper. Stir in ginger, mace, sugar and Bourbon. Cook stirring constantly, for 3 minutes. Remove the foil and fill the squash halves with the pear mixture. Cover again and bake for 10 minutes longer. Makes six servings.

Thursday

Crumbed Eggs with Tomato Sauce

Crumbed Eggs with Tomato Sauce
Green Beans and Scallions
French Fried Potatoes
Apple Custard Pie

8 hard-cooked eggs
1 3½-ounce can shrimp, drained and chopped
salt
1 teaspoon dry mustard
dash of Tabasco
approximately 2 cups fine dry bread crumbs
2 eggs
1 tablespoon water
⅓ cup melted butter
2 cups tomato sauce

Shell the eggs and cut into halves lengthwise. Scoop out the yolks. Mash them to a smooth paste with the shrimp, a little salt, mustard and Tabasco. Fill the halves with the mixture. Put the egg halves together again to form whole eggs. Carefully roll each egg first in some of the crumbs, then dip it in the beaten eggs and one tablespoon water and roll it again in crumbs. Place the crumbed eggs in a buttered shallow baking dish. Sprinkle with melted butter. Bake in a preheated 350° oven for 20 minutes or until crisp and golden. Serve with tomato sauce on the side. Makes four to six servings.

Friday

Savory Baked Fish a la Grecque

Savory Baked Fish a la Grecque
Potato Salad
Cucumber Salad
Apple Custard and Cookies

2 pounds firm white fish such as cod, halibut or haddock *or*
2 pounds frozen fish fillets, drained and dried
salt
freshly ground pepper
2 tablespoons fresh lemon juice
⅓ cup olive oil
4 medium onions, thinly sliced
1-2 garlic cloves, minced
1 cup minced parsley
3 tomatoes, peeled and chopped
¼ cup water or dry white wine
2 tomatoes, sliced
1 lemon, thinly sliced

Sprinkle fish with salt, pepper and lemon juice. Heat olive oil in a deep frying pan. Add onions, garlic and parsley. Cook, stirring constantly, for 3 minutes or until onion is soft. Add tomatoes and water or wine. Cook, stirring constantly, for about 3 minutes longer. Spread half of the sauce on the bottom of a shallow baking dish. Top with fish and top the fish with the remaining sauce. Arrange the tomato and lemon slices in overlapping rows on top of the fish. Bake in a preheated 350° oven for 30 minutes or until the fish flakes. If the fish looks dry while baking, add a little more hot water or bouillon, 2 tablespoons at a time. Serve hot or cool, but not chilled. Serves six.

Saturday

Chicken with Lemon Sauce

Chicken with Lemon Sauce
Rice
Buttered Whole Leaf Spinach
Vanilla Ice Cream with Hot Fudge Sauce

1 4-pound chicken or 2 2½-pound fryers, cut into pieces (no backs) or 3 pounds chicken pieces
6 tablespoons butter
salt
freshly ground pepper
1 cup hot water
6 bunches spring onions, well washed, white and green parts cut into 1½-inch pieces
grated rind of 1 lemon
2 eggs, well beaten
juice of 1 lemon
¼ cup minced parsley

Cut all fat off chicken pieces and if desired, remove the skins. Heat butter in a large heavy saucepan and cook chicken pieces until golden on all sides. Sprinkle with salt and pepper. Add hot water and scallions. Simmer, covered, over low heat for 35-45 minutes or until the chicken is tender. Beat together the lemon rind, egg yolks, and lemon juice. Drain about ½ cup broth from the saucepan with the chicken. Stir it into the egg mixture, beating to prevent curdling. Lower the heat under the chicken to lowest possible. Stir the egg mixture into the chicken. Stir vigorously for 1 minute to prevent curdling and do not allow to boil. Remove immediately from heat and sprinkle with parsley. Makes four to six servings.

ENTERTAINING

October

Sunday

Rice Torte

Hot Consommé with Sherry
Shrimp Salad
Spinach, Mushroom, and Bacon Salad with Tomato Slices
Rice Torte

½ cup long-grain or Italian rice (do not use instant or converted rice)
4 cups milk
the yellow peel of 1 lemon, cut in one long twist
½ cup finely diced candied orange peel
½ cup finely diced candied lemon peel
½ cup finely diced candied citron
½ cup brandy, Curacao, rum, or other liqueur
6 eggs, beaten
¾ cup sugar
½ cup shredded blanched almonds
1 teaspoon almond extract
fine dry bread crumbs
sifted confectioners' sugar

Combine rice, milk, and lemon rind in the top of a double boiler. Cook over boiling water, stirring frequently, until rice is very soft and has almost absorbed the milk. There should be just a little moisture left, so that the rice will stay moist in the cooling. Remove the lemon rind and throw it away. Cool. While the rice is cooling, put the orange, lemon, and citron peels into a small bowl and pour liqueur over them. Mix well. When the rice has cooled, beat in the eggs, the sugar, candied peels and their liquid, almonds and almond flavoring. Butter a 9-inch square or round baking dish or spring-form pan generously and sprinkle the bottom and the sides with bread crumbs. Turn the rice mixture into it. Bake in a preheated 300° oven for 1 hour or until a skewer inserted in the middle of the torte comes out clean. Cool the torte; it may be refrigerated or kept in the breadbox. Before serving, place a paper lace doily on it and sprinkle confectioners' sugar through the doily to make a pattern. Cut the torte into small helpings and serve with a dessert wine, such as port, Barsac, cream sherry, or Asti Spumante. Makes one nine-inch cake.

Monday

Baked Zucchini and Eggs

Baked Zucchini and Eggs
Cold Roast Chicken and Salad
Cheese Tray
Apples, Pears, and Grapes

8 large zucchini
salt
¼ cup olive oil
6 tablespoons butter
1 large onion, thinly sliced
3 slices white bread, crusts removed, soaked in milk and mashed
or
½ cup plain yogurt
4 eggs, beaten
⅓ cup freshly grated Parmesan cheese
⅓ cup minced parsley
3 tablespoons minced fresh marjoram or 2 teaspoons dried marjoram
freshly ground pepper
2 cups fine dry bread crumbs

Wash and trim zucchini, but do not peel. Cut into quarters lengthwise, and if very large, halve the quarters. Scrape off seeds with a sharp spoon. Cut strips into ¾-inch pieces. Lay the zucchini pieces on a clean kitchen towel on the counter. Sprinkle with salt, but not too heavily. Tie the four ends of kitchen towel together and hang over sink or put in a colander standing in the sink or in a dish. Let stand for about 30 minutes. The zucchini will start losing their moisture. Squeeze and twist towel to extract as much moisture as possible; you will be surprised how much there is — this is the secret of this dish. In a large, deep frying pan heat olive oil and 4 tablespoons of butter and cook onion until soft but still white. Add zucchini and cook, stirring frequently, over medium heat for about 7 minutes. Cool. Stir in bread or yogurt. Stir in eggs, Parmesan cheese, parsley, and marjoram. Check the seasoning — the zucchini may have enough salt in them — and add pepper. Blend mixture thoroughly. Coat a 12-inch baking dish lightly with olive oil and sprinkle with ½ cup bread crumbs. Turn the vegetable mixture into the dish. Sprinkle with remaining bread crumbs and dot with remaining 2 tablespoons of butter. Bake in a preheated 350° oven for 30 minutes or until well set. Serve, cut into slices, warm or cool, but never chilled. Serves six.

Tuesday

Mushrooms Pickled in Wine

Hot Cream of Watercress Soup
Lemon Grilled Chicken
Baked Potatoes
Mushrooms Pickled in Wine
Pumpkin Soufflé

2 cups dry white wine
1 cup olive oil
1 medium onion, minced
yellow rind of 2 lemons
6 whole cloves
1 tablespoon dried thyme or savory
4 bay leaves
12 whole peppercorns
1 teaspoon salt
2 pounds mushrooms, thickly sliced or quartered
2 tablespoons lemon juice
½ cup minced parsley

Combine the wine, olive oil, onion, lemon rind, cloves, thyme or savory, bay leaves, peppercorns, and salt in a saucepan. Bring to boil. Reduce heat to very low and simmer, covered, for 10 minutes. Strain into another large saucepan and bring back to simmering. Add the mushrooms. Simmer for 5 to 10 minutes (depending on the size of the mushrooms) until tender but still firm. Turn into a serving dish and chill. Before serving, pour off what is left of the marinade and stir in lemon juice. Sprinkle with parsley. Serves six.

Wednesday

Matrosenfleisch

Matrosenfleisch
Buttered Noodles Sprinkled with Toasted Poppy Seeds
Brussels Sprouts with Lemon Sauce
Watercress and Red Radish Salad
Vanilla Ice Cream with Brandied Fruit

3 pounds boneless sirloin
¼ cup lard or bacon fat
3 medium onions, thinly sliced
¼ teaspoon sugar
¼ cup cider vinegar
salt
freshly ground pepper
1 large garlic clove, mashed
2 bay leaves, crumbled
¼ teaspoon ground thyme
¼ cup butter
3 medium carrots, shredded
3 celery stalks, shredded
1 cup dry red wine
⅓ cup fine dry bread crumbs
½ cup hot water
⅓ cup capers

This dish sounds humbler than it is. Cut the meat into slices that are ¼ inch thick, 1 inch wide and 3 inches long. Heat lard in a large saucepan. Add onions, sprinkle sugar over the onions and cook them, stirring constantly, until soft and golden. Sprinkle vinegar over the onions. Add the meat and season with salt and pepper. Add the garlic, bay leaves, and thyme. Mix well and simmer, covered, over low heat until the meat is half tender. Cooking time will be about 10 minutes, depending on the meat. In another saucepan heat butter and cook the carrots and celery until they are soft. Add wine and cook for about 2 minutes longer. Add to the meat and stir in bread crumbs. Add water, stir and simmer, covered, for about 10 minutes or until the meat is tender. The sauce should be medium thick; if necessary, add a little more water to thin or a few more bread crumbs to thicken. Stir in capers and serve immediately. Serves six.

Thursday

Dried Apricot and Fresh Pear Compote

Belgian Endive and Avocado Salad
Beef Bourguignon
Boiled Potatoes
Broccoli Puree
Dried Apricot and Fresh Pear Compote
Heavy Cream

1 pound dried apricots
¼ cup cognac
4 large, firm pears
orange juice
sugar to taste
½ cup sliced blanched almonds

Soak apricots in cold water to cover, add cognac, and let stand for 24 hours. Since the apricots will not be cooked, they must be very soft, as if cooked. Not cooking them preserves their flavor. Peel and core pears and quarter them; if very large, cut into eighths. Drain the apricots and measure their liquid. Add enough orange juice to make 4 cups. Bring to boil and lower heat. Poach the pears, a few pieces at a time, until just soft. Transfer the cooked pears to a glass serving dish. Add the apricots to the pears. Add sugar to taste to the poaching liquid. Bring to boil and cook until reduced by about one-third. Pour the boiling juice over fruit. Chill thoroughly. Before serving, sprinkle with almonds. Serve with heavy cream. Serves six.

Friday

Beef en Daube

Melon with Lime
Beef en Daube
Saffron Rice
Red and Green Pepper Salad
Zucchini Salad with Green Sauce
Chocolate Mousse

4 pounds lean beef, such as bottom round
¼ cup fresh marjoram, leaves only
¼ cup fresh basil, leaves only
¼ cup fresh thyme, leaves only
¼ cup parsley heads
1 large garlic clove
12 slices bacon
8 medium onions, quartered
4 large carrots, sliced
salt
freshly ground pepper
2 ounces dried mushrooms, soaked in water to tenderize
8 bay leaves
1 cup port wine
1 cup dry red wine
1 tablespoon butter
1 pound mushrooms, quartered
¼ cup cognac
2 tablespoons flour

The secret is long, slow cooking in a tightly covered pot. Fresh herbs make all the difference. Trim every bit of fat, nerve, and gristle from meat; it is important that the meat be absolutely fat-free. Cut into 2-inch cubes. Mince together marjoram, basil, thyme, parsley, and garlic. Line a 4- or 5-quart heavy casserole with bacon slices. Scatter half of the onions, carrots, and herbs over it. Add meat and season with salt and pepper. Scatter remaining onions over meat and add dried mushrooms and their liquid and bay leaves. Add the port and red wine. Cover casserole with a sheet of aluminum foil tightly tied and cover foil with the lid of the casserole. It is essential that no steam escape during cooking time. Place casserole on middle shelf of a preheated 275° oven. Cook for 5 hours without lifting lid or foil. During last 10 minutes of cooking time heat butter in a heavy frying pan and cook quartered mushrooms over high heat, stirring constantly, for 5 to 7 minutes or until they have yielded their liquid and are dry. Pour cognac over mushrooms and flame. Stir in flour and coat mushrooms. Remove from heat. Untie the daube and stir in mushrooms. Let stand in oven for 5 more minutes before serving. Serves eight.

Saturday

Chili Party for Twelve

Chili Con Queso Dip, with Corn Crisps*
Bob Holleron's Chili Con Carne*
Mexican Rice
Refried Beans (Frijoles)*
Salsa (Uncooked Hot Tomato and Chili Pepper Sauce)*
Guacamole*
Almond Bavarian   Fresh Fruit Salad
Cookies
Drinks: Imported Beer, Preferably Mexican

A Chili Party is an excellent way of entertaining a group, especially one of sophisticated guests who yearn for a change from fancy French cooking. A well made chili is seldom found in restaurants. It is not a difficult dish to make, but one that requires careful preparation which can be quite lengthy, such as preparation of the meat. It may be made ahead of time and reheated, but not too often, because as in any stew (and chili is basically a stew) the meat must not be mushy. A proper chili does not use hamburger-ground meat. In Texas, you can buy a coarse grind of meat called Chili-ground hamburger, but even at that, it is best to cut the meat into ¼ to ½-inch cubes.

Chili Con Carne is not a Mexican dish, but a Tex-Mex one. Thanks to their proximity to the border and their liking for hot foods, the Texans have evolved a cuisine of their own based originally on Mexican cooking. Notwithstanding some opinions, a proper Chili Con Carne should not contain beans; these are served on the side, preferably re-fried, as in the following recipe.

A Chili party can contain more Tex-Mex and Mexican dishes, such as tacos, enchiladas and the like. But experience has shown to the authors that this is not necessary since guests prefer to concentrate on the chili proper. Unless one knows how hot a dish guests can tolerate, it is better not to make too hot a chili. A bottle of Tabasco or any other hot pepper sauce on the table will allow a guest to season his food to his own taste.

The dessert should be a smooth bland one, such as a Bavarian Cream, or fresh, as in a Fruit Salad made from fresh foods only.

As for drinks, beer is the only one that stands up to chili or to any heavily spiced food, such as curry. If absolutely necessary, serve an inexpensive rosé.

Frijoles or Pinto Beans

1 pound dried pinto beans, soaked overnight
5 cups water
1 medium onion, cut into 4 pieces
1 garlic clove, minced
1 teaspoon chili powder
½ pound ham hock or salt pork (optional)
salt to taste

Put beans into a heavy saucepan or kettle. Add the water, onion, garlic, chili powder and ham or salt pork. Bring to boil. Lower heat to very low and simmer, covered, for 2 hours. Stir occasionally. Add salt to taste and simmer for 1 hour longer. If necessary, add a little more water to prevent sticking. Remove the ham hock before serving. Serves six.

Frijoles Refritos or Refried Beans

Cook beans as in Frijoles and remove ham. With a potato masher, mash beans well. Stir in ½ to 1 cup bacon drippings or lard and mix well. Cook over medium heat, stirring constantly, until the beans are thickened and the fat has been absorbed. If desired, serve with shredded Cheddar or Longhorn cheese sprinkled over the beans.

Bob Holleron's Chili Con Carne

According to all who have eaten it, this is the best chili in the world. The inventor is a distinguished Texas (San Antonio) amateur cook. I give the recipe in his own words, because it makes the dish very clear. Preface: Essentially, Chili Con Carne, truly a Tex-Mex dish, is nothing more than a well-designed and well thought-out stew. Like other classic stews, certain ground rules are important. 1. The meat, chuck, sirloin or round, must be carefully trimmed. This means that if you want to come up with 6 pounds trimmed meat, you must buy 8 pounds. Every bit of fat, which would make the chili greasy, must be trimmed off. 2. The meat must be thoroughly dried. This means, it must be well browned. This takes quite a bit of time since the meat, at first gives out quite a lot of water. This water evaporates as the meat browns. 3. The meat is best browned in a good vegetable oil. The traditional fat to brown chili meat in is lard, which is all right if you like the flavor. You can also use rendered beef fat. When a large quantity of chili is made, as in this recipe, it is best to brown the meat in batches, using a heavy iron frying pan. The pan must be heavy.

6 pounds lean beef, such as round or lean chuck, trimmed weight
approximately ½ to ¾ cups salad oil
1 large onion, cut into tiny dice
1 large garlic clove, crushed
1 8-ounce can tomato sauce
2 cups hot water
6 tablespoons Gebhard's Chili Powder (available in Spanish-Mexican groceries) or other good quality chili powder
4 tablespoons ground cumin
1 tablespoon cracked black pepper
1 tablespoon salt
½ tablespoon paprika
1 generous dash Tabasco
3 tablespoons masa harina (available in Spanish-Mexican groceries) or flour
6 tablespoons warm water

Cut the beef, which must be absolutely free of all fat, into ¼-to ½-inch dice. Heat ¼ cup of salad oil in a heavy frying pan and brown part of the meat over medium heat until totally dry and there is no liquid in the frying pan. This takes longer than one thinks, at least five minutes, depending on the amount of meat in the frying pan. Transfer the browned meat to a heavy casserole. Repeat the process with more meat and more oil until all the meat is used up. Cook the onion and garlic in the frying pan until the onion is soft, but not browned. Add to the meat and mix well. Stir tomato sauce, water, chili powder, cumin, pepper, salt, paprika and Tabasco into the meat. Cover casserole. Simmer over very low heat for 1–2 hours, stirring frequently. Add a little hot water if there is danger of scorching. If the chili is thinner than desired, blend the masa harina or flour and the 6 tablespoons of water to a smooth paste. Stir the mixture into the chili and cook 10 minutes longer. Serves twelve.

Note: 1. If the meat was properly trimmed, there should be no fat in the chili. However, should there be some fat, skim it off with paper towels or refrigerate the chili and remove congealed fat. 2. Make sure that the spices are fresh, or the chili won't have any flavor. For a hotter chili, use more chili powder and Tabasco, for a milder one, use less. But the recipe as is has proved to be very successful.

Chili Con Queso

1 pound processed American cheese
½ cup tomato juice
1 4-ounce can hot green chili peppers, peeled, seeded and chopped fine
2 tablespoons of onion juice

A very popular dunk, to be scooped up with corn crisps. Cut cheese into small dice. Place diced cheese into a skillet. Add tomato juice, hot green chili peppers and onion juice. Mix well. Cook, stirring constantly, over moderate heat until the cheese has melted and the mixture is well blended, about 10 minutes. Serve hot, studded with corn crisps, with more corn crisps on the side. Makes about four cups.

Note: This is a good chafing dish recipe.

Salsa (Uncooked Hot Tomato and Chili Pepper Sauce)

2 large tomatoes, peeled and chopped fine
1 onion, minced
1 jalapeno pepper or more to taste, fresh or canned, drained, seeded and chopped fine
2 tablespoons salad oil
juice of 1 lemon
¼ teaspoon oregano
salt
pepper

Combine all the ingredients and mix well. Store in refrigerator until serving time. Makes about one and a half cups.

Guacamole

3 large ripe avocados
3 tablespoons lemon or lime juice, or to taste
salt
freshly ground pepper
1 tablespoon grated onion (optional)
2–3 canned hot green chili peppers, rinsed, seeded and minced or to taste (optional)

There are many variations of this favorite and very colorful salad. With corn crisps, it is also a dip. Cut the avocados into halves, remove the seed and peel or scoop out the pulp with a spoon. Mash the flesh with a fork and immediately add lemon juice to prevent darkening. The avocado flesh may be mashed very smoothly or left lumpy; it is a matter of personal preference. Mix in salt, pepper, onion and chili peppers, if used.

Note: Guacamole may be served on a bed of salad greens, topped with 1 small peeled tomato, chopped or tomato slices may be placed on a plate lined with salad greens and topped with guacamole. Another pretty way is to scoop cut small tomatoes and fill them with guacamole, to be used as a garnish for a meat platter or a salad.

NOVEMBER

Mercifully, more and more people are realizing that wine drinking is not an esoteric art, but something you do at meals, just like eating. After all, mankind has made wine for thousands of years, enjoying it along with food, as a mild stimulant and as a way to relax without harm. Of course I am talking of wine taken in judicious quantities — a glass or two at a meal, a little before bedtime as a soporific. There are so many good and inexpensive wines to choose from, for daily and for company drinking. Nothing beats the gallon and half gallon jugs that come from California, as do so many of the finer wines. When you serve wine to guests, give them what they will most appreciate. Save your best wines for the connoisseurs, and give the cocktail drinkers something sturdy. The rule is to have plenty of good wine at a dinner party, rather than a dribble of rare, noble wine. Enough good wine at the table will keep up spirits without drunkenness if the guests came to the table in a moderate mood, and there won't be that after-dinner let-down that deadens far too many a dinner party. And keep wine simple, you don't need a battery of glasses. An 8 or 10-ounce clear tulip shaped glass is all you need to drink wine in style with the most sophisticated of wine lovers.

NOVEMBER

FAMILY FARE

	LUNCHES	DINNERS
Sunday	Brandade de Morue* Scalloped Apple Slices Coffee Cake	Duck with Orange and Glazed Oranges* Boiled Dry Rice Avocado and Belgian Endive Salad Charlotte Russe
Monday	The Original Bale Onion Tart* Waldorf Salad Chocolate Cookies	Mushroom Risotto* Veal Scallopine Braised Cucumbers Cherry Tomatoes Creme de Menthe Bavarian
Tuesday	Swiss Mashed Potatoes Baked with Bacon* Green Salad Cheese and Apples	Roast Beef Baked Acorn Squash Leeks Vinaigrette French Chocolate Cake*
Wednesday	Grilled Ham Sandwiches Lettuce Wedges Brown Sugar Pudding*	Stuffed Breast of Veal* Parsleyed Potatoes Avocado Salad Creme Brulee
Thursday	Baked Fettucine* Marinated Carrots Gingered Applesauce	Russian Veal and Cherry Casserole* Yellow Rice Hearts of Palm and Leek Salad Pumpkin Mousse
Friday	Tuna Casserole with Artichokes* Buttered Noodles Orange and Watercress Salad Cookies and Fruit	Rosemary Veal* Buttered Noodles Braised Peas and Lettuce Cheese Pie
Saturday	Baked Eggs with Potatoes and Mozzarella* Orange Cranberry Compote	Quick Scallops in Vermouth* Green Rice Red Beet Salad Lemon Sponge

QUICK & EASY Dinners For Two	BUDGET DINNERS	ENTERTAINING
Sautéed Veal with Lemon* Mashed Potatoes Green Peas Cooked with Shredded Lettuce and Butter Cucumber Salad Chocolate Cake	Broiled Marinated Flank Steak Spinach Soufflé Scalloped Eggplant and Tomatoes Watercress Orange and Cherry Compote*	Prosciutto or Virginia Ham Platter Watercress Baked Idaho Potatoes with Black Caviar and Sour Cream Cream of Dried Apricots*
Italian Hamburgers* Spanish Rice Panfried Broccoli Frozen Strawberries with Frozen Pureed Raspberries	Easy Lamb Curry* Chutney Rice Cucumbers in Yogurt Lemon Chiffon Pie	Steak Mushroom Goulash* Tossed Green Salad Hot Chocolate Soufflé
Broiled Ham with Madeira Sauce Easy Cabbage with Cream* Homefried Potatoes Salad and Cheese	Spanish Pork Stew* Boiled Potatoes Steamed Cabbage Apple Crisp	Fresh Artichokes Vinaigrette Roast Lamb Eggplant Casserole* Spoon Bread Vanilla Bavarian with Apricot Sauce
Polish or Italian Sausages Black Bean Casserole Braised Leeks and Mushrooms* Baked Apples	Pork Chops with Sautéed Apples Potato and Egg Casserole* Buttered Spinach Apple Pie	Stuffed Baked Mushrooms Beef Stroganoff Wheat Pilaf Stir-Fried Snowpeas Grapefruit and Strawberries*
Venetian Liver with Onions* Parsleyed Potatoes Buttered Spinach Beet Salad Cheese Cake	Pork, Bacon and Sauerkraut Casserole* Choice of Mustards Boiled Potatoes Buttered Green Beans Mandarin Oranges and Cookies	Belgian Endive Spears Filled with Minced Ham Salad Chicken Casserole with Port* Buttered Fine Noodles Creamed Spinach Hot Apple Tart
Crab Meat Stew* Rice Belgian Endives and Red Beet Salad Stewed Pears and Cookies	Frittata with Onions Flemish Potatoes* Green Salad Baked Apples	Shrimp Pâté on Toast* Pheasant Braised in Madeira Wild Rice or Barley Pilaf Creamed Savoy Cabbage Ripe Pears with Brie Cheese
Italian Mozzarella and Bread-Cube Omelet* Stewed White Tuscan Beans with Tomatoes Green Salad Stewed Kumquats	Danish Pork Balls* Hashed Browned Potatoes Cucumber Salad Sugared Orange and Grapefruit Sections with Rum	Cold Boiled Artichokes with Green Sauce* Pollo Piccante (Piquant Chicken) Melting Potatoes Green Peas Cooked with Prosciutto Assorted Cheeses Mont Blanc of Chestnuts and Cream

FAMILY FARE LUNCHES

November

Sunday

Brandade de Morue

Brandade de Morue
Scalloped Apple Slices
Coffee Cake

2 pounds salt cod, covered with cold water and soaked for 24 hours
1 cup milk
cold water
1 large garlic clove, mashed
1½ cups olive oil or half olive, half salad oil
1⅓ cups heavy cream
salt
freshly ground pepper
cayenne pepper
toast triangles

A specialty from Provence, this dish of creamy salt codfish has the consistency of mashed potatoes. Traditionally, it is served piled up in the center of a serving dish, with toast triangles around the base. It can be eaten with a fork or spread on the toast.

Cut off tail and fins of cod and remove any skin and bones. Cut into 4 large pieces and put in saucepan. Add the milk and enough water to reach 1 inch above the cod. Bring to boil, then simmer for 10 minutes. Drain and shred cod. Grind as finely as possible and put in mixing bowl. Stir in garlic. Place the oil in one small saucepan and the cream in another. Heat both thoroughly but do not boil. At medium speed, alternately beat. Add small amounts at a time the oil and cream into the cod, beat continuously to obtain a smooth mixture. When all the oil and cream are beaten into the cod, season to taste with salt and pepper and a little cayenne. Can be served with toast triangles. Six servings.

Monday

The Original Bale Onion Tart

The Original Bale Onion Tart
Waldorf Salad
Chocolate Cookies

for the Pastry:
2 cups flour
½ teaspoon salt
½ cup butter
4 tablespoons ice water
  (approximately)
for the Filling:
1½ tablespoons butter
6 large onions, thinly sliced
½ teaspoon salt
⅓ cup diced bacon
2 cups milk or light cream
3 tablespoons flour
2 eggs, well beaten
2 cups shredded Swiss cheese

To make the pastry, sift flour with salt. Cut in butter until particles are the size of small peas. Stir in ice water, a little at a time, to make a stiff dough. Knead dough lightly on a floured baking board. Roll out to fit bottom and sides of a well-buttered deep, 10-inch pie pan. Chill. To make the filling, heat butter in frying pan and cook onions until soft and golden. Stir in salt and add bacon. Cook over medium heat, stirring constantly, for 2-3 minutes. Remove from heat. Stir milk gradually into flour in a large bowl. Beat in eggs and cheese. Add onions and bacon, including the pan juices, and mix well. Pour mixture into the pastry shell. Bake in a preheated 350° oven for 30 minutes. Then, at 400°, bake 5 minutes longer or until browned and bubbly. Serve hot. Makes six servings.

Tuesday

Swiss Mashed Potatoes Baked with Bacon

Swiss Mashed Potatoes Baked with Bacon
Green Salad
Cheese and Apples

2 pounds potatoes
¼ cup butter, softened
2 eggs, beaten
⅓ cup heavy cream
salt
freshly ground pepper
2 tablespoons grated onion
½ pound thickly sliced bacon,
  cut into ½-inch strips

Boil the potatoes in their skins. Peel. While still warm, force through sieve or food mill. Stir in butter. Beat eggs with heavy cream and stir into potatoes. Season with a little salt (the bacon will be salty) and pepper. Stir in onion. Spoon the potato mixture into buttered baking dish. Smooth the top with a spatula. Stick the bacon strips into the potatoes. Bake in preheated 350° oven for 15 - 20 minutes or until potatoes are browned and bacon is crisp. Serves four to six.

Wednesday

Brown Sugar Pudding

Grilled Ham Sandwiches
Lettuce Wedges
Brown Sugar Pudding

3 tablespoons butter
½ cup sugar
1 cup flour
2 teaspoons baking powder
1 teaspoon nutmeg
½ teaspoon salt
1 cup milk
½ cup chopped walnuts
1 tablespoon cornstarch
1 cup dark brown sugar
2 cups water
1 teaspoon vanilla extract
heavy cream

Cream 2 tablespoons of the butter until soft. Gradually beat in sugar until well blended. Sift together flour, baking powder, nutmeg and salt. Add to the butter mixture, alternating with the milk, beginning and ending with flour. Stir in walnuts. Combine cornstarch with brown sugar in saucepan. Stir in the water, add vanilla and remaining tablespoon of butter. Bring to a boil, then simmer 5 minutes until thick and shiny. Pour this syrup into buttered 1¼-quart baking dish. Top with the batter. Bake in preheated 350° oven for 1 hour. Serve warm, with cream. Six servings.

Thursday

Baked Fettucine

Baked Fettucine
Marinated Carrots
Gingered Applesauce

1 pound spinach noodles
2 tablespoons salt
2 cups light cream or
  Half and Half
1½ cups freshly grated
  Parmesan cheese
salt
freshly ground pepper

Cook noodles in water with salt until they are not quite tender. Drain. Put the noodles into a large bowl and toss with 1½ cups of the cream, 1 cup of the Parmesan cheese and salt and pepper to taste. Turn into a buttered 13 × 9-inch baking dish. Sprinkle with remaining ½ cup of Parmesan cheese. Cover with foil. Bake in preheated 350° oven for 15 minutes or until thoroughly heated through. Remove from oven. Sprinkle with remaining ½ cup of cream, return to oven and bake 5 minutes longer. Serve immediately. Six servings.

Friday

Tuna Casserole with Artichokes

Tuna Casserole with Artichokes
Buttered Noodles
Orange and Watercress Salad
Cookies and Fruit

5 tablespoons butter
2 tablespoons minced onion
1 tablespoon flour
salt
freshly ground pepper
⅛ teaspoon ground nutmeg
1¼ cups milk
1 cup shredded Swiss cheese
2 7-ounce cans chunk style tuna, drained
1 10-ounce package frozen artichokes, thawed and halved
¼ cup soft white bread crumbs

Heat 3 tablespoons of butter and cook onion for 2 minutes. Stir in flour, and salt and pepper to taste; go easy on the salt since the tuna may be salty. Stir in nutmeg. Gradually stir in milk. Cook, stirring constantly, until the sauce is smooth and thick. Remove from heat and stir in cheese until melted. Break tuna into bite size pieces, and add tuna and artichokes to the sauce. Turn into a buttered 1½-quart casserole. Sprinkle with bread crumbs and dot with remaining butter. Bake in preheated 350° oven for about 20 minutes. Serves six.

Saturday

Baked Eggs with Potatoes and Mozzarella

Baked Eggs with Potatoes and Mozzarella
Orange Cranberry Compote

3 medium potatoes, boiled, peeled and sliced
½ to ¾ pound Mozzarella, thinly sliced
6 eggs
½ teaspoon salt
freshly ground pepper
⅓ cup freshly grated Parmesan cheese
2 tablespoons butter

Place the sliced potatoes in a buttered shallow baking dish. Top with the Mozzarella slices. Carefully break the eggs over the Mozzarella. Season with salt and pepper and sprinkle with Parmesan. Dot with butter. Cook in a preheated 400° oven for 20 minutes. Serve immediately. Makes six servings.

FAMILY FARE DINNERS

November

Sunday

Duck with Orange and Glazed Oranges

Duck with Orange and Glazed Oranges
Boiled Dry Rice
Avocado and Belgian Endive Salad
Charlotte Russe

1 5-6 pound duck
salt
freshly ground pepper
1 orange cut into quarters (do not peel but remove seeds)
1 cup freshly squeezed orange juice
½ cup dry white wine
Orange Sauce
Glazed Oranges
Watercress

Since American ducks are much fatter than European ducks, it is essential to get rid of the fat before finishing the bird. Simmer the giblets and neck of the bird in 1½ cups water for 20 minutes. Drain and reserve broth for the sauce. Rub duck's cavity and skin with salt and pepper. Stuff with orange quarters. Truss and prick all over with a fork. Place on a rack in a shallow roasting pan. Roast in a preheated 450° oven for 10 minutes. Lower oven temperature to 350° and roast 20 minutes longer. Pour off all fat. Combine orange juice and wine. Roast the duck for about 45 minutes to 1 hour, depending on the age of the bird. Baste frequently with the orange juice and wine liquid. While the duck is roasting, make the Orange Sauce. Carve the duck and serve it heated on a serving platter. Dribble a little sauce over the duck and serve the rest separately. Arrange the Glazed Oranges and the watercress around the duck. Four servings.

Orange Sauce: Combine 1 cup of the reserved duck broth, 1 cup freshly squeezed orange juice, juice of ½ lemon, 2 tablespoons grated orange rind and 2 tablespoons brandy. Blend 2 tablespoons cornstarch with 3 tablespoons water and stir into the first mixture. Simmer over low heat, uncovered, for 10-15 minutes, stirring frequently, or until the sauce is thickened, smooth and hot. Add 1 peeled, seeded and coarsely chopped orange to the sauce and heat through.

Glazed Oranges

4 seedless oranges
½ cup sugar
½ cup water
2 tablespoons light corn syrup
6 cloves
1 2-inch piece fresh gingerroot, peeled or 1 teaspoon ground ginger

Remove all yellow and white peel from the oranges. Section them removing all membranes. Combine the sugar, water, corn syrup, cloves and ginger in a small saucepan. Bring to boil and cook over medium heat for 3 minutes. Remove cloves and ginger root with a slotted spoon and add orange sections. Simmer over low heat for about 5 minutes.

Monday

Mushroom Risotto

Mushroom Risotto
Veal Scallopine
Braised Cucumbers
Cherry Tomatoes
Creme de Menthe Bavarian

6 tablespoons butter
1 medium onion, minced
1 cup long grain rice
salt
freshly ground pepper
½ teaspoon saffron
2 cups hot chicken bouillon
½ pound mushrooms, thinly sliced
3 tablespoons dry sherry
juice of 1 lemon
¼ cup minced parsley
freshly grated Parmesan cheese

Heat 4 tablespoons of butter in a heavy saucepan and cook the onion until golden. Add rice. Cook over medium heat, stirring constantly, for 3-4 minutes or until rice is opaque. Season with salt and pepper. Stir saffron into the bouillon and add to the rice. Simmer, covered, over low heat for 20-25 minutes or until rice has absorbed the liquid and is tender but not mushy. Meanwhile, heat the remaining butter in a frying pan. Add mushrooms and cook, stirring constantly, for about 2 minutes. Stir in sherry and lemon juice. Cook for about 2 minutes longer. Add mushrooms and their pan juices to the rice and sprinkle with parsley. Serve with plenty of Parmesan cheese. Makes six servings.

Tuesday

French Chocolate Cake

Roast Beef
Baked Acorn Squash
Leeks Vinaigrette
French Chocolate Cake

4 squares (4 ounces) unsweetened chocolate
4 tablespoons water or coffee
½ cup butter, cut into small pieces
½ cup sugar
3 large or 4 small eggs, separated
1 tablespoon brandy or rum, or 1 teaspoon vanilla flavoring
½ cup ground almonds or walnuts
⅓ cup flour
apricot jam or currant jelly
chocolate frosting or whipped cream (1 cup unwhipped)
candied violets

Combine the chocolate and water in a heavy saucepan or in the top of a double boiler. Over very low heat, or over hot water, melt the chocolate, stirring constantly. Stir in the butter piece by piece, stirring after each addition until melted. Remove from heat and stir in sugar. Cool. Beat in egg yolks, one at a time, beating well after each addition. Blend in flavoring and nuts. Sieve the flour into the batter and mix thoroughly. Beat egg whites until stiff and fold them into chocolate mixture. Grease and flour 2 round 8-inch layer pans. Put half the batter into each pan. Bake in a preheated 350° oven for 20 minutes or until the cake shrinks away from sides of pans. Do not overbake; the cake should be on the moist side. When cool, spread one layer with jam or jelly and top with the other layer. Frost with any chocolate frosting or with whipped cream. Decorate with candied violets.

Wednesday

Stuffed Breast of Veal

Stuffed Breast of Veal
Parsleyed Potatoes
Avocado Salad
Creme Brulée

1 breast of veal, weighing about 4-5 pounds, cut with a pocket
half a lemon
4 tablespoons butter
1 medium onion, chopped
1 garlic clove, mashed
1 cup fresh white bread crumbs
1 egg
2 teaspoons dried rosemary, crumbled
2 teaspoons grated lemon rind
2 10-ounce packages chopped spinach, cooked, drained and squeezed dry
salt
freshly ground pepper
4 slices bacon
1 cup chicken bouillon or water

Rub breast of veal inside the pocket and outside with the cut side of lemon. Heat butter and cook the onion and garlic until the onion is soft and golden. Stir in bread crumbs and egg. Mix well. Stir in the rosemary, lemon rind and add the spinach. Season with salt and pepper. Mix thoroughly. Fill pocket of the breast of veal with mixture. Close opening with skewers or sew it closed. Place meat on a rack in a roasting pan. Cover with bacon slices. Pour bouillon in the bottom of the pan. Cover with foil. Cook in a preheated 325° oven for 1½ hours. Remove the foil and cook for 20 minutes longer. Carve by cutting between the bones so that each helping resembles a chop with bone, meat and stuffing. Four to six servings.

Thursday

Russian Veal and Cherry Casserole

Russian Veal and Cherry Casserole
Yellow Rice
Hearts of Palm and Leek Salad
Pumpkin Mousse

¼ cup butter
2 pounds boneless veal, cut into 1-inch cubes
2 tablespoons flour
4 green onions, white and green parts, chopped
2 cups drained sour cherries, stoned
⅓ cup golden raisins
⅔ cup chicken bouillon
½ cup port wine
1 teaspoon ground cardamom
1 teaspoon salt
freshly ground pepper
2 cups cooked drained canned flageolet beans or small white beans

Heat the butter in a 3-quart casserole. Over high heat, brown the veal on all sides. Then, under very low flame, sprinkle the meat with flour. Stir until meat is evenly coated with flour. Add all other ingredients except the beans and mix thoroughly. Simmer, covered, over very low heat for 1 hour or until meat is tender but not mushy. Check for moisture; if necessary, add a little more chicken bouillon. Add beans 10 minutes before serving time and heat through.

Note: If the sauce looks pale rather than a rich rosy red, add a drop or two of red food coloring.

Friday

Rosemary Veal

Rosemary Veal
Buttered Noodles
Braised Peas and Lettuce
Cheese Pie

4 tablespoons butter
½ pound mushrooms, sliced
2 garlic cloves
2 pounds boneless veal, either sliced or cut into 1½-inch cubes
flour
½ cup dry sherry
1 tablespoon dried rosemary, crumbled
salt
freshly ground pepper
½ to ¾ cup heavy cream

Heat butter in a large, deep frying pan and cook mushrooms, stirring constantly, for 3-4 minutes. The mushrooms should be firm. Transfer mushrooms to a casserole. In the same frying pan, brown the garlic for 2-3 minutes. Discard the garlic. Coat the meat with flour and shake off the excess. Cook over high heat, stirring constantly, for 4 minutes or until the veal is golden brown on all sides. Add veal to the mushrooms. Stir in sherry and rosemary. Simmer, covered, for 30 minutes or until veal is tender. Check for moisture; if necessary, add a little hot water, 2 tablespoons at a time. Season with salt and pepper. Stir in ½ cup of the cream. Cook for 5 minutes longer, but do not boil. The sauce should be the consistency of heavy cream. If too thick, stir in the remaining cream, 2 tablespoons at a time. Serves four to six.

Saturday

Quick Scallops in Vermouth

Quick Scallops in Vermouth
Green Rice
Red Beet Salad
Lemon Sponge

2 pounds scallops
½ cup butter
⅓ cup dry vermouth
salt
freshly ground pepper
lemon wedges

A simple and excellent dish. Cut the scallops into halves if they are large. Wash and dry them. Heat the butter in a frying pan. Add the scallops. Cook over medium heat, stirring gently with a fork, for 2-3 minutes. Add vermouth and cook for 1-2 minutes longer or until heated through. Remove from heat and season with salt and pepper. Serve with lemon wedges.

QUICK & EASY DINNERS FOR TWO

November

Sunday **Sautéed Veal with Lemon**

Sautéed Veal with Lemon
Mashed Potatoes
Green Peas Cooked with Shredded Lettuce and Butter
Cucumber Salad
Chocolate Cake

¾ pound boneless veal, in one piece
salt
freshly ground pepper
flour
1 tablespoon butter
1 tablespoon salad oil
juice of 1 large lemon
⅓ cup dry white wine
2 tablespoons minced parsley

A chicken breast, halved, skinned and trimmed of excess fat, can also be used in the same way. Adjust cooking time in this case. Trim gristle and any fat off the meat and cut into 1½-inch pieces. Season with salt and pepper. Coat with flour, and shake off excess flour. Heat butter and oil in a frying pan and, over high heat, brown the veal, stirring constantly. Lower heat and stir in lemon juice. Cover the frying pan. Cook over low heat, shaking the pan frequently, for 5-10 minutes, depending on the age of the veal, or until almost tender. Add the wine and check seasoning. Cook until the meat is tender. Sprinkle with parsley before serving.

Note: There should be only a little sauce in the dish.

Monday

Italian Hamburgers

Italian Hamburgers
Spanish Rice
Panfried Broccoli
Frozen Strawberries with Frozen Pureed Raspberries

¾ to 1 lb. lean, good quality hamburger
1 tablespoon minced parsley
1 small garlic clove, mashed
1 teaspoon anchovy paste (optional)
grated rind of ½ lemon
salt
freshly ground pepper
1 small egg
2 tablespoons dried bread crumbs
2-3 tablespoons olive oil

Combine all the ingredients except the olive oil. Mix well and shape into hamburger patties. Heat the olive oil in a frying pan, the amount depends on the size of the pan. Over medium heat, cook the hamburgers for 2-3 minutes, turn and cook on the other side.

Tuesday

Easy Cabbage with Cream

Broiled Ham with Madeira Sauce
Easy Cabbage with Cream
Homefried Potatoes
Salad and Cheese

½ small green cabbage, preferably a Savoy cabbage
½ cup water
salt
freshly ground pepper
⅔ to 1 cup heavy cream

The goodness of this dish is due to its plainness. Trim the cabbage, also cutting off the tough part of the stalks. With a sharp knife, cut it into thin strips. Wash and drain. Place the cabbage into a heavy saucepan. Add the water and season with salt and pepper. Over high heat, stirring frequently, cook the cabbage until it is almost soft. Lower heat and add the cream. Cook until the cabbage is soft, but not mushy and until there is only a little cream left in the pan, serving as a sauce.

Wednesday

Leeks and Mushrooms

Polish or Italian Sausages
Black Bean Casserole
Leeks and Mushrooms
Baked Apples

3-4 leeks
¼ cup olive oil
¼ cup water
juice of ½ lemon
1 garlic clove
1 bay leaf
½ pound fresh mushrooms, sliced
salt
freshly ground pepper

Remove the wilted leaves from the leeks. Cut white and green part into 2-inch lengths. Put leeks into a bowl filled with cold water and let stand a couple of minutes to loosen dirt. Change the water several times making sure no trace of dirt remains. Drain. Combine the olive oil, water, lemon juice, garlic clove and bay leaf in a saucepan. Bring to boil and cook for 2 minutes. Lower heat and add the leeks. Cook uncovered for 5 minutes or until the leeks are half done. Add the mushrooms. Season with salt and pepper. Mix well and continue cooking until the vegetables are barely done; they should be firm and almost all of the cooking liquid should have evaporated. Serve hot or at room temperature.

Thursday

Venetian Liver with Onions

Venetian Liver with Onions
Parsleyed Potatoes
Buttered Spinach
Beet Salad
Cheese Cake

½ to ¾ pound calf's liver
2 tablespoons butter
1 tablespoon olive oil
2 large onions, very thinly sliced
¼ cup dry white wine
salt
freshly ground pepper
juice of ½ lemon (or less)
minced parsley (optional)

The liver must be sliced very thin since the dish doesn't succeed unless it is cooked very quickly. Wash and dry the liver thoroughly but quickly. Cut into very thin 2-inch strips. Heat butter and oil in a frying pan and cook the onions until soft and golden. Add the wine and season with salt and pepper. Cook, stirring constantly, for 2 more minutes. Add the liver. Cook 1-2 minutes on each side, until just browned. Remove from heat and stir in the lemon juice and parsley. Serve immediately, on a hot platter and plates.

Friday

Crab Meat Stew

Crab Meat Stew
Rice
Belgian Endives and Red Beet Salad
Stewed Pears and Cookies

2 cups fresh or canned crab meat
½ cup dry sherry
2 tablespoons butter
¼ cup minced shallots or onion
1 tablespoon flour
1 cup drained canned tomatoes chopped, or fresh tomatoes
½ teaspoon dried thyme
½ to ¾ cup heavy cream
salt
freshly ground pepper

Pick over the crab meat and remove all fibers and membranes. Put the crab meat into a small bowl, add the sherry and soak for 10 minutes. In a casserole, preferably one that can go to the table, heat the butter. Add shallots and cook, stirring constantly, for 3 minutes or until soft and golden, but not brown. Stir in flour. Add the tomatoes and thyme and blend. Cook over medium heat, stirring frequently, for 3 to 5 minutes. Lower heat. Stir in the crab meat, the sherry in which it soaked and ½ cup of the cream. Season with salt and pepper. Cook 5 to 10 minutes longer, stirring frequently. If the stew gets too thick, add the remaining cream.

Saturday

Italian Mozzarella and Bread Cube Omelet

Italian Mozzarella and Bread Cube Omelet
Stewed White Tuscan Beans with Tomatoes
Green Salad
Stewed Kumquats

2 slices firm white bread
4 eggs, slightly beaten
salt
freshly ground pepper
4 ounces (½ package) Mozzarella cheese, diced small
3 tablespoons butter or olive oil

Trim the crusts from the bread and cut into ¼-inch cubes. Combine the eggs, salt, pepper and Mozzarella cheese. Heat the butter in a frying pan, but do not let it brown. Fry the bread cubes until they are golden. Add the egg mixture. Cook over low heat for 5 minutes or until firmly set, shaking the pan frequently. Turn over and cook until set. Serve hot.

Note: To turn an Italian omelet, hold a plate the size of the frying pan over the omelet and turn it over. The cooked side will be on top, the uncooked one at the bottom. Slip the omelet back into the frying pan to allow the uncooked side to be set and firm.

BUDGET DINNERS

November

Sunday

Orange and Cherry Compote

Broiled Marinated Flank Steak
Spinach Soufflé
Scalloped Eggplant and Tomatoes
Watercress
Orange and Cherry Compote

1 cup orange marmalade (preferably the bitter kind)
½ cup fresh orange juice
grated rind of 1 orange
2 tablespoons dry sherry
4 oranges, peeled, thinly sliced and seeds removed
2 cups drained canned Bing cherries
¼ cup toasted slivered almonds

Heat the marmalade in a small saucepan. Stir in orange juice and orange rind. Cool. Stir in sherry. Arrange the oranges and cherries in a glass bowl in 2 or 3 layers. Pour the orange sauce over the fruit. Chill thoroughly. While chilling, baste the fruit twice with some of its own juice. Sprinkle with almonds before serving. Makes six servings.

Monday

Easy Lamb Curry

Easy Lamb Curry
Chutney
Rice
Cucumbers in Yogurt
Lemon Chiffon Pie

2 tablespoons butter
2 large onions, thinly sliced
1 garlic clove, minced
1 tablespoon curry powder
¼ cup golden or seedless raisins
1 large apple, peeled, cored and chopped
salt
2 medium tomatoes, peeled and sliced *or*
  1 cup canned tomatoes, drained
2 pounds boneless lamb, fat trimmed off,
  cut into 1-inch cubes
1 cup boiling water
2 cups tomato juice

Heat the butter in a large, heavy saucepan. Add the onions and garlic. Cook, stirring constantly, for 2 minutes or until soft. Stir in curry powder and cook 1 minute longer. Add the raisins, apple and salt to taste. Cook, stirring constantly, for 3-4 minutes. Add the tomatoes and cook 3 minutes longer. Add the meat and water. Simmer, covered, over low heat for 30 minutes, stirring occasionally. Add the tomato juice and simmer for 30 more minutes. Stir occasionally and if necessary to prevent sticking, add a little more water or tomato juice, 2 tablespoons at a time. Six servings.

Tuesday

Spanish Pork Stew

Spanish Pork Stew
Boiled Potatoes
Steamed Cabbage
Apple Crisp

2 pounds lean boneless pork,
  cut into ½-inch slices
salt
freshly ground pepper
flour
⅓ cup olive or salad oil
1 large onion, sliced
1 garlic clove, minced
1 cup drained canned plum or
  Italian style tomatoes
1 cup dry white wine
1 teaspoon cinnamon
2 hard-cooked eggs, chopped fine
¼ cup minced parsley

Sprinkle the meat with salt and pepper. Coat with flour and shake off excess flour. Heat olive oil in a large frying pan. Over high heat, cook the pork until browned on both sides. Transfer the meat to a casserole. Add the onions and garlic. Cook over medium heat, stirring constantly, until the onion is soft. Add the tomatoes, wine and cinnamon. Cook for 3 minutes. Pour the sauce over the meat. Simmer, covered, over low heat for 1 hour or until the pork is well done. Sprinkle with chopped eggs and parsley. Serve very hot in the same dish. Makes six servings.

Wednesday

Potato and Egg Casserole

Pork Chops with Sautéed Apples
Potato and Egg Casserole
Buttered Spinach
Apple Pie

1 tablespoon butter
6 slices bacon, chopped
6 medium potatoes, cooked, peeled and sliced
6 hard-cooked eggs, sliced
salt
freshly ground pepper
4 tablespoons minced parsley
⅔ cup sour cream

Combine butter and bacon in a frying pan and cook until the bacon is crisp. Drain the bacon and reserve the fat. Place alternate layers of potatoes, eggs and bacon in a 1½-quart casserole. Season with salt and pepper and sprinkle with parsley. Stir the reserved bacon fat into the sour cream. Pour over the potato mixture. Bake, covered, in a preheated 350° oven for 20 minutes or until golden and hot. Makes four to six servings.

Thursday

Pork, Bacon and Sauerkraut Casserole

Pork, Bacon and Sauerkraut Casserole
Choice of Mustards
Boiled Potatoes
Buttered Green Beans
Mandarin Oranges and Cookies

6 thick bacon slices (they must be thick)
1 quart sauerkraut, drained, rinsed and drained
6 ¾-inch thick pork chops, excess fat trimmed off
1 large onion, thinly sliced
12 whole black peppercorns
2 cups chicken bouillon
1 cup dry white wine

Put the bacon slices in the bottom of a large saucepan or a large, deep frying pan. Top with sauerkraut. Arrange the pork chops on top of the sauerkraut and top with onions. Sprinkle the peppercorns over the sauerkraut and onions. Pour bouillon and wine over chops. Simmer, covered, over low heat for 1 to 1¼ hours. To serve, place the sauerkraut in the middle of a heated serving dish and surround with the bacon slices and pork chops. Makes six servings.

Friday

Flemish Potatoes

Frittata with Onion
Flemish Potatoes
Green Salad
Baked Apples

2 tablespoons bacon fat
1 large onion, thinly sliced
5 medium carrots, sliced
salt
freshly ground pepper
⅛ teaspoon ground nutmeg
⅓ cup water
5 medium potatoes, cut into 1-inch cubes
beef bouillon or water
¼ cup minced parsley

An excellent combination of two familiar vegetables. The dish should be soft, but not soupy. Heat bacon fat in a large saucepan and cook the onion until soft but not browned. Add the carrots, salt, pepper and nutmeg. Stir to mix. Add water. Cook, covered, over low heat for about 5 minutes. Add the potatoes and enough beef bouillon to reach halfway up the vegetable mixture; amount depends on the size of the saucepan. Cook, covered, over low heat 10 to 15 minutes or until the vegetables are tender. Check the cooking liquid. If there is too much, cook uncovered to let it evaporate. It too little, add a little more bouillon, 2 tablespoons at a time. At serving time, stir the vegetables with a fork to mix and sprinkle with parsley. Six servings.

Saturday

Danish Pork Balls

Danish Pork Balls
Hashed Browned Potatoes
Cucumber Salad
Sugared Orange and Grapefruit Sections with Rum

2 pounds lean pork, ground
½ cup flour
1 egg
1 tablespoon grated onion
salt
freshly ground pepper
⅛ teaspoon ground nutmeg
½ cup soda water or cold water
6 tablespoons butter
½ cup to ¾ cup light cream or milk
3 large onions, thinly sliced

Combine the pork, flour, egg, grated onion, salt and pepper to taste and nutmeg. Blend thoroughly with a fork. Stir in soda water and mix well. The soda water adds lightness to the dish. Using hands, shape into meatballs. Heat 3 tablespoons of butter in a large frying pan. Over medium heat, brown the pork balls on all sides. Lower the heat to very low. Continue cooking the pork balls for 20 minutes, turning occasionally. To prevent possible scorching, add a little water if necessary, 3 tablespoons at a time. Transfer the pork balls to a heated serving dish and keep hot in low oven (200°). Add the cream to the pan juices, scraping up all the brown bits at the bottom. Keep the sauce warm. In another frying pan, heat the remaining butter and cook onions until soft and golden brown. Pour the sauce over the pork balls and top with onions. Serves four to six.

ENTERTAINING

November

Sunday

Prosciutto or Virginia Ham Platter
Watercress
Baked Idaho Potatoes with Black Caviar and Sour Cream
Cream of Dried Apricots

Cream of Dried Apricots

2 cups dried apricots (tightly packed)
grated rind of 1 small lemon
juice of 1 lemon
½ cup sugar, or sugar to taste
1 cup heavy cream, whipped

Soak the apricots for a few hours or overnight in water to cover. Put them in a saucepan with their water, and, if necessary, add more water to cover them abundantly. Add grated lemon rind. Simmer slowly until the apricots are very soft. Remove from heat. Stir in lemon juice and sugar to taste. Cool completely. Puree in a blender or press through a sieve. Mix together the apricot puree and whipped cream. Place in a glass dish and chill before serving. Serves four to five.

Note: This simple dessert can be made with any dried fruit. If it has to be stretched, add more whipped cream.

Monday

Mushroom Goulash

Steak
Mushroom Goulash
Tossed Green Salad
Hot Chocolate Soufflé

4 tablespoons butter
2 medium onions, thinly sliced
1 to 2 tablespoons sweet paprika
2 pounds firm mushrooms, thinly sliced
½ cup water
2 medium tomatoes, peeled, seeded, and chopped
salt
freshly ground pepper
½ cup sour cream

Heat butter in a casserole that can go to the table and cook onions until soft and just golden. Stir in paprika. Cook, stirring constantly, for about 2 minutes. Add the mushrooms and water. Cook, stirring frequently, over medium heat for about 5 minutes. Add the tomatoes and season with salt and pepper. Cook 5-10 minutes longer; the mushrooms should be tender but still firm. Remove from heat and stir in sour cream. Return to heat and heat through, but do not boil. Six servings.

Note: If a thicker sauce is wanted, sprinkle the mushrooms with 1-2 tablespoons flour before adding the water.

Tuesday

Eggplant Casserole

Fresh Artichokes Vinaigrette
Roast Lamb
Eggplant Casserole
Spoon Bread
Vanilla Bavarian with Apricot Sauce

1 big eggplant, peeled and cut into 1-inch cubes (6 to 8 cups)
2-3 tablespoons salt
½ cup olive oil
3 medium sweet green peppers, seeded and cut into strips
3 small onions, thinly sliced
2 cups peeled and chopped tomatoes or drained Italian-style plum tomatoes, chopped
2 whole garlic cloves
salt
pepper
½ teaspoon dried thyme or oregano or basil
⅓ cup minced parsley
⅓ cup currants, plumped in water, *or* ½ cup pitted black olives, halved

Put eggplant into a strainer and sprinkle with 2 to 3 tablespoons salt. Place strainer over a bowl. Let stand at room temperature for about 1 hour, stirring and squeezing eggplant with the hands, in order to extract moisture. The eggplant will be mushed up, but this does not matter. Heat olive oil in a drying pan.The flavor trick is to sauté the vegetables separately in olive oil before cooking them with the tomatoes. Over medium heat cook pepper strips, stirring frequently, until semi-soft. Using a slotted spoon, transfer pepper strips to a casserole. In the same hot oil cook eggplant for 3-4 minutes. Transfer eggplant to casserole. Now cook onions and garlic in remaining oil until semi-soft and barely golden. Add onions to vegetables in casserole. Add tomatoes, salt, pepper, thyme, oregano or basil, parsley and currants or olives to the casserole. Mix well. Simmer over low heat for about 20 minutes, or until tender but not overcooked. Check occasionally for moisture; if necessary, add a little hot water, one tablespoon at a time, to prevent scorching. Serves four to six.

Wednesday

Grapefruit and Strawberries

Stuffed Baked Mushrooms
Beef Stroganoff
Wheat Pilaf
Stir-Fried Snowpeas
Grapefruit and Strawberries

8 large grapefruits
1 cup sugar, or to taste
3 10-ounce packages frozen strawberries, thawed

Peel the grapefruits carefully. Section them by removing all the membranes and keeping the segments intact. Pile the segments neatly in a serving dish. Sprinkle with sugar. Puree the strawberries in a blender. Pour over the grapefruit and chill before serving. Serves six.

Thursday

Chicken Casserole with Port

Belgian Endive Spears Filled with Minced Ham Salad
Chicken Casserole with Port
Buttered Fine Noodles
Creamed Spinach
Hot Apple Tart

1 3½-pound chicken, cut into serving pieces
2 tablespoons butter
2 medium onions, thinly sliced
1 garlic clove, minced
1 tablespoon flour
½ cup port wine
¼ cup chicken bouillon
1 tablespoon mild vinegar
½ teaspoon ground ginger
1 cup peeled chopped tomatoes
salt
freshly ground pepper
1 package frozen artichoke hearts, thawed and cut into quarters
juice of 1 lemon
¼ cup minced parsley

Remove the skin and all fat from chicken pieces. Heat butter in a frying pan and brown the chicken pieces on all sides. Transfer the chicken pieces to a 3-quart casserole. Brown onion and garlic in the frying pan juices. Stir in flour, port, chicken bouillon, vinegar, and ginger. Bring quickly to boil and pour over the chicken pieces. Simmer, covered, over low heat for about 20 minutes, stirring frequently. Add tomatoes, salt, and pepper. Simmer, covered, for 10 more minutes. Add the artichokes and cook for 5-10 minutes longer. Remove from heat and stir in lemon juice. Sprinkle with parsley. Serves four to five.

Friday

Shrimp Pâté on Toast

Shrimp Pâté on Toast
Pheasant Braised in Madeira
Wild Rice or Barley Pilaf
Creamed Savoy Cabbage
Ripe Pears with Brie Cheese

¾ to 1 cup olive oil
1 pound small shrimp, cooked, shelled, deveined, and chopped
¼ cup fresh lemon juice
grated rind of 1 lemon
1 teaspoon freshly ground pepper
salad greens

Put all the ingredients, beginning with ¾ cup olive oil, into the blender. Puree at low speed, scraping down the sides and adding the remaining olive oil in a trickle if the mixture is too thick. Line a serving dish with salad greens and pile the paté lightly on it. Serve with toast for spreading. Makes six servings.

Saturday

Italian Dinner for Four to Six

Cold Boiled Artichokes with Green Sauce
Piquant Green Blender Sauce*
Pollo Piccante (Piquant Chicken)*
Melting Potatoes
Green Peas Cooked with Prosciutto
Assorted Cheeses
Mont Blanc of Chestnuts and Cream
**Recipe in book*

Italian food is more than spaghetti or rice. When served at a meal, spaghetti or other pasta and the rice dish are the first course, eaten by themselves in moderate quantities since there is more to come. The Spaghetti dinner, beloved by Americans, with nothing but a tossed salad, cheese and fruit to follow, is unknown in Italy. Pasta and rice are never served as side dishes, as they are in America, with the single exception of rice accompanying Osso, Buco, veal shank.

A salad is not a course in itself as in America. It is served instead of a vegetable with the meat, and eaten on the same plate. The dressing is a simple one of olive oil and vinegar, salt and pepper. The Italian hostess, who does not feel like making dessert because desserts are party food only, will be praised for buying hers at one of the first class patisseries found in any Italian town. Fresh fruit is usually the end of an everyday meal.

The wine, should be on the robust side, since both the first and second courses are apt to overpower it. Italy has an ample choice of such wines, both red and white.

Wines:

White: Dry Orvieto, Verdicchio di Jesi
Red: Barolo, Frecciarossa, Quality Chianti (Black Roosher or Reserve Label)

Pollo Piccante (Piquant Chicken)

4 large chicken breasts, split
flour
3 tablespoons butter
3 tablespoons olive oil
6 anchovy fillets, drained and mashed
3 garlic cloves, mashed, or garlic to taste
1 cup dry white wine
¼ cup white or white wine vinegar
¼ cup drained capers (if large, chopped)
salt
freshly ground pepper
2 large sprigs fresh rosemary, or 1 tablespoon dry rosemary, crumbled
½ cup minced parsley

Remove the skin and all fat from chicken breasts. Wash and dry thoroughly. Roll the chicken breasts in flour and shake off excess. Heat butter and oil in a frying pan and over medium heat, cook chicken breasts until golden. Drain on paper towels. Transfer chicken breasts to a casserole. Pour out all but 1 tablespoon of the fat from the frying pan. Add mashed anchovies and the garlic. With a wooden spoon, stir together to make a paste. Cook for about 1 minute. Add wine and bring to boil. Add vinegar and cook for 2-3 minutes, stirring constantly to make a smooth sauce. Add capers. Taste the sauce before seasoning with salt and pepper; the anchovies may be very salty. Pour sauce over chicken breasts, making sure that each piece gets some sauce. Cover and cook in a preheated 350° oven for 30 minutes or until done; cooking time depends on the size of chicken breasts. Baste frequently. Transfer chicken breasts to a heated serving platter, pour the sauce over them and sprinkle with rosemary and parsley before serving. Serves four to six.

Note: Chicken breasts vary in size. If they are very large, increase the sauce ingredients to 8 anchovy fillets, garlic to taste, and additional ½ cups of dry white and ⅓ cups of vinegar. If a more piquant dish is wanted, increase the vinegar and capers to taste. The sauce should reduce in cooking so that the dish is on the dry side.

Piquant Green Blender Sauce

2 tablespoons drained capers
1 tablespoon chopped onion
1 garlic clove
1 anchovy or 1 teaspoon anchovy paste
2 cups parsley heads without stems, tightly packed
1 teaspoon dried basil or fresh basil to taste
¾ cup olive oil (it must be olive oil)
juice of 2 lemons
1 teaspoon salt
½ teaspoon freshly ground pepper

This sauce is good for all boiled and grilled seafood, boiled meats, hard-cooked eggs and cooked vegetable salads. Combine all the ingredients in a blender top. Blend until smooth. Keep under refrigeration. Makes about one and a quarter cups.

Variation: For a thicker sauce, add a chopped hard-boiled egg or a small cooked potato to the mixture and blend. The sauce should reduce in cooking so that the dish is on the dry side.

DECEMBER

Even non-believers in Christmas should consider this a season when it behooves us to think of others. Apart from contributing to the general holiday feeling — a worthy thing in these uncertain times — it is good for the soul to bake a cookie for a child or take a flower to an old lady who is alone, or to cook a meal for a stranger away from home. Holidays are difficult times for many of us, reminding us of happy days gone forever. But contentment, if not happiness, is largely of our own making. Forget the past and salute the present in doing something for somebody else. How well I know that this makes one feel better at once.

DECEMBER

FAMILY FARE

	LUNCHES	DINNERS
Sunday	Cheeseburgers French Fries Apricot Cream*	Ukrainian Borsch* French Garlic Bread Cheese Tray Dried Figs, Raisins, Almonds and Walnuts
Monday	Egg Curry* Rice Ring Chutney Sliced Oranges and Grapefruit with Honey	Carbonnades Flamandes* Buttered Noodles Broccoli Vinaigrette Pumpkin Pie
Tuesday	Great Macaroni and Cheese* Buttered Spinach Stewed Vanilla Pears	Baked Lamb Shanks* Braised Celery Potato Balls Cheese Cake
Wednesday	Frankfurters with Cheese and Bacon* Orange and Onion Salad Chocolate Cookies	Calf's Liver with Onion Rings and Apples* Boiled Potatoes Red Radish and Cucumber Salad Apple Tart with Cream
Thursday	Belgian Endives and Ham au Gratin* French Bread Brie and Boursin Cheeses	Tipsy Beef Stew* Boiled Potatoes Creamed Peas, Carrots and Onions Green Salad Cheese and Fruit
Friday	Tomato, Egg and Cheese Toasts* Apple Brown Betty	Baked Cod Creole Green Rice Cauliflower Polonaise Grasshopper Pie*
Saturday	La Tourtiere* Cranberry Relish Hermits	Steak au Poivre* Shoestring Potatoes Belgian Endive, Raw Mushroom and Watercress Salad Cold Tart Lemon Soufflé

QUICK & EASY Dinners For Two	BUDGET DINNERS	ENTERTAINING
Lamb Chops Hashed Brown Potatoes Brussels Sprouts with Lemon Sauce Belgian Endive Salad Arabian Oranges*	Roast Beef Baked Potatoes Braised Artichokes and Peas Orange Pie with Whipped Cream*	Artichoke and Shrimp Curry* Rice Chutney Cucumbers in Yogurt Lemon Meringue Pie
Spinach and Rice Soup* Fried Chicken Potato Salad Red Radishes, Carrots Fresh Applesauce and Cookies	Dried Pea Soup* French Bread Cheese French Apple Cake	Cold Ham and Chicken Mushroom and Potato Pie* Lettuce and Avocado Salad Apple Tart and Cream
Eggplant Broiled with Mozzarella* Spanish Rice Green Salad Chocolate Pudding	Chicken Adobo* French Fried Potatoes Stewed Peppers and Tomatoes Fresh Fruit Salad	Tournedos Flambé* Potatoes Anna Sautéed Cherry Tomatoes Belgian Endive Salad Orange Slices in Port Cookies
Sautéed Chicken with Sherry* Cracked Wheat Pilaf Green Bean Salad Lemon Meringue Pie	Frankfurter Skillet Dish* Home-fried Potatoes Green Beans Vinaigrette Poached Pears and Cookies	Grapefruit with Ginger Roast Ham Artichoke and Rice Casserole* Pickled Beets Apple Crisp with Cream
Pork Chops Savory Potato Galette* Red Cabbage with Apples Cut-Up Grapefruit and Oranges Cookies	Lemon-Braised Lamb Shanks* Rice Braised Red Radishes Hot Gingerbread and Ice Cream	Wild Mushroom Soup* Pheasant Cooked with Sauerkraut Boiled Potatoes Buttered Brussels Sprouts Fresh Pineapple with Kirsch Cookies
Garlic Broiled Shrimp* Risotto Green Peas in Cream Watercress Cheese and Apples	Peanut Soup* Egg Salad Sandwiches Tossed Green Salad Chocolate Cream Pie	Pâté Maison Roast Duck with Oranges Pilaf with Pignoli Nuts Lettuce and Avocado Salad La Delice de Lausanne*
Eggs with Mushrooms* Chick-Pea Casserole Cucumber Salad Apple Brown Betty	Meat Loaf Scalloped Potatoes Baked Acorn Squash Watercress and Avocado Salad Dutch Lemon Whip*	Spiced Cider Punch A Variety of Decorated Cookies Sugar Gingerbread* Almond Butter Stars* Pencil Wreaths*

FAMILY FARE LUNCHES

December

Sunday

Cheeseburgers
French Fries
Apricot Cream

Apricot Cream

1 pound dried apricots
2 cups water
½ cup sugar
2 tablespoons fresh lemon juice
2 cups heavy cream, whipped

This dish is easy and excellent. Cook the apricots in the water for about 20 minutes, or until very tender. If necessary, add a little more water. Stir in the sugar. Cool and stir in the lemon juice. Puree the apricots in a blender or force through a food mill. Fold the cream into the apricot puree. Turn into a glass serving dish and chill thoroughly. Makes six servings.

Monday

Egg Curry

Egg Curry
Rice Ring
Chutney
Sliced Oranges and Grapefruit with Honey

4 tablespoons butter
1 tablespoon Madras curry powder or to taste
¼ cup minced onion
1 large garlic clove, minced
1 tablespoon tomato paste
¾ cup water
1 teaspoon salt
1 tablespoon fresh lemon juice
6 large hard-cooked eggs, cut in halves lengthwise

Heat the butter in a heavy casserole. Stir in the curry powder. Cook over medium heat, stirring constantly, for about 2 minutes. Add the onion and garlic. Cook, stirring all the time, for 3–4 minutes or until the onion is soft. Stir in the tomato paste, water, and salt. Cook for 3–4 minutes. Stir in the lemon juice. Cook for about 1–2 minutes or until the sauce is medium thick. Carefully add the halved eggs. Cook until they are heated through thoroughly. Serve in the center of a rice ring. Makes six servings.

Tuesday

Great Macaroni and Cheese

Great Macaroni and Cheese
Buttered Spinach
Stewed Vanilla Pears

2 cups (8 ounces) elbow macaroni
3 tablespoons butter
¼ cup minced onion
3 tablespoons flour
½ teaspoon salt
¼ teaspoon freshly ground pepper
1 cup heavy cream
½ cup dry white wine
2 cups (½ pound) grated sharp Cheddar

Cook the macaroni in plenty of rapidly boiling salted water until not quite tender. Drain and reserve. Heat butter in a saucepan and cook the onion until tender but not browned. Stir in flour, salt and pepper. Slowly add the cream and wine. Cook over low heat, stirring constantly, until thickened. Add cheese and stir until melted. Combine the macaroni and the cheese sauce in a large bowl and mix well. Put into a buttered 1½-quart casserole. Bake in a preheated 350° oven for 15–25 minutes, or until thoroughly heated through and bubbly. Four to six servings.

Wednesday

Frankfurters with Cheese and Bacon

Frankfurters with Cheese and Bacon
Orange and Onion Salad
Chocolate Cookies

8 frankfurters
8 thin slices Cheddar or Swiss cheese
4 slices bacon, cut into halves

Cut the frankfurters lengthwise three-quarters of the way to the bottom and split them open. Roll the cheese slices and place 1 roll into each frankfurter. Bring the frankfurters together again. Wrap ½ a bacon slice around frankfurter and secure it with toothpicks or small skewers. Broil about 4 inches away from the heat until the cheese is melted and the bacon crisp. Serve on buttered rolls. Makes four to six servings.

Thursday

Belgian Endives and Ham au Gratin

Belgian Endives and Ham au Gratin
French Bread
Brie and Boursin Cheeses

8 large firm Belgian endives
1 tablespoon lemon juice
1 teaspoon salt
2 tablespoons butter
2 tablespoons flour
1¼ cups milk
½ cup grated Swiss cheese
1 egg yolk
salt
freshly ground pepper
⅛ teaspoon ground nutmeg
8 slices boiled ham
¼ cup grated Parmesan cheese

Trim the endives at the stalk and remove any brown-edged leaves. Wash and dry them. Put the endives into a large saucepan. Add lemon juice, salt and just enough water to cover. Simmer, covered, for 10 minutes or until the endives are just tender but still firm. Drain the vegetables and dry them. Heat butter in a saucepan and stir in flour. Cook, stirring constantly for about 2 minutes. Add milk. Cook, stirring all the time until the sauce is thickened and smooth. Add Swiss cheese and stir until melted. Remove from heat and stir in the egg yolk. Season with salt and pepper and stir in nutmeg. Wrap the endives in ham slices and place them in one layer in a shallow buttered baking dish. Spoon the cheese sauce over vegetables and sprinkle with Parmesan cheese. Bake in a preheated 350° oven for 15 minutes or until very hot and golden brown and bubbly on the top. Serves four.

Friday

Tomato, Egg and Cheese Toasts

Tomato, Egg and Cheese Toasts
Apple Brown Betty

2 tablespoons butter
1 small onion, minced
3 cups drained canned Italian plum tomatoes
salt
freshly ground pepper
½ teaspoon sugar
½ cup grated Cheddar cheese
3 eggs, beaten
8 slices buttered toast

Heat butter in a frying pan. Add the onion and tomatoes. Cook uncovered over medium heat for 10–15 minutes, or until the mixture is thick. Stir very frequently. Season with salt and pepper and stir in sugar. Stir in the cheese and cook until the cheese is melted. Stir in the eggs and cook, stirring constantly, until thick. Spread on buttered toast. Makes four servings.

Saturday

La Tourtiere

La Tourtiere
Cranberry Relish
Hermits

1½ pounds lean boneless pork, ground
1 teaspoon salt
freshly ground pepper
¼ teaspoon ground nutmeg
½ teaspoon ground mace
1 tablespoon cornstarch
1 cup beef bouillon or water
pastry for a 2 crust 8-inch pie

Combine all the ingredients except the pastry in a saucepan and mix well. Simmer, covered, over low heat for about 20 minutes, stirring frequently. Cool. Roll out the pastry. Use half of the rolled-out pastry to line the bottom of an ungreased 8-inch pie pan. Spoon the meat mixture into the pie pan. Cover with the remaining pastry and seal the edges with water. Prick with a fork to allow steam to escape during baking. Bake in a preheated 425° oven for 10 minutes. Reduce heat to 350° and bake for 20 more minutes or until the top crust is browned lightly. Serve hot or cold. Six servings.

FAMILY FARE DINNERS

December

Sunday **Ukrainian Borsch**

Ukrainian Borsch
French Garlic Bread
Cheese Tray
Dried Figs, Raisins, Almonds and Walnuts

1 pound beef chuck, sliced
8 cups beef bouillon
salt
freshly ground pepper
2 bay leaves
2 tablespoons butter
1 medium onion, chopped
2 medium carrots, sliced
3 medium raw beets, peeled and shredded
½ medium cabbage, shredded
2 tablespoons minced parsley
1 8-ounce can tomato sauce
1–2 tablespoons vinegar
2 medium potatoes, cubed
3 tablespoons grated raw beets
3 tablespoons minced dill weed
sour cream

This substantial soup lends itself to be the main course at a meal. Put the meat into a large heavy kettle and add bouillon, a little salt and pepper and the bay leaves. Bring to boil and skim. Reduce heat to very low. Simmer, covered, for about 30 minutes. In another saucepan heat butter. Over medium heat cook the onion, carrots, beets, cabbage and parsley for 5 minutes. Stir constantly. Reduce heat to low. Add the tomato sauce and vinegar. Simmer, covered, for about 10 minutes. Add to the meat and bouillon together with the potatoes. Simmer, covered, over very low heat for about 1 hour. Skim when needed and stir frequently. Check the seasoning. Ten minutes before serving time, stir in the grated beets, to color the soup. Remove the meat to a separate platter and serve separately, if desired, and serve the soup in a bowl or serve meat and soup in large heated bowls, with a sprinkling of dill weed. Serve with sour cream on the side. Six servings.

Monday

Carbonnades Flamandes

Carbonnades Flamandes
Buttered Noodles
Broccoli Vinaigrette
Pumpkin Pie

¼ cup butter
6 medium onions, thinly sliced
1 garlic clove, minced
2 pounds lean boneless round, cut into 2-inch strips
½ teaspoon dried thyme
⅛ teaspoon ground nutmeg
3 cups beer or ale
salt
freshly ground pepper
beurre manié made by kneading together 1 tablespoon butter with 1½ tablespoons flour
1 teaspoon sugar

Heat 2 tablespoons of butter in a large frying pan and cook the onion and garlic until soft and golden. Transfer the onion and garlic to a heavy casserole. Add the remaining butter to the frying pan. Over high heat and stirring constantly, brown the meat until it is dark brown, but not burned. Add the meat and pan juices to the onions and garlic. Add the thyme, nutmeg, beer and season with salt and pepper. Bring to boil and turn heat to lowest possible. Simmer, covered, for about 1½ hours. Drop the beurre manié in pea-size pieces into the stew, stirring well after each addition. Stir in sugar and cook for 5 more minutes. Makes six servings.

Tuesday

Baked Lamb Shanks

Baked Lamb Shanks
Braised Celery
Potato Balls
Cheese Cake

4 large lamb shanks
2 medium onions, chopped
2 garlic cloves, minced
juice of 1 lemon
1 cup canned, drained, chopped plum tomatoes
¼ cup minced parsley
2 teaspoons dried basil
salt
freshly ground pepper
1 cup dry white wine
1 tablespoon flour
1 cup sour cream

Trim all fat off the lamb shanks. Place them in a deep, large 3–4 quart casserole. Sprinkle the onions, garlic, lemon juice, tomatoes, parsley and basil over the lamb. Season with salt and pepper. Pour wine over the meat. Cover tightly with foil. Cook in a preheated 350° oven for about 1–1½ hours. Drain the pan juices into a small saucepan. Over high heat, reduce them to about ⅔ cup. Stir flour into the sour cream and add to the reduced pan juices. Mix well and heat through thoroughly, cooking over low heat for about 2–3 minutes. Put the lamb shanks into a deep serving dish and spoon the sauce over the meat. Four servings.

Wednesday

Calf's Liver with Onion Rings and Apples

Calf's Liver with Onion Rings and Apples
Boiled Potatoes
Red Radish and Cucumber Salad
Apple Tart with Cream

8 tablespoons butter
2 large onions, thinly sliced and separated into rings
salt
freshly ground pepper
6 medium tart cooking apples, peeled, cored and sliced crosswise into ¼-inch rings
1½ pounds calf's liver, cut into ¼-inch slices
flour

This is a very popular recipe from Berlin and a change from the usual ways of cooking liver. Heat 2 tablespoons of butter in a large, heavy frying pan and cook onions over medium heat, stirring constantly, until golden brown. Season with a little salt and pepper. Transfer onions to a large heated plate, cover with foil and keep warm in a 200° oven. Add 2 more tablespoons of butter to frying pan and cook half of the apple rings until golden on both sides but still firm. Transfer them to the plate with the onions and keep warm. Cook remaining apple slices in 2 more tablespoons of butter and add them to the others. Keep apples and onions warm while cooking liver. Coat the liver slices lightly with flour. Add the remaining 2 tablespoons of butter to the frying pan. Over moderate heat, stirring constantly, cook the liver slices for about 2 minutes on each side, or until browned. Do not overcook. Season with a little salt and pepper. Serve the liver on a heated serving dish, topped with onion and apple rings. Serve immediately. Serves six.

Thursday

Tipsy Beef Stew

Tipsy Beef Stew
Boiled Potatoes
Creamed Peas, Carrots and Onions
Green Salad
Cheese and Fruit

3 pounds chuck or stewing beef
2 tablespoons butter
1 tablespoon oil
3 large onions, thinly sliced
1 tablespoon flour
2 tablespoons brandy
2 cups beef bouillon
1¼ teaspoons dried thyme
salt
freshly ground pepper
2 bay leaves
½ cup dry Madeira
¼ cup minced parsley

Trim beef of all fat and gristle. Heat butter and oil in a large, heavy frying pan. Brown meat over high heat, in small amounts at one time. Do not crowd frying pan or meat will not brown properly; it should be the color of dark wood. Do not burn it. Transfer meat to a 4-quart casserole. If necessary, add a little more butter to the frying pan and cook onions until golden brown. Add onions to meat. Stir flour into frying pan juices and scrape up all the brown bits at the bottom. Stir in brandy, beef bouillon and thyme. Bring to boil and pour over meat. Taste for saltiness; if necessary, add more salt, pepper, and bay leaves. Cover and cook in a preheated 325° oven for 1 hour. Stir in Madeira. Cook, covered, for 30 more minutes or until meat is tender. Sprinkle with parsley before serving. Serves six.

Friday

Grasshopper Pie

Baked Cod Creole
Green Rice
Cauliflower Polonaise
Grasshopper Pie

Graham Cracker Crust:
1½ cups graham cracker crumbs
¼ cup confectioners' sugar
⅛ teaspoon ground mace
6 tablespoons melted butter

Put enough crackers through the medium blade of a meat grinder to give 1½ cups. Combine the cracker crumbs, confectioners' sugar and ground mace in a bowl and mix well. Stir in melted butter. Pat the mixture firmly on the bottom and sides of a generously buttered deep 9-inch pie pan. Bake in a preheated 375° oven for about 15 minutes. Cool before filling.

Creme de Menthe Filling:
1 envelope unflavored gelatin
⅓ cup water
3 egg yolks
¼ cup sugar
2 cups heavy cream
⅓ cup crème de menthe
1 or 2 drops green food coloring
1 square bitter or semi-sweet chocolate, grated or shaved

In a little bowl, sprinkle the gelatin over water and stir to mix. Place bowl into a pan with hot water. Over medium heat, cook until gelatin is dissolved. Remove from pan with hot water and cool. Beat egg yolks and sugar with an electric beater or mixer until very thick and lemon colored. Stir cooled gelatin into the egg mixture. Whip 1 cup of cream until fluffy. Fold into the egg mixture, stir in crème de menthe, and add 1–2 drops green food coloring. Turn the mixture into the graham cracker crust shell. Refrigerate until set. Whip the remaining cup of cream and spread over the top of the pie. Sprinkle with grated chocolate. Makes one nine-inch pie.

Saturday

Steak au Poivre

Steak au Poivre
Shoestring Potatoes
Belgian Endive, Raw Mushroom and Watercress Salad
Cold Tart Lemon Soufflé

4 tablespoons crushed pepper or to taste
4 minute steaks, about 1-inch thick
4 tablespoons butter
salt
4 tablespoons brandy
2 teaspoons Bovril or other meat glaze
1 cup heavy cream

Press the crushed pepper into steaks with the heel of your hand or the round side of a soup spoon. Let stand at room temperature for 1 hour. Heat butter in a large heavy frying pan. Over medium heat, turning once, sear the steak on both sides. Turn down the heat slightly and continue cooking to the desired degree of doneness. Season with a little salt. Pour brandy over the steaks and flame. When the flames have died down, add Bovril or other meat glaze to color the steaks dark brown. Turn the steaks quickly to brown on the other side. Transfer the steaks to a hot platter and keep hot. Add cream to the frying pan and, over medium heat, cook down to about ½ cup. Spoon over the steaks and serve immediately. Makes four servings.

QUICK & EASY DINNERS FOR TWO

December

Sunday

Lamb Chops
Hashed Brown Potatoes
Brussels Sprouts with Lemon Sauce
Belgian Endive Salad
Arabian Oranges

Arabian Oranges

2 large navel oranges
¼ cup shredded blanched almonds (they come canned)
4 dates pitted and chopped
⅓ cup freshly squeezed orange juice
2 tablespoons brandy or Kirsch

Peel the oranges, removing all of the yellow and white skins. On a plate (to save the juice), cut the oranges into thin slices. Place them in a glass serving dish. Add the almonds, dates, orange juice and brandy. Toss carefully with two forks. Chill for 10 minutes in the freezing compartment of the refrigerator.

Monday

Spinach and Rice Soup

Spinach and Rice Soup
Fried Chicken
Potato Salad
Red Radishes, Carrots
Fresh Applesauce and Cookies

1 pound fresh or 1 10-ounce
  package chopped frozen spinach
4 cups chicken or beef bouillon
¼ cup rice
salt
freshly ground pepper
dash of grated nutmeg (optional)
freshly grated Parmesan cheese

With kitchen scissors cut off the coarse stems of the spinach and cut the leaves into shreds. Wash in several waters to get rid of all the sand. Bring bouillon to boil. Add rice. Simmer, covered, until the rice is almost tender. Add the fresh or frozen spinach. Season with salt, pepper and nutmeg. Cook 3 minutes longer; the spinach should be still firm. Serve hot with grated Parmesan cheese.

Tuesday

Eggplant Broiled with Mozzarella

Eggplant Broiled with Mozzarella
Spanish Rice
Green Salad
Chocolate Pudding

1 small eggplant
about 8 ounces Mozzarella cheese
salt
freshly ground pepper
4 tablespoons olive oil

Peel the eggplant. Cut crosswise into ½-inch thick slices. Cut the Mozzarella into the same number and size slices as the eggplant. Place the eggplant slices side by side in a broiler pan. Season with salt and pepper and brush with about half the olive oil. Turn the slices, season and brush with remaining oil. Broil for 3–4 minutes or until light brown. Turn and broil for 2–3 more minutes. Top each eggplant slice with a slice of Mozzarella. Broil until the cheese melts. Serve very hot.

Wednesday

Sautéed Chicken with Sherry

Sautéed Chicken with Sherry
Cracked Wheat Pilaf
Green Bean Salad
Lemon Meringue Pie

1 large chicken breast, halved
salt
freshly ground pepper
4 tablespoons butter
⅓ cup dry sherry

Skin the chicken halves and trim off any fat. Season with salt and pepper. Heat butter in a frying pan. Add the chicken. Over high heat, brown the chicken breasts on both sides. Lower heat and add sherry. Cover and simmer over low heat for about 8–10 minutes, turning over once or twice.

Thursday

Savory Potato Galette

Pork Chops
Savory Potato Galette
Red Cabbage with Apples
Cut-Up Grapefruit and Oranges
Cookies

4 to 5 medium potatoes
½ cup butter
1 cup hot beef consommé
salt
freshly ground pepper
½ teaspoon ground thyme or crumbled rosemary or more to taste
1 medium onion, minced

This recipe can be easily doubled or tripled. Preheat the oven to 350–400°F. Peel the potatoes, cut into pieces and cook in salt water to cover until soft. Drain potatoes and mash while still hot. Beat in ½ of the butter, the consommé and salt and pepper to taste. Go easy on the salt, the consommé may be quite salty itself. Beat in thyme. Heat 2 tablespoons of the remaining butter and cook onion until soft. Do not let it brown. Stir onion into the mashed potatoes. Turn the potatoes into a buttered 1-quart casserole. Bake until the top has become a golden brown crust; baking time depends on the heat of the oven.

Friday

Garlic Broiled Shrimp

Garlic Broiled Shrimp
Risotto
Green Peas in Cream
Watercress
Cheese and Apples

1 pound raw shrimp
2 minced garlic cloves
½ cup olive oil
2 teaspoons salt
¼ cup chopped parsley
juice of 2 large lemons
lemon wedges

Shell the shrimp. If the black veins down their spine are very visible, remove them with the point of a knife. Place the shrimp in a shallow baking pan. Sprinkle with garlic, olive oil, salt, and parsley. Let stand at room temperature or refrigerate for about 10 minutes. Broil about 4 inches from the source of heat for about 3–4 minutes on each side, depending on size. Transfer to a serving dish and sprinkle with lemon juice. Serve with lemon wedges.

Saturday

Eggs with Mushrooms

Eggs with Mushrooms
Chick-Pea Casserole
Cucumber Salad
Apple Brown Betty

2 tablespoons butter
¼ pound fresh mushrooms, sliced
1 tablespoon brandy
1 tablespoon flour
⅓ cup hot beef or chicken bouillon
2 slices ham
4 eggs
salt
freshly ground pepper
2 tablespoons minced parsley

In a small saucepan, heat 1 tablespoon of the butter and cook mushrooms, stirring constantly, for about 2 minutes. Sprinkle with brandy and stir with the flour. Stir in bouillon. Cook, stirring frequently, for 5 minutes, or until the sauce is rather thick. While mushrooms are cooking, heat the remaining butter in a frying pan that can go to the table. Add the ham, placing the slices side by side. Cook until golden, turning once. Lower the heat. Carefully break eggs over the ham, two for each ham slice. Season lightly with salt and pepper. Cover and cook for a minute or two, or until the whites are beginning to set. Top the eggs with mushroom sauce. Cover again and cook until the eggs are firmly set. Sprinkle with parsley and serve with buttered dark bread.

BUDGET DINNERS

December

Sunday

Roast Beef
Baked Potatoes
Braised Artichokes and Peas
Orange Pie with Whipped Cream

Orange Pie with Whipped Cream

1 envelope unflavored gelatin
¼ teaspoon salt
½ cup sugar
2 eggs, separated
1¼ cups fresh orange juice
2 tablespoons fresh lemon juice
grated rind of 2 oranges
¼ teaspoon cream of tartar
1 cup heavy cream, whipped
1 baked 9-inch pie shell
1 square (1 ounce) unsweetened or semi-sweet chocolate or bitter chocolate
whipped cream

Combine the gelatin, salt and 6 tablespoons of the sugar. Beat together the egg yolks and orange juice. Stir the gelatin mixture into egg mixture and beat well. Cook over very low heat, stirring constantly for 5 minutes, or until the gelatin is melted and the mixture slightly thickened. Remove from heat and stir in lemon juice and orange rind. Chill until just beginning to set. Beat the egg whites with cream of tartar until stiff. Gradually beat in the remaining sugar. Beat until very stiff, as for a meringue. Fold the whipped cream into the gelatin mixture. Then gently fold the egg whites. Blend carefully but thoroughly. Spoon into pie shell and chill until set. Grate chocolate directly over the top of the pie. Garnish with additional whipped cream. One nine-inch pie.

Monday

Dried Pea Soup

Dried Pea Soup
French Bread
Cheese
French Apple Cake

1 pound green or yellow split peas
3 quarts water
1½ tablespoons salt
½ teaspoon freshly ground pepper
¼ teaspoon ground allspice
¼ teaspoon dried marjoram
2 pounds spareribs, cut into 2-inch pieces, all fat trimmed off
3 medium onions, thinly sliced
1 cup chopped celery
1 pound Italian or Polish sausage, peeled and thinly sliced

Put the peas and the water into a large kettle. Bring to boil and lower heat to very low. Simmer, covered, for about 1 hour. Add the salt, pepper, all spice, marjoram, spareribs, onions and celery. Bring to boil and skim. Lower heat to low. Simmer, covered, for about 20 minutes, or until the meat is almost tender. Add the sausage and cook 10 minutes longer. Makes six servings.

Note: For a small touch of elegance, fish the spareribs out of the soup before adding the sausage. Cut off the meat, discard the bones, return the meat to the soup and continue cooking.

Tuesday

Chicken Adobo

Chicken Adobo
French Fried Potatoes
Stewed Peppers and Tomatoes
Fresh Fruit Salad

3 pounds chicken pieces
salt
freshly ground pepper
2 garlic cloves, minced
2 bay leaves
½ cup cider vinegar
2 cups chicken bouillon or water
juice of 1 lemon

Combine all the ingredients in a large, deep frying pan. Bring quickly to boil. Lower heat and simmer, uncovered, for 40 minutes or until all the pan juices have evaporated. Increase the heat to medium. Brown the chicken well on all sides, turning frequently. Sprinkle with lemon juice before serving.

Note: There will be enough fat clinging in the frying pan to allow the chicken to brown.

Wednesday

Frankfurter Skillet Dish

Frankfurter Skillet Dish
Home-fried Potatoes
Green Beans Vinaigrette
Poached Pears and Cookies

2 bacon slices, chopped fine
2 medium onions, minced
1½ pounds frankfurters, sliced
2 large green peppers, cut into strips
12 black olives, pitted and halved
1–2 tablespoons drained capers
salt
freshly ground pepper
½ teaspoon dried thyme
6 eggs
2 tablespoons milk
2 tablespoons minced parsley

Cook the bacon in a large, deep frying pan until it begins to crisp. Add the onions and cook, stirring constantly, for 3 minutes. Add the frankfurters and green peppers and cook for 5 minutes. Add olives and capers. Taste and season with a little salt, if necessary, pepper and thyme. Cook for 2 minutes longer. Beat the eggs with milk and pour over the frankfurter mixture. Cook over medium heat, stirring frequently, until the eggs are set. Sprinkle with parsley. Makes six servings.

Thursday

Lemon-Braised Lamb Shanks

Lemon-Braised Lamb Shanks
Rice
Braised Red Radishes
Hot Gingerbread and Ice Cream

6 lamb shanks
salt
freshly ground pepper
¼ cup flour
2 teaspoons paprika
3 tablespoons salad oil
¾ cup chicken bouillon
1 garlic clove, minced
2 bay leaves
grated rind of 1 lemon
1 cup fresh lemon juice
¼ cup minced parsley

The secret of this dish is plenty of *fresh* lemon juice. Trim any excess fat off meat and season with salt and pepper. Combine flour and paprika. Coat the lamb shanks with the mixture on all sides and shake off excess. Heat oil in a large, deep frying pan or in a large casserole. Over high heat, brown the meat on all sides. Add the chicken bouillon, garlic, bay leaves, grated lemon rind and lemon juice. Bring quickly to boil. Lower heat to very low. Simmer, covered, for 1½ hours or until the meat is tender. Check occasionally for moisture; if necessary, add a little more bouillon, ¼ cup at a time. Skim off fat as it rises during cooking. Sprinkle with parsley before serving. Six servings.

Friday

Peanut Soup

Peanut Soup
Egg Salad Sandwiches
Tossed Green Salad
Chocolate Cream Pie

1 pound shelled dry roasted peanuts
6 cups beef or chicken bouillon
¼ cup grated onion
1 tablespoon cornstarch or flour
2 cups Half and Half or
  1 cup milk and 1 cup light cream
salt
freshly ground pepper
Tabasco to taste or ½ teaspoon
  dried red pepper flakes
⅓ cup minced parsley

The superiority of this Peanut Soup over other peanut soups comes from the fact that real peanuts are used rather than peanut butter. Grind the peanuts, a few at a time, in an electric blender. Do not over blend or the result will be a paste rather than finely ground nuts. Heat bouillon in a large saucepan. Stir in onion and ground peanuts. Bring to boil. Lower heat and simmer uncovered for about 30–45 minutes. Stir frequently. Return to the blender and puree, then return to the saucepan. In a separate bowl, stir the cornstarch into the Half and Half. Gradually stir into the hot soup, stirring constantly. Cook over very low heat, stirring all the time, for about 10 minutes. Season with salt, pepper, and tabasco to taste. Sprinkle with parsley before serving. Eight servings.

Saturday

Dutch Lemon Whip

Meat Loaf
Scalloped Potatoes
Baked Acorn Squash
Watercress and Avocado Salad
Dutch Lemon Whip

4 large eggs, separated
½ cup sugar
grated rind of 1 lemon
¼ cup lemon juice
¾ cup dry white wine
1 lemon, peeled, thinly sliced

This is quick and on the non-fattening side. In the top of a double boiler, beat egg yolks with sugar and lemon rind until thick and fluffy. Use an electric beater at medium speed. Stir in lemon juice and wine. Cook over, not in, boiling water, stirring constantly, until thickened. Cool and refrigerate until serving time. At serving time, beat the egg whites until very stiff. Fold them gently into the egg mixture. Spoon into a glass dish. Garnish with lemon slices. Serves six.

Note: If desired, sprinkle about ¼ teaspoon of sugar on each lemon slice. Do not let the finished whip stand; it will separate. This is why the egg whites have to be added to the whip at the last minute.

ENTERTAINING

December

Sunday

Artichoke and Shrimp Curry
Rice
Chutney
Cucumbers in Yogurt
Lemon Meringue Pie

Artichoke and Shrimp Curry

1½ to 2 pounds shrimp
2 large artichokes, sliced
2 tablespoons butter
2 tablespoons salad oil
1 large onion, thinly sliced
½ cup minced parsley
2–3 teaspoons curry powder or to taste
4 medium tomatoes, peeled, seeded, and chopped
1 cup hot chicken bouillon
salt
juice of ½ lemon

Shell and devein the shrimp. Slice artichokes. Heat butter and oil together in a deep frying pan or asserole Add the onion and parsley. Cook, stirring constantly, until the onion is soft. Stir in curry powder. Cook 3 minutes longer. Add the artichokes, tomatoes, and bouillon. Over low heat simmer, covered, for 10 minutes or until the artichokes are about ¾ cooked. Add the shrimp. Simmer, covered, for 5 minutes or until the shrimp are cooked pink and the artichokes tender. Add salt if needed. Do not overcook. Remove from heat and stir in lemon juice. Makes six servings.

Monday

Mushroom and Potato Pie

Cold Ham and Chicken
Mushroom and Potato Pie
Lettuce and Avocado Salad
Apple Tart and Cream

3 cups rich mashed potatoes
1½ cups fresh mushrooms, sliced
¼ cup minced onion
2 tablespoons butter
1 teaspoon lemon juice
¼ teaspoon salt
⅛ teaspoon pepper
½ cup sour cream

The combination of potatoes and mushrooms is an excellent one. Place half the mashed potatoes in a layer in a well-buttered 9-inch pie pan. Sauté the mushrooms and the onion in hot butter. Stir in lemon juice, salt, and pepper. Top the potatoes with the mushrooms and sour cream. Cover with the remaining potatoes. Bake in a moderate 350° oven for about 35 minutes. To serve, cut into wedges. Makes six servings.

Tuesday

Tournedos Flambé

Tournedos Flambé
Potatoes Anna
Sautéed Cherry Tomatoes
Belgian Endive Salad
Orange Slices in Port
Cookies

4 tournedos, 1 to 1½ inches thick
¾ teaspoon salt
½ teaspoon freshly ground pepper
½ teaspoon dried thyme
5 tablespoons butter
⅓ cup minced shallots
¼ cup brandy
Dijon mustard
1¼ cups Pinot Noir or good-quality burgundy
6 tablespoons dry Madeira
¼ pound mushrooms, sliced
⅔ cup heavy cream
2 tablespoons minced parsley

The interest of this dish depends on the flavor combination of the wines and brandy. Have the butcher tie the tournedos with string so they won't come apart in cooking, or secure them yourself with toothpicks. Sprinkle meat on both sides with salt, pepper, and the thyme. Heat 4 tablespoons of butter in a large, heavy frying pan. Cook shallots until soft and golden, but do not let them brown. Push shallots to one side of frying pan. Add the tournedos. Cook over high heat for 1 minute on each side. Sprinkle with brandy and flame. When the flames have died down, transfer the tournedos to a heated platter. Spread both sides of each tournedo with just a touch of mustard. Keep warm. Pour wine and Madeira into the liquid in the frying pan. Cook until reduced to about ¾ cup of liquid. Meantime, in a small frying pan, heat the remaining tablespoon of butter and cook mushrooms, stirring constantly, for about 2 minutes; they must remain firm and white. Add the mushrooms, cream, and parsley to the reduced liquid in the big frying pan. Return the tournedos to the frying pan. Cook over medium heat for 4–5 minutes on each side or to desired doneness. Serves four.

Note: Do not cook more than four tournedos at one time. If you are doubling the recipe, use two frying pans.

Wednesday

Artichoke and Rice Casserole

Grapefruit with Ginger
Roast Ham
Artichoke and Rice Casserole
Pickled Beets
Apple Crisp with Cream

3 tablespoons butter
2 tablespoons olive oil
2 large or 4 small artichokes, sliced
1 large tomato, peeled, seeded, and chopped
1 garlic clove, minced
1 teaspoon dried basil
2 cups (approximately) hot chicken bouillon
1 cup long-grain rice
1 teaspoon salt
freshly ground pepper
¼ cup minced parsley
freshly ground Parmesan cheese

Heat 2 tablespoons of butter and the olive oil in a heavy saucepan. Add artichokes. Cook, stirring constantly, for 3 minutes. Add the tomato, garlic, basil, and ½ cup of the bouillon. Simmer, covered, over low heat until artichokes are half tender. Heat the remaining tablespoon of butter in a 2-quart casserole. Add rice. Cook over medium heat, stirring constantly, until rice is yellow and opaque. Add the remaining 1½ cups of bouillon, salt, and pepper. Simmer, covered, over lowest possible heat until rice is three-quarters cooked. Check for moisture and, if necessary, add a little more hot bouillon, a few tablespoonfuls at a time. The dish should not be soupy. Add artichokes to rice and mix well. Simmer, covered, until both rice and artichokes are done. Again, check for moisture. Sprinkle with parsley and serve with plenty of freshly grated Parmesan cheese. Serves four to six.

Thursday

Wild Mushroom Soup

Wild Mushroom Soup
Pheasant Cooked with Sauerkraut
Boiled Potatoes
Buttered Brussels Sprouts
Fresh Pineapple with Kirsch
Cookies

¼ pound (4 ounces) dried imported mushrooms
8 cups strong beef bouillon
1 medium onion, chopped
6 tablespoons butter
2 tablespoons flour
salt
sour cream

This most flavorful soup is made with the imported dried mushrooms found in all gourmet stores and most supermarkets. Wash the mushrooms quickly under running cold water to remove any dust. Soak the mushrooms in beef bouillon overnight. Add the onion, 4 tablespoons of the butter and bring to boil. Reduce heat and simmer, covered, for 1 hour. Puree in a blender. Blend together the remaining 2 tablespoons butter with flour. Drop small pieces, the size of a hazelnut, into the hot soup, stirring well after each addition. Add salt if needed. Cook for 5 minutes longer without boiling. When served, top each serving with a tablespoon of sour cream. Six servings.

Note: For a thinner soup, use 1 tablespoon butter and 1 tablespoon flour, or no thickening at all.

Friday

La Delice de Lausanne

Pâté Maison
Roast Duck with Oranges
Pilaf with Pignoli Nuts
Lettuce and Avocado Salad
La Delice de Lausanne

2 cups strong espresso coffee, very hot
1 bar (4 ounces) sweet cooking chocolate, crumbled
1 tablespoon sugar, or sugar to taste
3 tablespoons light rum or Kirsch
2 cups heavy cream, whipped stiff and very cold

This rich concoction combines dessert and coffee. Pour the coffee into a saucepan. Over very low heat and stirring constantly, dissolve the chocolate and sugar in the coffee. Be sparing with the sugar. Do not let the mixture boil. Stir in the rum or Kirsch. Chill thoroughly. Just before serving, whip the cream and fold it into the coffee mixture. Spoon into wine or sherbet glasses and serve immediately. If allowed to stand, the mixture separates. Makes six servings.

Saturday

Cookie Tree Party

Spiced Cider Punch
A Variety of Decorated Cookies
Sugar Gingerbread*
Almond Butter Stars*
Pencil Wreaths*

Children love parties, and they can learn at an early age to become gracious hosts. A Cookie Tree Party given shortly before Christmas is a delightful way for children to say Merry Christmas to their friends and to take part in the holiday preparations.

This particular party appeals to younger children, nursery school through second grade. Beyond that age, children expect more than a cookie at a party.

Start making cookies way ahead and freeze them. Send out invitations specifying the hours: mid to late afternoon. Invite the mothers as well. You can't handle all those children alone, and the presence of their mothers also insures that the children won't stay for an inordinate length of time.

Put up a small tree, preferably in a playroom or in the kitchen, because the depth of cookie crumbs on the floor will be considerable. The cookies are loosely tied to the tree with colorful strings. The tree should be well covered with cookies. After the usual games and entertainment, have one or two grown-ups cut down the cookies and distribute them to the children.

Serve the Spiced Cider Punch warm in paper cups, pouring from pitchers. If the mothers want a little rum or bourbon in their cider, that's all right too, as is vodka or whatever a grown-up body fancies with cider.

Sugar Gingerbread Cookies

¾ cup butter
1 cup sugar
1 egg
2½ cups flour
2 tablespoons ground ginger
½ teaspoon baking soda
1 tablespoon cream

The more decorative shapes, the better. A large number of imaginative cookie cutters may now to be found in household stores. Decorate the cookies with sprinkles, silver balls, and the like, or paint them with food colors and colored sugars. Have the children help you with the decorating. Cream butter and sugar until the mixture is very smooth. Beat in the egg and mix well. Beat in flour and ground ginger. Dissolve the soda in cream and beat into batter. Stir and knead the dough until it holds together, turn onto waxed paper and chill thoroughly. Roll out on a floured board to the thickness of ¼ inch. Cut into decorative shapes. Transfer the cut-outs to greased and floured baking sheets. Bake in a preheated 350° oven for about 10 minutes. Transfer the cookies onto racks. While still warm, using a skewer or an ice pick, make a hole in the top of each cookie for the string from which it is to be hung on the tree. Cool and decorate.
Note: The oven temperature increases after the baking of the first batch. Check and if necessary, decrease the length of baking time.

Almond Butter Stars

¾ cup butter
¼ cup sugar
½ teaspoon almond extract
2 cups flour
¼ teaspoon salt
1 egg white, unbeaten
granulated sugar

Preheat the oven to 350°. Cream together the butter and sugar until light. Beat in the almond extract, flour and salt. Work the dough with the fingers until it holds together. Make a ball and wrap in waxed paper. Chill for at least 3 hours or until firm. On a floured board, roll the dough, about ¼ at a time, to the thickness of ⅛ inch. Cut into star shapes of various sizes. Place the cookies on greased and floured baking sheets. Brush with the egg white and sprinkle heavily with sugar. Bake for 8 minutes or until just golden. Cool a little, but while the cookies are still warm, puncture a hole for string in one of the points, using a skewer or an ice pick. Makes about sixty cookies.
Note: If you don't have any metal star cutters of more than one size, make your own cardboard patterns and cut around them.

Pencil Wreaths

1 cup butter
½ cup sifted confectioners' sugar
½ teaspoon vanilla extract
½ teaspoon almond extract
2½ cups flour
¼ teaspoon salt
¼ teaspoon red food coloring
¼ teaspoon yellow or green food coloring

Preheat oven to 350°. Cream together the butter, sugar, vanilla and almond extracts, until light. Beat in flour and salt. Work the dough with the fingers until it holds together. Divide the dough into halves. To one half, knead in red food coloring. To the other half, knead in yellow or green food coloring. Snip off about 1 teaspoon of each colored dough, press them together and roll between your hands into pencil shapes. Form each dough pencil into a wreath and press the ends together well. Place on greased and floured baking sheets. Bake for 8 minutes. Makes about sixty cookies.

INDEX

A

B

C

F

M

N

O

P

Q

R

S

T

U

V

W

XYZ